Expert Systems for the Technical Professional

Expert Systems for the Technical Professional

DEBORAH D. WOLFGRAM
TERESA J. DEAR
CRAIG S. GALBRAITH

JOHN WILEY & SONS

New York / Chichester / Brisbane / Toronto / Singapore

This publication is designed to provide accurate and
authoritative information in regard to the subject
matter covered. It is sold with the understanding that
the publisher is not engaged in rendering legal, accounting,
or other professional service. If legal advice or other
expert assistance is required, the services of a competent
professional person should be sought. *From a Declaration
of Principles jointly adopted by a Committee of the
American Bar Association and a Committee of Publishers.*

Library of Congress Cataloging in Publication Data:

Wolfgram, Deborah D., 1959–
    Expert system for the technical professional.

    Bibliography: p.
    Includes index.
    1. Expert systems (Computer science)   I. Dear,
Teresa J., 1957–   . II. Galbraith, Craig.
III. Title.
QA76.76.E95W65   1987   006.3'3   86-33970
ISBN 0-471-85645-2

Printed in the United States of America

10 9 8 7 6 5 4 3 2 1

Knowledge is Power.

Those who can interpret
a tremendous amount of knowledge
have the potential to hold
a tremendous amount of power.

Expert systems provide a vehicle
to harness this knowledge.

—Deborah D. Wolfgram—

Preface

Expert systems have arrived in force. They are rapidly proving their financial and economic worth, demonstrating that we are on the cutting edge of a phenominally powerful artificial intelligence computer age. Expert systems represent a powerful growth industry in today's world, an industry that will likely revolutionize virtually every facet of organizational life—from research and development, to production, to finance, to sales, and to strategic planning. Often, in a dynamic industry like expert systems, state-of-the-art knowledge races ahead at a blinding pace. The early important papers of expert systems are often presented at little known, poorly attended professional meetings. New ideas are typically traded through informal networks and much of the interesting development is proprietary and internal.

This book was written specifically as a compilation and summarization of current knowledge regarding expert systems as they apply *today*. We have drawn on a wide variety of sources ranging from informal and formal, to written and verbal. Also a variety of fields is represented, which include computer science, management information science, psychology, engineering, and management. This book is directed toward the technical professional and the student of expert systems. Some background of computer systems assists greatly in the synthesis of this knowledge. This book discusses current and valuable issues important to every organization involved with or considering becoming involved with expert systems.

The book begins with a brief history combined with an introduction to the definition, components, and stages of development of expert systems. We intimately discuss methodologies and strategies for storing, representing, manipulating, massaging, and interpreting this knowledge, that is, the "brain" of an expert system.

Next, the hardware and software used for expert system development and execution is discussed. The advantages and disadvantages of specialized symbolic processing machines and conventional computing machines are detailed and the various types of expert system software; artificial intelligence programming languages, development tools or "shells," and prepackaged expert systems are carefully examined.

The total process of developing and implementing an expert system is known as knowledge engineering. While knowledge engineering is discussed in bits and pieces in various forums, we have sought to bring this important information together by documenting not only the responsibilities of the knowledge engineer; but also the important technologies and tools used by the knowledge engineer to extract critical knowledge from the experts. Once knowledge is acquired, the expert system can then be developed. Using five different development tools, we construct five expert systems to illustrate the range of expert system technology.

This book is complete and self-contained for those who want to learn more about expert systems, the hardware used, the software employed, how knowledge is acquired, and finally how it all comes together in the construction of an expert system. We have tried to be consistent in terminology, employing the most prevalent nomenclature used today. While the issues and concepts regarding expert systems are generic, we have strived to discuss also the actual programs currently available in the industry. It is our belief that a careful study of this book will provide the reader with the basic foundation to be a more than competent knowledge engineer.

It is not yet clear as to the full extent that expert systems will impact the organization and in what ways. Today, many of these issues are at the mercy of an infant industry and the pioneers willing to brave these unknowns.

The masculine pronoun has been used throughout in order to facilitate ease in reading, no slight is intended toward women in the profession.

A book like this requires the help of many people. We wish to thank Roxanna Camen, for insight on knowledge acquisition; Mr. and Mrs. July Dear, whose support will last a life-time; Bennett Dear, where competition was not the key, but support and understanding. We would also like to thank Jean Galbraith, who spent countless hours proofreading; Oliver and Nannette Galbraith, of Galbraith Forensic and Management Sciences, Ltd; John Maginnis, with his continual enthusiasm and support; and Douglas Wolfgram, whose undying ambition and thirst for knowledge has always been an inspiration.

DEBORAH D. WOLFGRAM
TERESA J. DEAR
CRAIG S. GALBRAITH

Irvine, California
Irvine, California
Mission Viejo, California
April 1987

Contents

PART FOUR–CONSTRUCTION OF AN EXPERT SYSTEM

PART FIVE–CONCEPT TO REALITY

Expert Systems for the Technical Professional

PART ONE

INTRODUCTION TO EXPERT SYSTEMS

Over the past several decades, society has had an infatuation with trying to breathe life or intelligence into machines. We no longer want computers to just add, subtract, multiply, or divide, but to act human, to think. Imagine the endless possibilities of intelligent machines: computer systems that recommend profitable financial and marketing strategies, eagerly perform dangerous and monotonous manufacturing or exploration tasks, create new designs in the automobile or semiconductor industries, and quickly monitor and diagnose a patient's health. An entirely new research effort dedicated to the development of artificial intelligence (AI) evolved, growing in significance to become a virtual growth industry in today's world.

Chapter 1 provides an initial framework and vocabulary for discussing expert systems to be expanded on in later chapters. Chapter 2 discusses in detail 12 examples of expert systems applications in different industries. Each of these expert systems is either in advanced development stages or currently in use.

1

Introduction to Expert Systems

What is *intelligence*? According to *Webster's Second College Edition New World Dictionary*, intelligence is "the ability to learn or understand from experience; the ability to acquire and retain knowledge; mental ability; the ability to respond quickly and successfully to new situations; the use of the faculty of reason in solving problems, directing conduct, etc., effectively." What is *artificial intelligence*? Applied epistemology—the practical application of the study or theory of knowledge with its cognitive limits. As researchers started to explore these issues, a new branch of AI developed that combined knowledge representation with problem-solving techniques. Today this field is known as knowledge-based expert systems. Other branches of AI include robotics, natural language processing, speech recognition, voice synthesis, cognitive modeling, automatic programming, visualization systems, and symbolic processing computers (Figure 1.1).

WHAT ARE EXPERT SYSTEMS?

Expert systems are computer systems, comprising both hardware and software that mimic an expert's thought processes to solve complex problems in a given field (domain).

An expert system manipulates vast amounts of information with the intention of solving a particular applicational problem. What makes

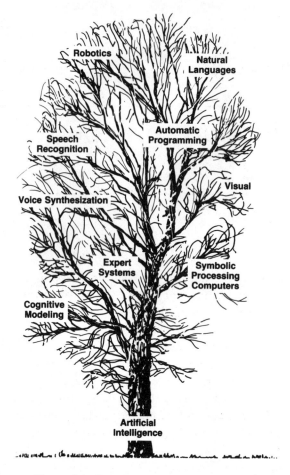

Figure 1.1. Branches of artificial intelligence.

expert systems unique is the *way* they approach and solve problems (combining knowledge representation and problem-solving algorithms) and the different *types* of problems they can solve (heuristic
problems vs. conventional problems). Expert systems attempt not only
to apply conventional mathematical and Boolean operators (e.g., $+$,
$-$, $/$, $*$, AND, OR), but to incorporate typical human reasoning processes such as "rules of thumb" and "shortcuts" to solving problems.
The goal of an expert system is to mimic an expert's thought processes
in solving a problem.

Expert systems have the capacity to manipulate problem statements
and integrate relevant pieces of knowledge from a knowledge base

(a collection of information) using reasoning techniques, commonly known as heuristics, to emulate the expert. By their very nature, expert systems address and solve knowledge-intensive problems (large information sets) that can have multiple correct or acceptable answers.

BRIEF HISTORY

No book is complete without mentioning the early and still viable expert systems that paved the way to where we are today. In 1965, researchers at Stanford University began work on the grandfather of all expert systems, DENDRAL. DENDRAL, based on an algorithm developed by Nobel Prize-winning chemist Joshua Lederberg, was designed to analyze information from a spectroscopic analysis on chemical compounds to determine their molecular structures. Using an efficient variant of a generate-and-test search technique in its problem solving, DENDRAL outperformed some of the finest human experts in the field. Approximately 15 work-years were spent in developing DENDRAL—extracting heuristic information from expert chemists; formulating the experts' reasoning rules into formal rules, and implementing and testing the final system. Programmed in LISP (LISt Programming language), DENDRAL is a good example of a rule-based system, storing much of its knowledge in "If–Then" production rule statements.

In 1970, CADAUCEUS was developed at the University of Pittsburgh to aid physicians in the diagnosis of human internal diseases. Seventeen years later, this system has approximately 100,000 programmed relationships which represent 85% of all relevant knowledge in this particular domain. CADAUCEUS analyzes by initially examining the problem using a bottom-up problem-solving strategy and then switching to a top-down strategy, thus squeezing in on the diagnosis.

MACSYMA was written in the late 1960s as part of Project MAX (the original name of MIT's Laboratory of Computer Science). By 1971 it was being successfully employed in sophisticated symbolic mathematical analysis. MACSYMA surpasses most human experts by performing differential and integral calculus symbolically and simplifying symbolic expressions. Comprising more than 300,000 lines of LISP program code, MACSYMA represents approximately 100 work-years of development time.

MYCIN was developed at Stanford University in 1972. One of the most publicized and famous expert systems, MYCIN assists with the diagnosis and treatment of infectious blood diseases. Based on production rules, its knowledge base currently has approximately 400 rules. From MYCIN stemmed TIERESIAS in 1976. Also from Stanford University, TIERESIAS is a knowledge acquisition tool that assists with entering and updating the MYCIN knowledge base by utilizing meta-knowledge. TIERESIAS uses a subset of natural languages to interface with the expert.

Around 1978 the development tool EMYCIN evolved from MYCIN. EMYCIN contains all of the logical structure of MYCIN, with the exception of its knowledge of infectious blood diseases, hence the name "Empty MYCIN." Thus was born the expert system shell, a program containing logical structures and thinking strategies, but without the knowledge base of a specific domain.

Then came PUFF, a diagnostic consultation expert system for pulmonary function diseases. PUFF is a derivative of EMYCIN with a pulmonary function diseases knowledge base added. Test equipment measures the volume of the lungs and their ability to get oxygen into the blood and carbon dioxide out of the blood. These measurements assist in the determination of the existence and severity of lung disease. PUFF records data directly from the pulmonary function test equipment. It is a goal-directed, backward-chaining, rule-based system. Unfortunately, PUFF cannot perform analogies in order to recognize patterns in "like" cases—something physicians often look for.

About the same time, the Stanford Research Institute (SRI) constructed the PROSPECTOR expert system. It is a rule-based system that assists with the analysis of information related to geological exploration. Funded by the U.S. Geological Survey and the National Science Foundation, PROSPECTOR was created specifically to provide consultation to geologists in the early stages of locating a site for ore-grade deposits. Its data structure is based on a semantic network.

In 1980, XCON, developed by Digital Equipment Corporation, became the first expert system to be used successfully on a daily basis in a commercial environment. XCON performs the difficult job of configuring a customer's request for a VAX computer system. Digital Equipment Corporation reports that XCON saves the corporation approximately $200,000 per month in staff costs alone, not to mention savings in manufacturing costs.

Parallel with the growth of expert systems was the development of expert system tools, which are designed to make the complicated task of building expert systems easier. TIERESIAS and EMCYIN were already mentioned. ROSIE, developed by the Rand Corporation, provides a general-purpose developing environment based on production rules and was the first system designed to support a wide range of expert system applications. OPS, HEARSAY-II, KAS, RLL, and AGE all stemmed from the need to assist with modeling the expert.

CHARACTERISTICS OF EXPERT SYSTEMS

By definition, expert systems are used to solve problems or make decisions. What applications are suitable for expert systems? First, expert systems operate on a processing level higher than that of conventional programs. They function like a thought process—they make inferences and guesses and ask questions for additional information. Suitable applications for expert systems are those that fall into one of the following categories.

Interpreting and Identifying

Explaining summarized results from input information.

Applications include identifying: geological structures (PROSPEC-TOR), ship types (HASP/SIAP, Stanford and Systems Control Technology), computing needs for customers (Infomart), credit policy, corporate capital expenditures, and marketing data.

Predicting

Inferring likely consequences of given or hypothetical situations.

Applications include predicting: discount airline seating (ASA, Northwest Orient Airlines), crop damage (PLAND/CD, University of Illinois), crop irrigation needs, stock market movement, petroleum demand, and electric power demand.

Diagnosing

Identifying causes, given symptoms.

Applications include diagnosing: infectious diseases (MYCIN, Stanford University), hydrostatic sterilizers (Campbell Soup), corrosion failures (Westinghouse Research), locomotives (DELTA, General Electric), telephone networks (ACE, Bell Laboratories), epitaxial reactors (IMP, Texas Instruments), human poisoning, and electronic circuit problems.

Designing

Configuring objects into systems, given constraints.

Applications include designing: computer system configurations (XCON, Digital Equipment Corporation and Carnegie-Mellon University), oil well drilling mud (NL Baroid and Carnegie-Mellon University), gene clones, organic molecules, computer microchips, and factory floor layouts.

Planning

Devising a method for making or doing something in order to achieve an end.

Applications include planning: bombing missions (TATR, DARPA and Rand Corporation), battle management (FRESH, DARPA), construction projects, regular delivery routes, manufacturing schedules (Westinghouse), and dispatching taxicabs.

Monitoring

Comparing observations with established standards.

Applications include monitoring: nuclear reactors (REACTOR), space shuttle computers (NAVEX, NASA and Inference Corporation), manufacturing plants, robot welding, and power plants.

Debugging and Testing

Prescribing remedies for malfunctions.

Applications include testing: electronic circuit boards (Texas Instruments) and printed circuit boards (Sperry).

Instructing and Training

Educating and transferring information.

Applications include instructions for: selecting therapies for infections (GUIDON), selecting metallurgical materials (Westinghouse), how to repair hydrostatic sterilizers (Campbell Soup), selecting appropriate welding materials (WELDSELECTOR, Colorado School of Mines), and training in disaster management.

Controlling

Regulating or guiding the operation of a machine, apparatus, or system.

Applications include controlling: the treatment of patients in intensive care (VM, Stanford University), autonomous land vehicle navigation (DARPA), and vehicular traffic flows.

Expert systems are appropriate where there are no established theories, where human expertise is scarce or in high demand, and where the information is "cloudy" or "fuzzy." Applications not suitable for expert systems are those that are calculative or deterministic in nature, where a "magic" formula or model exists, and where human experts are plentiful. The use of expert systems in these areas would be overkill and unnecessarily expensive. For example, a poor application would be to calculate mortgage payments for a home loan.

But are expert systems a form of decision support systems? They are not classified as such. Decision support systems are more mechanistic; that is, they operate under basic mathematical and Boolean operators in their execution. They are passive tools used to model and forecast matrix-type problems, such as pro forma financial statements, which assist decision making. Examples of decision support systems are spreadsheets used for applications such as financial investment analysis, capitalization and depreciation schedules, and financial budgeting. To gain a better understanding about what expert systems really are, it is useful to compare them with the broad classes of decision support systems and conventional programs. Characteristics unique to expert systems are listed in Table 1.1.

1. Expert systems perform difficult tasks at "expert" levels of performance, whereas decision support systems perform at a more "mechanistic" level of execution. In other words, an expert system takes the place of a human expert in a problem-solving environment by interpreting knowledge, making inferences, and reasoning in ways similar to those of the human expert. An example of this difference would be an expert system designed for weather forecasting versus a decision support system designed for inventory control.

Table 1.1. Comparison of Characteristics Between Expert Systems, Decision Support Systems, and Conventional Programs

EXPERT SYSTEMS	DECISION SUPPORT SYSTEMS	CONVENTIONAL PROGRAMS
Domain		
1. Specific area of expertise	General, mechanistic areas	General, mechanistic areas
Reasoning and Search Techniques		
2. Heuristic reasoning	Mechanistic/monotonic reasoning	Mechanistic/monotonic reasoning
3. Symbolic manipulation	Numeric and alphabetic manipulation	Numeric & alphabetic manipulation
4. Dynamic decision process	Static decision process	Static decision process
5. Remembers information	Doesn't remember information	Doesn't remember information
6. Prediction and inference	What-if scenarios	If-Then scenarios
7. Data pattern driven	Control driven	Control driven
8. Multiple solutions	Single solution	Single solution
9. Search intensive	Computation intensive	Computation intensive
10. Recursive	Iterative	Iterative
11. Certainty factors	Truths or falseness	Truths or falseness
Data Characteristics		
12. Uncertain & incomplete data	Exact & factual data	Exact & factual data
13. AI data structures	Fixed, hierarchical data structure	Fixed, hierarchical data structure
14. Dynamic and static variables	Static variables	Static variables
User Interface		
15. Natural language dialogue	Menu/command interface	Menu/command interface
16. Generates and reviews summaries	Generates summaries	Generates summaries
17. Quantitative and qualitative	Quantitative	Quantitative
System Maintenance		
18. Expert or Knowledge Engineer developed	User maintained	Programmer maintained
19. Expert or Knowledge Engineer maintained	User maintained	Programmer maintained

2. Expert systems are able to handle formidable problems through symbolic manipulation in a real-world domain.

3. Expert systems can incorporate sets of values called certainty factors, confidence factors, and probabilities which represent the definitude of a statement. These values represent the most common ways for the expert system to deal with uncertainty.

4. Expert systems are qualitative rather than quantitative in their results. Expert systems do not simply generate answers; they analyze and present the "best" possible answer with advice and recommendations. For example, an expert system can not only identify a mechanical failure in a piece of machinery, it can also identify potential sources of the failure with their associated certainty factors, which indicate the strength of each recommendation.

5. Expert systems are designed to solve one or more problems simultaneously while considering a tremendous amount of information. This implies that there may be several nondefined or unknown components of a problem. In this instance the expert system may be required to solve one or more problems not directly related to the problem at hand, but whose solution will affect its problem-solving process.

6. Expert systems base their reasoning process on symbolic manipulation and heuristic inference procedures—the type of reasoning human experts employ. Conventional programs and decision support systems recognize only numeric or alphabetic (string) manipulation.

7. Problems addressed by expert systems can have multiple solution paths, one solution path, or no solution path. Expert systems have some knowledge of the basic principles in the problem domain; they know how they operate and how they arrive at the results. Conventional programs and decision support systems simply execute according to the predefined direction of the program. They have only one solution path.

8. Expert systems are capable of reconstructing inference paths for explanation and justification purposes. This provides what is called an "audit trail" for the end user. The end user cannot ask a conventional program to explain how it derived its answer. For example, MYCIN provides an elaborate discussion of its reasoning strategies when queried, allowing the physician to understand its reasoning processes.

9. Expert systems are able to reformulate the problem, that is, work the problem backwards, when necessary; conventional programs cannot.

10. Expert systems are more flexibly designed than conventional programs. This allows for modifications as problems become better defined and additional data becomes known. Since the environment of an expert system is never static, an expert system must be capable of manipulating dynamic variable inputs. Dynamic variables are those that are constantly changing, such as the stock market prices. An expert system employing stock prices must be flexible enough to easily incorporate the continuous changes.

11. Expert systems are search intensive rather than computation intensive. Expert systems compare and analyze relationships among numeric and nonnumeric data, versus straightforward algebraic computation of numeric data.

12. Expert systems are recursive, versus iterative in nature. During its problem-solving process, once an expert system has read in information, it is not necessary to read in the information again. Information is remembered. An example of this is a subroutine in a conventional program that is called numerous times throughout the execution of the program. An expert system would need to call the subroutine only once.

13. Expert systems are pattern directed, versus control directed. Conventional programs execute according to a predefined data flow, no matter what type of data is inputted. Expert systems follow a flow determined by the relationship of the inputted data and the current contextual environment. There is no predefined execution path.

14. Expert systems tolerate imprecision when interfacing with the user. Expert systems are designed to have a "natural language" dialogue with the user, versus menus or command screen prompts.

15. Some expert systems are self-modifying. If during, or after, a program run, the expert system determines that a piece of its data or knowledge base is incorrect, or no longer applicable because the environment has changed, it has the capacity to update the information. Consequently, if the same set of parameters were reentered, the expert system might deduce a different answer.

16. Expert systems model a task that has already been performed by a specialist. They emulate experts, whereas conventional programs do not.

17. Expert systems are generally maintained by the experts or knowledge engineers, whereas conventional programs are generally maintained by programmers.

COMPONENTS OF AN EXPERT SYSTEM

The four basic components of an expert system are (1) the knowledge base, (2) the inference engine, (3) the interface, and (4) the development engine (Figure 1.2).

Knowledge Base

The knowledge base of an expert system houses the information used by the expert system in pursuit of a solution to a problem. A knowledge base is a step above a conventional database in that a knowledge base not only contains static data as in a database, but also contains relational information. A third area of the knowledge base is working memory. Working memory is used only during processing and is the resident space for information manipulation.

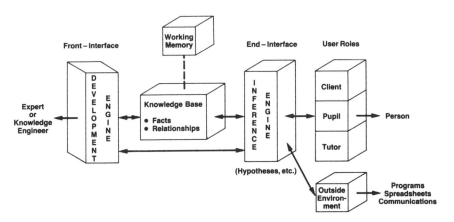

Figure 1.2. Basic components of an expert system.

The Database

This includes the facts of the problem, both related and unrelated. This is a passive area of the expert system—simply a storage space for data and formulas. The information included encompasses the given and unchanging knowledge about the problem and domain. For example, this area might contain formulas for integral calculus or equations for amortized loan payments.

The Knowledge Base

This includes the related and unrelated relationships of the data of the problem and domain. Production rules, the basis of most expert systems, are located here. An example of a production rule is: "If a person purchases a stock with a beta greater than 1.7, then he is considered risk aggressive."

The Working Memory

Here the knowledge base is modified by the inference engine as situations and data change—a much more interactive area of the expert system than the database. Working memory takes data from the database, knowledge from the knowledge base, and combines them with the information supplied from the user to then be massaged by the inference engine in pursuit of a solution.

An expert system may be described by others as having a database or a knowledge base. We maintain that the knowledge base of an expert system has both. We differentiate them here primarily to illustrate the degree of passiveness of these separate groups of information referenced by the expert system. However, categorically, for the remainder of the book these components will be referenced in their entirety as the "knowledge base."

Inference Engine

The inference engine is the workhorse of the expert system. It consists of the processes that work the knowledge base, do analyses, form hypotheses, and audit the processes according to some strategy that emulates the expert's reasoning. The inference engine massages new information, combines it with the knowledge base, considers the relationships in the knowledge base, and proceeds to solve the problem in working memory using its established reasoning and search strategies. In other words, the inference engine is the "thinker" of a problem-solving system; it provides overall control.

Interface

Numerous interfaces are used in the creation and operation of an expert system. Interfaces include a terminal (TTY screen), graphical representations (visuals), multiple character windows, and multiple graphic windows. These interfaces operate in three situations. The first situation is where the user acts as a client. Here the user wants answers to problems. The second situation is where the user acts as a tutor to enhance the expert system. Here the user, primarily the knowledge engineer, wants to improve or increase the knowledge of the expert system. The third situation is where the user acts as a pupil of the expert system. In this situation the user wants to harvest the knowledge base.

Development Engine

A development engine, also called an editor or knowledge acquisition subsystem, is vital in the creation of the expert system in that it allows the knowledge engineer to create, modify, add, and delete information from the knowledge base. The development engine is not always resident within the expert system software.

The strength and power of an expert system lie in the knowledge base. Expert systems are usually successful if they are rich in knowledge, even if they have poor problem-solving capabilities (i.e., reasoning and search strategies). This knowledge is largely heuristic—judgmental, experimental, and uncertain. Expert systems are complex programs to construct and maintain, but in return offer tremendous problem-solving power and efficiency.

An expert system is actually a knowledge system. A knowledge system is a less specific problem-solving system that has all the characteristics of an expert system, but the knowledge and reasoning strategies used are not considered to be equivalent to those of a human expert. A knowledge system is a computer system that symbolically represents knowledge and manipulates it to solve problems. An expert system is a knowledge system that performs at such a high level of

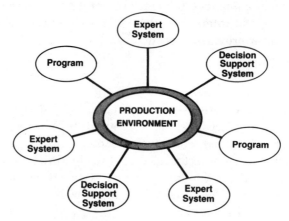

Figure 1.3. Integrating expert systems.

human expertise that it is considered a specialist or expert. This leads to a discussion of "What is the definition of an expert?" in later chapters. Throughout the remainder of the book, we will address both knowledge systems and expert systems simply as *expert systems*.

Expert systems are not stand-alone systems. They are usually linked together with other expert systems, programs, and decision support systems to form a complex and sophisticated integrated system (Figure 1.3). For example, a possible application for an integrated system would be to devise a corporate strategy regarding a new product introduction. This total system might include several experts and their expert system in (1) advertising and packaging, (2) industry and competitor analysis, and (3) distribution, combined with advanced deterministic mathematical models to generate economic forecasts and spreadsheet applications for pro forma computations. Thus the integrated expert system brings together and analyzes expertise from various areas throughout the organization in an efficient and effective manner.

STAGES OF EVOLUTION

The stages in the evolution or construction of an expert system are similar in concept to the stages in the evolution of virtually any computer program (Figure 1.4).

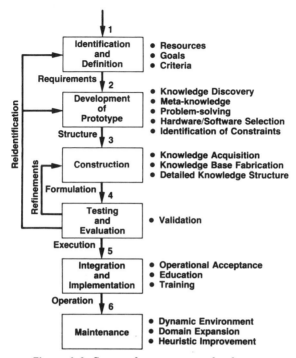

Figure 1.4. Stages of expert system development.

Stage 1: Identification and Definition of the Problem

This stage details the identification and determination of the scope of the problem and its characteristics. It entails the identification of the expert(s) required, the resources needed (such as money, hardware, software, personnel, and development time), and the goals of the expert system. It is important to recognize whether the problem can actually be addressed by an expert system. Some problems may not be appropriate because they may be too simplistic or diverse. There also may not be an expert or a definable domain in which to model the problem. At this stage it is imperative to identify clearly the goals and criteria of the system—what is it supposed to do? These considerations provide an initial guideline for direction in the development of the expert system prototype and should be documented through an *Expert System Project Study*.

If an organization is looking to enter the realm of expert systems and is attempting to identify a problem for the application, there are competing views as to the type of problem that should be considered. Dr. Edward A. Feigenbaum of Stanford University argues that the organization should choose a problem with high associated costs and economic value and/or savings. It should be a vital and highly visible area for the organization's successful operation. Feigenbaum maintains that the organization should attack the problem with intensity, not skimp on equipment and labor, and secure knowledgeable consultants for at least the initial stages of development to ensure success. Conversely, Paul Harmon of Harmon & Associates firmly maintains that initially an organization should address smaller applications, thus gradually acquiring the expertise needed to pursue larger problems. He also suggests that it is not always possible to find the "big" high-cost problems. It may be smarter to start smaller, with lower costs and investment, and work up the ladder of expertise and complexity.

There is no clear-cut answer. The answer is a complicated function of the organization's available resources, operations, or timetable and the organizational ability to accept new technology and innovations. Regardless of the approach taken, problem identification is extremely important and is oftentimes the determining factor in the application's success. Currently, a popular method of problem identification is to present expert system examples to sections of the work force and discuss what expert systems can potentially do. The workers are then encouraged to submit expert system application proposals on which they are knowledgeable. Often, the best suggestions for expert system applications come from the actual workers. This "bottom-up" approach to problem identification has proven extremely fruitful in the past.

Stage 2: Development of the Prototype

This stage entails finding the basic concepts which represent knowledge via key metarules, relations, and identifying the flow of information needed to describe the problem-solving process. Decisions are made as to the appropriate hardware and software. Also, the formats for representing the knowledge of the system are established. This requires the mapping of key concepts, subproblems, and information flow characteristics, isolated into a representation, given various categories of expert system software. The data gathering process is designed, initiated, and coordinated to comply with the software and hardware requirements of the expert system. Data may be inputted manually or electronically (for example, from an ASCII-format data file). Equally important is the identification of any major constraints to the problem and the development of the expert system (such as cost and time requirements). This stage, and ensuing stages, is done by knowledge engineers or specially trained internal personnel.

In the prototype, the knowledge engineer must begin to identify and document the reasoning processes of the expert. This is called *knowledge discovery*. These processes are the heart of the operation of the expert system and provide the "human-like" thought aspect to solving the problem. The expert's knowledge is documented in a *knowledge handbook*, which becomes the base for future, more detailed knowledge acquisition.

Once the prototype is in place, it is a working model, or submodel, of the planned complete expert system. It is at this stage that, after careful testing and review, a decision is made whether to continue the project and construct the complete expert system or abandon the project.

Stage 3: Construction of the Expert System

Here, the detailed rules that embody the knowledge are concretely formulated and refined by combining and reorganizing the knowledge from the prototype. This stage also entails the primary data gathering process, formally called *knowledge acquisition*. Not only is the knowledge base dramatically expanded, but the front and end user interfaces are carefully designed. The front interface deals with the input, modification, and maintenance of the information in the knowledge base. The end interface deals with the user and how the system will run (i.e., menu driven) and what features will be available to the user (such as "help" mode or the ability to review the reasoning of the system). The end of the construction stage begins the tedious and time-consuming testing stage where the system is reviewed and checked repeatedly.

Stage 4: Testing and Evaluation of the Expert System

The expert system is tested and retested in many different ways. Everything is checked, from the construction of the front interface, to the clarity, communication, and ease of use of the end interface, to the accuracy of problem outcomes. The reasoning techniques and data structures are carefully validated and finely tuned. The assignments and combinations of the certainty factors, if used, are also scrutinized.

The initial verification of the expert system is against the notes of the knowledge engineer to check for obvious errors in the expert system. From there, the expert system is presented to the expert for verification. The most common method is to give problem examples to both the expert and the expert system and compare results. As a good target, the expert system should agree with the expert in at least 90% of the examples.

Any modifications required for correction are completed here, and then the sequence loops back to restart testing and verification again. This continuous loop of testing—modification—testing is essential since one change can have numerous repercussions which may not be immediately identifiable, particularly with large and complex systems. The loop continues until all testing is complete, at which point the expert system is ready for use.

Stage 5: Integration and Implementation of the Expert System

This stage is an often overlooked and unattended stage of expert system development. Here, the expert system is integrated into the day-to-day operations of the organization. This entails education, training, and operational procedure changes. Resistance may be met, which compounds the difficulty of system integration. If the intended users of the expert system refuse to use the system (due to poor training or hesitancy or if the expertise is of no assistance in solving their problem), then the expert system may have been developed in vain. The possible magnitude of problems associated with the integration of the expert system should not be taken lightly, and the integration phase should be carefully planned and organized with full training, support, and documentation.

Stage 6: Maintenance of the Expert System

The refinements of an expert system are never complete, due primarily to the dynamic environment of information and the ability of expert systems to be continuously updated with new rules and heuristics. The maintenance of the expert system entails the continual process of reviewing, modifying, expanding, and upgrading the knowledge base, hardware, and software.

EXPERT SYSTEMS AS A BUSINESS SOLUTION

One key question asked today is: "Are expert systems a viable business solution?" Many industry analysts estimate that currently only 10% of potential expert system applications are being recognized, and a 75% annual growth in the industry is expected over the next five years. The timeline from research to business for any product or technology has many milestones. A product or technology starts in research with an idea or vision. As the technology is made available to the commerical market, it gains "substance" but is still in the exploratory stages of acceptance by the market. Full commercial integration occurs when businesses assume accountability for any action the product or technology performs during the course of business. Of all the branches of AI, expert systems is the furthest along in terms of real-world business applications (Figure 1.5). Although the commercial application of expert systems is still in its infancy, the industry is rapidly becoming a growth business.

Most companies are still exploring the concept of expert systems, attempting to define areas where expert systems can make profitable contributions to the organization. Only since 1984 have expert systems become readily available to the commercial user, thanks in large part

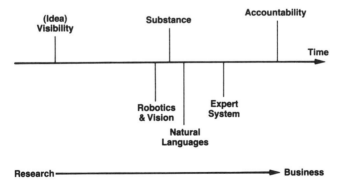

Figure 1.5. Expert system technology transfer—research to business.

to the emergence of develoment tools which assist in the construction of an expert system.

Given the recent commercial availability of expert system software, the issue of appropriate applications in the organizational environment is becoming a relevant topic of discussion for today's professionals. Although expert systems have tremendous potential to make profitable contributions to an organization, it is important to be aware of the organizational and social impacts that accompany expert systems.

2

Applications of Expert Systems

Expert systems have been in existence for over 10 years, but their early applications were basically limited to research and development. These early systems while pushing forward a new frontier of AI, required large amounts of resources, to model decision making, and thus could be afforded by only a few Fortune 500 companies and the government. Since modeling an expert is considered a proprietary and integral part of the strategic plan of many organizations, depending on the sensitivity of the application, nobody really knows the amount of time or money that has actually been spent developing these systems. Only a few, more developed systems have been fully disclosed to the commercial world. Yet within the last couple of years, due primarily to the emergence of expert system software for the microcomputer, there has been a virtual explosion in the number of expert systems developed on a much smaller scale, with substantially lower costs.

Although the details of most expert systems are considered proprietary, most companies have been willing to at least disclose that they are actively involved in expert system development. These firms span such industries as medicine, automotive, oil/petroleum/natural gas, computers and telecommunications, space exploration, national defence, airlines, chemicals, banking, public utilities, transportation, and finance.

This chapter briefly summarizes a variety of current, state-of-the-art applications to give a better feel for how expert systems are being used today and concludes with a detailed list of expert system applications indexed across industries. This list was compiled from a variety of published sources, including press releases, commercial announcements, and public statements. Where available, the application program name and company name are listed in parentheses. Appendix A details companies involved in expert systems across the same and other industries.

WESTINGHOUSE CORPORATION

The Westinghouse Research and Development Center in Pittsburgh, Pennsylvania, has developed an expert system to assist it in its research on metal corrosion. Two Westinghouse engineers, Dr. Neil Pessall and Dr. Jan Schreurs, developed the system to capture some of the broad knowledge used daily at the Westinghouse facility. The engineers had three demonstrations prototyped in one week using Texas Instruments' PERSONAL CONSULTANT development tool.

The function of the expert system is to evaluate critical points in steam generators, which are often corroded by impurities in water. There are four types of corrosion that are analyzed in steam generators: pitting (usually caused by local acidic conditions), denting (caused by corrosion products squeezing the tube), stress corrosion cracking, and thinning (the general corrosion of metal). The system analyzes the four possibilities based on a series of questions that leads to a conclusion and recommendation for alternative choices of alloy.

By committing his knowledge to an expert system, Dr. Pessall believes his understanding of the field has improved. In an interview with Texas Instruments, he states,

> The process of developing these systems can actually improve the expertise of the expert. He is forced to organize his knowledge and logic, which in turn can indicate critical gaps in the knowledge base and trigger new ideas. Our approach to the development of expert systems is aimed *not* at replacing the expert, but at developing an environment that will make him more efficient and his knowledge more accessible to others. The use of expert system technology can provide a common link between engineers and scientists from different disciplines. The resulting cross-fertilization of methodology through research and development would clearly improve productivity by minimizing repetition of effort. (*AI Interactions*, Texas Instruments Data Systems Group, Dec. 1985, pp. 2–5)

AIRLINE INDUSTRY

The Federal Aviation Administration is funding the Flight Transportation Laboratory of MIT to develop an expert system to aid airport tower controllers in assigning runways at busy airports. The applications process is to evaluate numerous variables that affect runway choices and sort them out to provide recommendations. These variables include weather, traffic, changes at other airports affecting inbound aircraft, runway repair, noise, and preferential runway standards. The first group of experts for this rule-based expert system will be the watch controller supervisors at Boston's Logan Airport. The system will then be modified for other airports according to their particular environments. Obviously, the system will be cautiously developed and carfully tested since, in this application, human safety is at stake.

CAMPBELL SOUP

Soup canning is one of the unheralded quality control wonders of the food industry. At low cost and high speed, the industry produces tens of billions of perfectly preserved units (cans of soup) year in and year out. Defective units are "as rare as broken anvils."

The process is highly automated from start to finish, which makes it susceptible to occasional minor malfunctions. Any down time, however, is expensive and quickly disrupts shipping schedules. So, Campbell Soup management decided that an expert system could help its repair and maintenance workers to anticipate and prevent malfunctions and diagnose them faster when they do occur.

Their initial application was the diagnosis of malfunctions that occur in cooker systems (formally called hydrostatic sterilizers). Cookers are the working heart of every Campbell canning plant, and the plants are spread throughout the world. The cooker's job is to sterilize the food in the cans. Elaborate conveyor systems load and unload the cookers.

Campbells plant operators and maintenance workers are capable of handling the day-to-day operation of the cookers and correcting common malfunctions. Occasionally, though, difficulties arise that demand diagnosis by an expert—someone thoroughly versed in the design, installation, and operation of the cookers. This expert is Aldo Cimino. Campbell wanted to capture his expertise in an expert system. Thus even the smallest plant would have his knowledge immediately available. It would also free him to concentrate on design improvements and new processes. A secondary objective was to use the system as a training tool for new maintenance personnel.

The first expert system, developed with PERSONAL CONSULTANT, took about six months from initial contact with the human expert to field testing. Following another year of testing and modifications, the system contained 151 rules, plus start-up and shut-down procedures, and was being distributed to other Campbell plants for installation. Campbell Soup sees five primary benefits from this effort:

1. Aldo Cimino's expertise is distributed across all of the plants simultaneously, providing quicker malfunction diagnosis.
2. Cimino's time will now be freed to design new equipment.
3. Cimino's expertise will be retained as corporate knowledge, especially after he has left the organization.
4. Campbell Soup realizes financial rewards for less down time.
5. This expert system should be able to handle 95% of the problems encountered.

INSURANCE INDUSTRY

The UNDERWRITING ADVISOR is a prepackaged expert system that consolidates senior underwriters' judgment, knowledge, intuition, and even subtle reasoning on both common and obscure underwriting factors. It was developed by Syntelligence in conjunction with American International Group (AIG), the St. Paul Companies, and Fireman's Fund Insurance Company.

Massive underwriting losses—totaling $24 billion industry wide in 1985—are forcing commercial insurance leaders to investigate better methods of managing and controlling the underwriting process and to address several key needs:

- *Better Access to Expert Advice.* Inexperienced underwriters—the average industry tenure is three years—do not have ready access to seasoned professionals in making potentially costly decisions.

- *More Consistent Application of Company Directives.* Bulky under-writing manuals are rapidly outdated and inconvenient to refer to, and are often used incorrectly in the field.

- *Improved Tracking of Decisions.* The recording of how and why particular underwriting decisions are made is handled locally on a person-by-person basis; paper files are not easily retrievable by management.

- *Enhancing the Efficiency of Underwriting.* Underwriting is one of the few areas in the insurance industry for which direct computer support has not been able to increase individual productivity.

The UNDERWRITING ADVISOR system provides specific features that address these needs, including

- *Preliminary Assessment.* It rapidly advises whether a potential piece of business merits additional evaluation, which enhances productivity of inexperienced underwriters.

- *Systematic Evaluation of Exposures.* It identifies and helps evaluate specific hazards for each risk, including which factors should be examined more closely, restructured, or excluded; provides assistance in pricing.

- *Analysis of Decisions.* On demand, provides the underwriter with the reasoning behind judgments and maps the steps taken to reach a decision.

- *Integrated Data Processing.* It can exchange data with existing IBM-based software programs, including on-line access to key databases and customer files.

- *Initial Customization and Ongoing Updates.* Standard encoded expertise is customized for each customer to reflect the standards and procedures of each company's management. Tools and training are provided to permit the customer to handle updates independently over time.

Syntelligence estimates that an insurance company whose annual commercial premiums average $250 million can achieve a total savings of $35 million over a five-year period.

INFOMART

Infomart in Dallas, Texas, is the world's first information processing market center. Infomart planners wanted a way to help direct first-time buyers of computer systems through the maze of selections. SNAP (Simplified Need Assessment Profile), created using the PERSONAL CONSULTANT development tool, is a 170-production-rule expert system. Debbie Hinkle, Coordinator of Infomart's Resource Center, states,

> SNAP helps first-time purchasers identify their computer needs. It helps them decide what they want a computer to do. Based on that, it makes general recommendations—no brand names involved. SNAP does the job of a good salesman and documents the results for the customer. This relieves the customer of having to repeat all of the information to each manufacturer he talks to. (Artificial Intelligence Letter, Texas Instruments System, Group, Dec. 1985, p. 2)

The process is simple. The customer takes a seat in front of 1 of 12 personal computers (all connected by a local area network). Each of the computers has its own resident knowledge base internal to the machine. The consultation begins with some examples designed to familiarize the customer with cursor controls and types of responses. With the basics out of the way, it is time to begin.

SNAP asks whether the customer is interested in obtaining a personal computer or an office computer, in receiving information on computers, or in getting greater performance from a current system. Next, it asks what business the customer is in (e.g., business, insurance), what types of applications are desired (e.g., spreadsheets, payroll, accounting), and what his future computing needs will be.

When the consultation is completed, SNAP produces a printed report summarizing the session and outlining general recommendations. In its first five months of operation, SNAP was used by more than 3300 customers. According to Hinkle, "the response has been favourable." The system is being expanded to cover additional business areas, such as manufacturing and computer graphics.

PILOT'S ASSOCIATE

The Pilot's Associate is a DARPA (Defense Advanced Research Projects Agency) funded government program designed to

- Monitor an aircraft's system, in the role of a flight engineer
- Provide mission planning and replanning in flight
- Provide external situation assessment, based on information obtained from the aircraft's radar and other sensors
- Act as a tactical manager to rapidly devise an optimum strategy for coping with external threats

The maintenance of aircraft system information includes mission requirements, navigation monitoring, fuel management, threat avoidance, and route replanning. The tactical assistance includes internal systems monitoring, fault diagnosis/isolation, fault compensation, and emergency response. Four interactive expert systems will control these functions. The situation assessment manager will evaluate such external factors as weather, terrain, targets, and resources; the system status manager will be responsible for monitoring the status of all internal systems; the mission planning manager will provide rapid revision or adaptation of the mission plan, reflecting the changing situation; and the tactical planning manager will make recommendations regarding weapons, tactics, and so on, based on the current combat situation. In essence, these systems are intended to supply the pilot of a single-seat fighter with the expertise of an entire flight crew.

In a conventional cockpit system, raw data—not organized information—are available to the pilot. He must then collect, interpret, and digest these data into a useful form which allows him to make decisions about which commands to give the plane through manual control mechanisms (switches, buttons, etc.). In the projected "integrated cockpit," the four expert systems will work together to convert these data into organized information, thereby facilitating decision making; the pilot will then be able to implement his decisions by giving the machine a general action plan—a mission—that it can carry out on its own.

An example of a Pilot's Associate project is the F-16 Emergency Procedures expert system. It monitors the aircraft's alarm systems, evaluates fast-changing emergency situations, and displays recommendations to the pilot in real time. If the pilot is disabled or distracted, the system will control the automatic flight control system of the aircraft. The primary contractors for this program are McDonnell-Douglas and Lockheed-Georgia.

BATTLE MANAGEMENT

Battle Management is another DARPA-funded government program. The intention of this application is to create an automated decision system which provides expert knowledge in machine form for decision making in the field. It is designed primarily to provide tactical planning assistance in military operations. One example of a battle management application is FRESH (Fleet Readiness Expert System Hawaii), developed by Texas Instruments, which monitors changes in military situations and gives strategic tactical planning recommendations to naval commanders. The system also predicts the results of scenarios, given particular decision inputs. It detects significant changes in the readiness of an entire fleet of ships and will help assign replacement ships. In its early version, the system will be evaluated as to its usefulness in helping military operations staffs to determine a fleet's capability to undertake various operations, considering current battle operations and ship types available.

Another part of the battle management program is the development of the Compact LISP Machine (CLM) chip by Texas Instruments. This compact chip will allow expert systems to be placed in thousands of vehicles for use in system monitoring and emergency procedures—vehicles such as fighter planes, space shuttles, military helicopters, and tanks.

BANKING INDUSTRY

Like the insurance industry, commercial banks are examining ways to relieve considerable pressure on profits due to loan losses. With loan write-offs, nonaccruals, and collection expenses already averaging between 1 and 2% of assets, commercial banks have become increasingly concerned with loan quality. Nearly half of all loan officers have less than three years of experience. While their work is reviewed by senior loan officers, many losses are still due to specific oversights resulting from their limited experience. Bank officers have also indicated that improved loan monitoring could substantially reduce the costs of reviewing loans and cut losses by allowing banks to identify problem loans early.

Syntelligence, working with development partners Wells Fargo

Bank and First Wachovia Bank, has completed the LENDING ADVI-
SOR system to assist commercial banking professionals in analyzing
"middle market" loans to companies with sales between $5 million and
$100 million.

The LENDING ADVISOR system helps banks achieve these savings
in several ways:

- *Preliminary Assessment.* By rapidly determining whether a company's loan application has the potential to merit additional
  work, productivity of inexperienced lending officers is enhanced.

- *Systematic Risk Analysis.* A detailed credit risk analysis of financial, management, and strategic factors is generated to assist in
  determining the degree of risk associated with an applicant. It
  also considers the purpose and appropriateness of the loan and
  makes recommendations for restructuring alternatives.

- *Industry Analysis.* Proprietary industry databases are being developed by Syntelligence to allow banks to monitor and evaluate
  industry conditions and changes that can affect the ability to pay,
  both at the time of the application and on an ongoing basis.

- *Training and Efficiency.* The LENDING ADVISOR system will
  assist the lending officer in providing inputs as well as the reasoning behind judgments. The system will permit communication
  with existing software and provide an organized credit memo and
  loan review.

Using the LENDING ADVISOR system, the reputed average net
gain over five years is $3 million for banks with $5 billion in assets. For
a $30 billion bank with below-average performance, the average net
gain is estimated at about $15 million over five years.

AUTONOMOUS LAND VEHICLE

The Autonomous Land Vehicle (ALV) project is probably the most
ambitious AI undertaking by DARPA, headed by Martin-Marietta
Aviation. Autonomous systems such as the ALV are intended to perform intelligent tasks on their own without direct human intervention, thereby offering the potential of carrying out life-endangering

missions without casualties. The ALV is an unmanned vehicle that can be used in such areas as reconnaissance, operations in contaminated areas, and dangerous missions. It uses a color television camera as its basic sensor and an expert system as its intelligence. It has the ability to determine the edges of an asphalt road and drive a vehicle down the center. In May 1985 the ALV traversed a 2.2-km road, went around a curve, and following a preprogrammed plan, pivoted 180 deg under the control of its vision system, renavigated the road, and returned to its starting point.

When the vehicle was unsure of the road's outer boundaries, it would slow down, much like a human when driving in a heavy storm. The visual perception part of the control system not only informs the control portion of the vehicle where it believes the center of the road is, but also offers a quantitative measure of its confidence in its determination.

Ultimately, the ALV will span all areas of AI and allow the vehicle to adjust to its environment without intervention, doing such things as detecting enemy sensors, using evasive tactics, and even lying in ambush. Unfortunately, current AI technology is limiting the true implementation of the ALV by the speed of existing computers; a dramatic increase in computing speed is required—estimated as much as 10,000 times faster. As a consequence, DARPA is also funding research efforts in novel computer architectures. One of these projects is the BBN Butterfly machine (discussed in Chapter 11). It is a symbolic multiprocessor which can be configured with up to 256 microprocessors.

DIGITAL EQUIPMENT CORPORATION

Perhaps one of the most well-known applications of expert systems is Digital Equipment Corporation's XCON. XCON stands for eXpert CONfigurer. Developed jointly by researchers at Carnegie-Mellon University and Digital Equipment Corporation, XCON configures VAX and PDP-11 computer systems. It is a forward-chaining rule-based system, developed in OPS5, embodying over 4200 rules. Interestingly enough, XCON does not employ certainty factors or probabilities. Components under consideration are either included or excluded.

The procedure begins by requiring the user to input a customer's order. Considering more than 400 components, XCON then builds a customized configuration. The system first checks for gross errors and unbundles the order to a configuration level recognized by the other subtasks. It begins by adding the primary components to the central processing unit (CPU). Next, the rest of the peripheral components are added to the CPU cabinet and configured. Finally, a floor room layout is made to determine cabling connections. These diagrams display the spatial relationships among the components in the customer's order which are used in assembling the system. The itemized list of components is also a valuable input for materials requirement planning (MRP).

XCON has numerous users:

1. Technical editors who are responsible for ensuring that only configurable orders are committed to manufacturing
2. Assemblers and technicians who work at the plant assembling the units
3. Sales personnel who use XCON with XSEL (XSEL is an expert system that prepares accurate quotes on configurations produced by XCON)
4. Scheduling personnel who examine the output to determine the most efficient configuration for combining options
5. Technicians who perform the installation at the customer's site

XCON has assisted in significantly reducing the number of personnel required for VAX configurations, thus freeing personnel to concentrate on specialized problems too complex for XCON to solve. "XCON is saving us roughly $18 to $20 million per year in manufacturing costs," says Joel Magid, Senior Product Manager of Digital Equipment Corporation's AI Technology Group (Davis, July 1986).

MEDICAL INDUSTRY

MYCIN was designed to play a role similar to that of a human specialist in infectious diseases. Infectious diseases include bacteremia (infections that involve bacteria in the blood) and meningitis (infections that involve inflammation of the membranes that envelop the brain and spinal cord). The system interacts with a physician to collect all of the relevant information that is available about a patient under consideration, and then examines this information for evidence upon which to base a diagnosis and recommendation for therapy. These diseases impress the need for the physician to act quickly, and unfortunately, positive identification of an infectious disease normally takes 24–48 hours. In many cases the physician must begin treatment before definitive test results are available. These diseases are complex enough to require the assistance of MYCIN as soon as possible.

The procedure that MYCIN follows in diagnosing a patient is

1. First, it collects relevant information about the patient through an interactive dialogue with the physician—information such as vital statistics (e.g., body temperature, age, sex, blood pressure), laboratory results (e.g., fluid analysis), and symptoms that the patient is exhibiting. Other information may be unknown or uncertain to the physician, which MYCIN can take into consideration. To accommodate uncertainty, all information given to MYCIN can be accompanied by a certainty factor.

2. If, during this process, further information is required, the system will either try to infer the information from the data it has already acquired, or it will ask the physician.

3. As soon as a reasonable diagnosis can be made, MYCIN will compile a list of possible diagnoses, therapies, and drug treatments.

MYCIN is a backward-chaining rule-based system, containing approximately 400 rules to date. As mentioned earlier, centainty factors may be associated with every rule to provide an heuristic technique for combining uncertain and incomplete data with experts' rules of inference. The inference engine employs an exhaustive search strategy (thereby considering all possible premises of all possible actions), augmented by a numerical heuristic combining function to rank competing hypotheses. MYCIN incorporates an explanation program to allow physicians to examine the reasons for the conclusions and also trace MYCIN's entire diagnostic trail.

The success of MYCIN has been evident over time, with a high occurrence of correct diagnoses and therapy recommendations. MYCIN has compiled a current, comprehensive, and extremely detailed knowledge base. It will never jump to conclusions or fail to ask for key pieces of information. When MYCIN was evaluated against several different panels of medical experts, MYCIN's performance was judged as good as, or superior to, that of all others.

> MYCIN's success proved that expert systems technology was strong enough to leave the laboratory, with its academic and well-circumscribed problems, and enter commercial environments with their incomplete and uncertain information, skeptical users who demand justification, and domains where substantial amounts of knowledge are the prerequisite of good judgment. (Harmon and King, 1985, p. 21)

COLORADO SCHOOL OF MINES

The Colorado School of Mines in Golden, Colorado, has constructed an expert system called WELDSELECTOR to assist welding engineers in the selection of the proper material for welding. The science of welding encompasses hundreds of base metals and welding electrodes (the materials used to join base metals together) and approximately 100 welding processes. The right choice is critical to the strength and safety of objects ranging from high-rise buildings to automobiles and jets—the commomplace structures in which we travel, work, and live. In an interview with Texas Instruments, Dr. Jerald Jones, Deputy Director of the Center for Welding Research, states, "When you consider that roughly 50 percent of the Gross National Product of the United States depends upon products that involve welding processes, you can see how important welding is in virtually every industry."

WELDSELECTOR, developed using PERSONAL CONSULTANT, is initially concentrating on three welding processes that Jones estimates comprise 15–20% of all welding performed—shielded metal arc welding, gas metal arc welding, and flux core arc welding. WELDSELECTOR asks the user a series of questions regarding the welding to be performed, pursuing the same line of reasoning as an expert welding engineer. As the user answers the questions, WELDSELECTOR searches the database to find suitable welding electrodes, based upon the user's input. As the questioning continues, WELDSELECTOR narrows the list of possibilities, until it presents its final recommendations.

WELDSELECTOR contains critical information on each base metal, such as the ASTM (American Society for Testing of Material) designation, and chemical and physical properties; the properties of the base metals to be joined help determine the welding electrode. But, just as important, it considers variables such as the position of the weld. Jones explains, "If you are welding overhead, you must use a rapidly solidifying material with a flux that holds the weld deposit in place. It's very different from welding flat on top of a table."

Another consideration is atmospheric contamination. "Liquid metal will rapidly absorb hydrogen from the atmosphere, which can cause very serious damage to the weld." WELDSELECTOR asks the user whether hydrogen cracking will be a problem and factors this answer into the final recommendation.

Jones sees the benefits from WELDSELECTOR to include reducing the chance of error in designing welds, improving the safety and stability of welded structures, reducing decision-making time by inexperienced engineers, and saving money through a more efficient materials selection.

OTHER EXPERT SYSTEM APPLICATIONS

What follows is a list of expert system applications across various industries. Some applications have the name of the expert system and/or the name of the company employing the system (enclosed in parentheses). These systems are either in use or in the prototyping stages of development. Considering the industry's continuous state of flux, the list is not complete, but will suffice to illustrate the breadth of applications of expert systems. It will quickly become evident that expert systems can be found in many industries, with the emergence of new expert systems a weekly experience.

Advertising
Media buying

Aerospace
Communication network diagnosis
Deep space station designer
Diagnosis of airplane engines
Fault isolation in Avionic
Helicopter repair (Boeing)

Navigator for reentry control (NAVEX, NASA)

Spacecraft malfunction diagnosis

Agriculture

Control of disease in winter wheat crops (WHEAT COUNSELLOR, ICI)

Controlling plant life in ponds (North Texas State University)

Crop rotation

Management of apple orchards (POMME, Virginia Polytechnic Institute)

Rice disease diagnosis

Chemical

Chemical synthesis planning (SYNCHEM, SUNY at Stony Brook)

Disease of Metals (Westinghouse Electric Company)

Herbicide advisor (British Gas)

Screener for new chemicals (Shell Institute)

Structure elucidation (DENDRAL, Molecular Design Ltd.)

Welding material selector (WELDSELECTOR, Colorado School of Mines)

Computers and Communications

Analyze VMS dump files after system crash (CDX, Digital Equipment Corporation)

Analyze telephone switching systems (COMPASS, GTE)

Assist circuit designers with logic design (DAS-LOGIC, Digital Equipment Corporation)

Check order entry (CONAD, Nixdorf)

Computer configuration (XCON, XSEL, and XSITE, Digital Equipment Corporation)

Configuring system layouts (Hitachi)

Database management system selection

Diagnose circuit fabrication lines (PIES, Fairchild)

Diagnosing failures in data processing equipment (DIAG8100, Travellors)

Diagnosing failures in disk drive (FAULTFINDER, Nixdorf)

Diagnosing failures in tape drives (AI-SPEAR, Digital Equipment Corporation)

Diagnosis of Cyber NOS-VE system (CDC Dump Analysis, Control Data Corporation)

Hardware diagnosing interpretation (DOC, Prime Computer)

Managing resources for chip designers (CALLISTO, Digital Equipment Corporation)

Monitoring MVS operating systems (YES/MVS, IBM)

Robot sensor interpretation

Sequence steps in PC board assembly (HI CLASS, Hughes Electro-Optical & Data Systems)

Software job costing (COCOMO 1, Level Five Research)

Software selection consultant

Software system troubleshooter

Troubleshooting photolithography steps in circuit fabrication (PHOTOLITHOGRAPHY ADVISOR, Hewlett-Packard)

Troubleshooting Ethernet networks (NTC, Digital Equipment Corporation)

Troubleshooting telephone lines (ACE, Southwest Bell)

Troubleshooting digital voltage sources (DIG VOLTAGE TESTER, Lockheed)

Troubleshooting communication hardware (BDS, Lockheed)

Drilling

Analysis of oil well logging datas (DIPMETER ADVISOR, Schlumberger)

Diagnosing drilling problems (MUDMAN, N.L. Industries)

Problem analysis on drill bits (SECOFOR, Elf-Acquitaine)

Education

Debugging PASCAL programs

Expert general library reference (Drexel University)

Learning disability classification advisor

Speech pathology advisor

Student behavior consultant

Technical engineering education

Test result interpreter

Textbook selection advisor

Tutor designers in design checking (DECGUIDE, Lockheed-Sunnyvale)

Tutoring users of VMS operating system (Digital Equipment Corporation)

Worksheet generator

Engineering

Carburetor fault diagnosis

Construction project planning and evaluation

Design of foundations for bridges and buildings (Carnegie-Mellon University)

Design of motor components

Engineering change order manager

Fastener selection

Front end for engineering design package

Linear programming system (American University)

Machine room safety

Material handling equipment selector (North Carolina State University)

Material selection

Road barrier requirements

Site planning for chemical plant

Statistical analysis tool selector

Statistical consultant (Carleton College)

Symbolic integral calculus (MACSYMA, M.I.T.)

Troubleshooting steam propulsion plants (STEAM, Navy Research Center)

Weight estimator for evolving designs

Environment

Environmental regulations

Mineral deposit relationships (PROSPECTOR, SRI)

Water discharge permit review (Environmental Protection Agency)

Weather forecasting

Financial Services

Advise in disclosure of confidential information (EDDAS, Environmental Protection Agency)

Advice on insurance underwriting

Analysis of risk insurance (UNDERWRITING ADVISOR, Syntelligence)

Assess commercial insurance risks

Bank services advisor

Brokerage legislation

Claim estimation

Commodity buying

Conflict-of-interest consultant

Credit approval (LENDING ADVISOR, Syntelligence)

Electronic banking services

Financial analysis (Palladin)

Financial planning advisor (PLANPOWER, Applied Expert Systems)

Financial statement analysis

Foreign exchange rates

International tax crediting

Legal analysis of contract claims

Loan application assistant

Performance evaluation of dealerships

Predicting business insolvency (University of Texas at Dallas)

Staff loan scheme

Stock broker marketing advice

Stock exchange regulations

Tax advisor

Management

Analyze battlefield intelligence (TRW)

Business productivity tool (GURU, Micro Data Base Systems)

Contingency planning

Corporate distribution analysis (INET)

Corporate structure

Corporate takeover

Creating documents (DOCUMENT MODELER, Model Office Company)

Database management system purchase advisor (Boeing)

Internal auditing

Inventory management advisor

Management portfolio expert

Management training

Naval acquisition management (ACQUISITION MANAGER ASSISTANT, U.S. Army)

Personnel planning and processing (U.S. Army)

Project management

Process management and information systems (MOD 300, Taylor Institute)

Qualitative reasoning for long-range planning (ROME)

Quality assurance standards

Tactical mission planning

Manufacturing

Analysis and prevention of mechanical failures (Duke University)

Chemical material selection

Continuous-process manufacturing advisor

Control railroad train braking system

Detecting cracks in billets (Kawasaki Steel)

Diagnosis of electronic controls

Diagnosis of computer board faults (ITT)

Diagnosis of hydrostatic sterilizers (Campbell Soup)

Diagnosis of railroad locomotives (DELTA, General Electric)

Drilling advisor for machining

Electrical system fault diagnosis

Fault diagnosis for auto subsystem

Gas turbine engine fault diagnosis

Maintenance advisor for hydraulic system

Maintenance of epireactor (IMP, Texas Instruments)

Newspaper layout design (Composition Systems)

Optimum performance maintenance (Ingalls Shipbuilding)

Power supply fault diagnosis

Process control applications (PICON, Lisp Machine, Inc.)

Refinery process control

Sensor verification for power plant

Sequencing computer board assembly (HI CLASS, Hughes)

Tooling selection for machining

Troubleshooting circuits (Hewlett-Packard)

Troubleshooting paper plants (ACID)

Medical

Adverse drug reaction

Arthritis and rheumatism expert (AI/RHEUM, Knowledge Research)

Cancer management (ONOCOCIN, Stanford University Oncology)

Diagnosis of poisoning via telephone hotline (Johns Hopkins University)

Diagnosis of learning disabled (CLASS. LD, Utah State University)

Diagnosis of pulmonary diseases (PUFF, Pacific Medical Center)

Diagnosis of infectious diseases (MYCIN)

Health care billing advisor (Ohio State University)

Learning to use MYCIN (GUIDON, Stanford University)

Medical expert (CADAUCEUS)

Serum protein analysis (Helena Laboratories)

Ordering Systems and Marketing

Configures VAX orders (XCON, XSEL, AND XSITE, Digital Equipment Corporation)

Order checking (OCEAN, NCR Corporation)

Order entry checking (Nixdorf)

Promotions of goods (PROMOTER, MDS)

Sales

Guide to selling methods

Pricing of custom products

Sales support

Sales commission and bonus

Scheduling

Airline crew scheduling

Job shop scheduling (Westinghouse)

Optimal airline seating (Northwest Orient Airlines)

Production management system (ISIS)

Scheduling manufacturing orders (ISA)

Teaching

Careers advice

Child abuse identification

Classroom systems

Course selection

Transportation

Airport runway assignment (M.I.T.)

Chemical transport legislation

Shipping charges

Freight transport

Most of the applications to date for expert systems have been diagnostic. This area is ideally suited for expert systems. As the AI industry matures, and the available hardware and software become more sophisticated, a much wider breadth of applicational areas will be seen.

STRUCTURES OF EXPERT SYSTEMS

Part Two is an overview of the various models used to document the thought processes of the expert. It describes the constructs of the knowledge base and the various lines of reasoning (problem-solving strategies) that can be used in the inference engine. Although it is not necessary to completely understand everything presented in Part Two in order to work with expert systems, a basic understanding will give insight to the complexity of "computer modeling" an expert.

Chapter 3 discusses the various models used to represent knowledge in an expert system. Models such as semantic networks, frames, production rules, and predicate calculus are the most widely used representations. Semantic networks are the most general representational form. Their basic construct is easy to understand and apply. However, they can rapidly become very large, inelegant, and complex. Frames are an enhancement over semantic networks in that they provide a natural, useful grouping of relations (in the semantic networks) into units (called frames of reference). Frames provide a more formal partitioning of knowledge, but the grouping can be nebulous. Production rules are the easiest to model the expert with because the expertise is generally described in an "if this occurs, then do this" manner. However, production rules impose a rigid, uniform structure of representation that can make it difficult to sort out the forest from the trees. Predicate calculus is a precise and modular mathematical representation of knowledge and thought—no gray areas of interpretation exist.

Models based on predicate calculus can lead to an exponential explosion of inferences as the data domain grows.

The best representation model is the one that closely mimics the domain organization of the expert for ease of encoding and debugging the expert system. The Dow Jones Industrial Index is modeled in the various data structures to illustrate the similarities and differences between each model. "Representation of knowledge is a combination of data structures and interpretive procedures that, if used in the right way in a program, will lead to 'knowledgeable behavior'" (Barr and Feigenbaum, 1981). The data structure is not the knowledge, but the source of knowledge. The interpretive procedure makes the inferences by "intelligently" analyzing the data structure.

Chapter 4 discusses how different types of problems are represented and subsequently solved. To solve a problem, the inference engine employs reasoning and searching strategies that manipulate the information in the knowledge base according to a predefined strategy. These strategies impose order upon the inference engine in the problem-solving process to deduce logically, infer, or prove why a problem occurred and/or how to solve a problem. The inference engine must also know where to begin solving a problem and be able to resolve any conflicts that might arise during the problem-solving process. For this reason the inference engine is often referred to as the "control strategy" part of an expert system.

The problem is generally described in a state-space or problem reduction representation that the inference engine understands how to solve. State-space representation models all of the attainable states for a given problem, starting with the initial conditions and ending with the goal state, a "state" being a snapshot of conditions at one moment in time. Problem reduction representation breaks the problem down into subproblems until no further subdivision is necessary. Emulating human thought processes is not easy, as computers are algorithmic and human problem-solving is heuristic. Problem-solving emulation is a four-step process. (1) Model the problem into a computer representational model. (2) Define a basic searching technique such as depth-first, breadth-first, or best-first, to explore the defined problem representational model. (3) Define a control strategy or reasoning technique that will direct the search, that is, tell what to do next. Does the search start with the answers and look for reasons why, or does it start with the reasons why and search for the answers? Reasoning techniques are the drivers of the inference engine. (4) Apply additional techniques such as certainty factors, assumptions, or constraints to deal with the anomalies of the real world of unreliable knowledge, incomplete knowledge, a large solution space, varying amounts of detail, or 50/50 guessing.

3
Knowledge Representation Models

Knowledge representation models describe the various architectures used to represent the expert's knowledge in an organized and consistent manner by faithfully imitating the domain of the expert. Although several methodologies currently exist in AI which can be used as data structures for the knowledge base, expert systems are most frequently represented by one of the following five models:

- Semantic networks
- Frames
- Production rules
- Predicate calculus
- Hybrid of the aforementioned

Each knowledge representation model has its advantages and disadvantages. Naturally, the hybrid attempts to incorporate the best of all models without the inherent disadvantages. Microcomputers commonly use production rules, primarily for ease of understanding and implementation. The remaining models, typically more complex, are currently seen more often on minicomputers and mainframes. However, as computer power increases and cost decreases, these models will become more common on microcomputers.

The objective is to select the knowledge representation model that most closely mimics the real-world application. For each particular problem, the expert already has a predefined structure or conceptual model of the domain, even though it may not be explicit. The selection of the knowledge representation model closest to the expert's world lends itself to easier encoding of the knowledge. In addition, debugging and testing the expert system will not be so cumbersome with a knowledge representation model that naturally fits the expert's viewpoint. For this reason, knowledge representation models, and the selection of the inference engine as described in the next chapter, are important considerations when evaluating the application and selecting appropriate expert system software.

SEMANTIC NETWORKS

Semantic networks (also called semantic nets) are the most general representational structure and serve as the basis for other knowledge representations. Semantic networks, alone, are never directly used to model the knowledge. The lack of formal definitive structural rules makes semantic networks very inelegant to use; however, they need to be understood since they are the theoretical underpinnings for other data representational methodologies (e.g., frames, production rules). A semantic network is a collection of objects (commonly referred to as nodes) that are linked together by a relationship. Nodes not only represent objects, but concepts and situations as well, and they are shown graphically by dots, circles, or boxes. Relationships between objects are expressed as arcs or links and are represented graphically by an arrow between the two nodes for which the relationship is intended to be expressed. Semantic nets are identifiable when meaning, contextual meaning, or an implicit or explicit relationship is expressed between two nodes.

As an illustration of semantic nets, Figure 3.1 represents knowledge of the Dow Jones Industrial Index. In the financial world the Dow Jones Industrial Index is a financial market index used for market indication and financial analysis. Its value is calculated from 30 specific industrial stocks and its movement (or trend) is essentially nonpredictable, due to the daily market forces of buying and selling. Notice that the Dow Jones Industrial Index and the Financial Market Index are located in circles representing two concepts. The arc *IS-A*, which connects these two circles, describes the relationship between

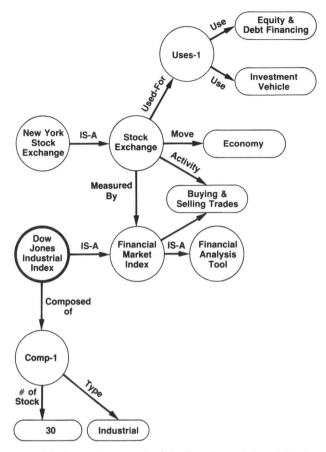

Figure 3.1. Semantic network of the Dow Jones Industrial Index.

the two. This linkage illustrates that the Dow Jones Industrial Index *is a* financial market index. Another example is the relationship between the nodes Financial Market Index and Buying and Selling Trades, expressed by the arc *Measures*; that is, the Financial Market Index *measures* buying and selling trades.

Flexibility is the major *advantage* of semantic networks through the ability to add, modify, or delete new nodes and arcs where appropriate. Suppose we want to add and express the statement "Financial analysis tools are being studied by graduate students." To do this, the arc *Studied By* is drawn between the nodes Financial Analysis Tool and Graduate Students, as illustrated in Figure 3.2. Entire networks can be

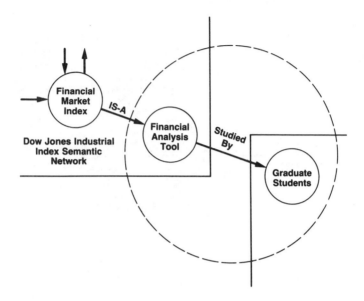

Figure 3.2. Adding to the Dow Jones Industrial Index.

combined by one arc to create a larger network of relationships (Figure 3.3) linking graduate student information with the Dow Jones Industrial Index. If the *School-1* information is not relevant to the understanding of the Dow Jones Industrial Index, the arc does not have to be established.

Another benefit of semantic networks is their ability to inherit relationships from other nodes—more specifically, the ability to reason and make assertions about one node and its relationship with another node where no direct arc exists between the two nodes. This inheritance is illustrated in Figure 3.1 by the statement "The Dow Jones Industrial Index is a financial analysis tool." Inheritance has two forms: (1) inheritance hierarchies as described previously where the relationship can be determined by tracing through several arcs, and (2) property inheritance that describes the representation of knowledge about properties (attributes) of objects (commonly represented by an *IS-A* arc). It is assumed that if an object is a member of a certain class, the object will also inherit all of the attributes of that class. In Figure 3.1 the Dow Jones Industrial Index inherits all of the attributes of a financial market index. If the Financial Market Index had more relationships expressed in the semantic network, the Dow Jones Indus-

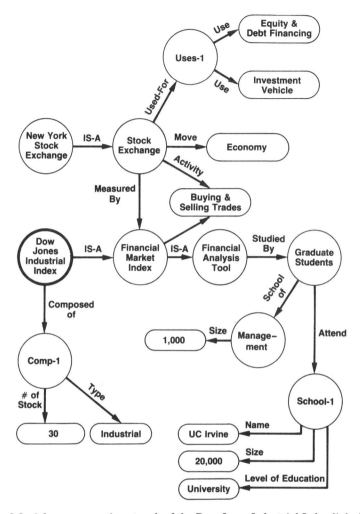

Figure 3.3. A larger semantic network of the Dow Jones Industrial Index linked with graduate students.

trial Index would also inherit a relationship with the other nodes connected to the Financial Market index by virtue of its *IS-A* arc. Also notice that semantic networks have the ability to create sets of arcs from one node, as illustrated by the Comp-1 and Uses-1 nodes in Figure 3.1. Comp-1 is a generic node that ties (1) the number of stocks (in this case 30), and (2) the types of companies (industrial) to identify the composition of the Dow Jones Industrial Index. Another example of a

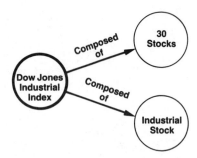

Figure 3.4. Another valid representation of the "composed-of" relationship for the Dow Jones Industrial Index.

generic node is Uses-1, which describes two uses of a stock exchange as (1) an equity or debt financing source, and (2) as an investment vehicle.

One of the *disadvantages* of semantic networks is that there is no formal representation structure. No standard rules exist by which to define unique nodes or relationships. For example, we could have defined the *"Composed Of"* relationship of the Dow Jones Industrial Index in Figure 3.1 with two relationships: (1) the Dow Jones Industrial Index is composed of 30 stocks and (2) the Dow Jones Industrial Index is composed of industrial stocks, as seen in Figure 3.4. Both representations are valid.

Also, it is difficult to distinguish between an individual inheritance and a class of inheritances. For example, in Figure 3.3 suppose the financial analysis tools of financial market indexes are being studied by graduate students. The semantic network in Figure 3.3 leads the analyst to infer that since the Dow Jones Industrial Index is a financial market index being studied by graduate students, then the Dow Jones Industrial Index is also being studied by graduate students. But it is not necessarily the case that graduate students are studying the Dow Jones Industrial Index now or at any time. Semantic networks have the ability to capture the semantics of a situation in a specialized and efficient manner, but only if few exceptions exist. If the problem under review has many exceptions, the number of nodes and arcs needed to describe the various exceptions becomes very large, making the structure of the semantic network inelegant and complex. Figure 3.5 is a small example of how quickly semantic networks can become complex, as we illustrate the beginnings of knowledge representation models.

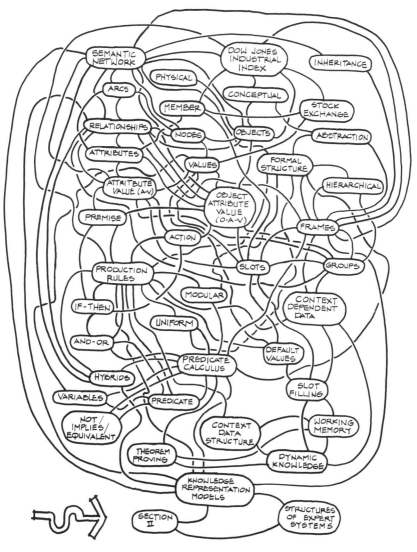

Figure 3.5. A complex semantic network. A small portion of knowledge representation models.

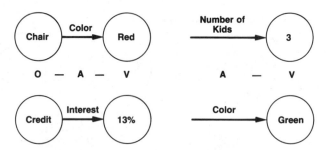

Figure 3.6. O–A–V and A–V representation examples.

Several varieties of semantic networks exist, but one most commonly used in expert systems is the object–attribute–value (O–A–V) triplet, exhibited in Figure 3.6. Objects are considered physical or conceptual entities (e.g., chair or credit loan) and are represented graphically as nodes. Attributes are the general properties or objects (e.g., color or interest rate) and are designated by arcs or links. Values are also represented by nodes and are the specific quantity or description of an attribute for an object (e.g., red or 13%).

The additional structure imposed on a semantic network by the O–A–V triplets makes the net more operational. Triplets allow semantic networks to be organized in tree graph form, allowing a starting point (called a root) for reasoning and gathering information. This is not to say the tree will not become tangled, as Figure 3.5, but at least some direction is given. Relationships are also expressed by attribute–value (A–V) pairs where they represent explicit definitions within a given domain and no inheritance is possible. As discussed in the remainder of this chapter, other representations such as frames and production rules stem from O–A–V or A–V representations.

FRAMES

Frames, as in frames of reference, consist of a collection of slots that contain attributes to describe an object, a class of objects, a situation, an action, or an event. Frames provide a concise, structural representation of useful relations that capture the way an expert typically thinks about the data in the knowledge base. They are an elaboration of semantic networks. In semantic networks, values describing an object can be dispersed randomly throughout the knowledge base.

Frames differ from semantic networks in that these values are grouped together into a single unit called a frame. Consequently, frames can encompass entire situations, complex objects, or a series of events in one unit, versus having to use several O–A–V triplets to describe the same situation (as with semantic nets). Data are organized in the frame representation to direct attention and facilitate recall and inference processes.

Frames represent explicit commonsense knowledge, assumptions, what things to look for, and in what ways to look for them, in a predefined internal representation. This organization facilitates expectation-driven processing: looking for items based on the context one thinks it is in (context of the frame). Frame-based reasoning is based on seeking confirmation of expectations or "filling in the slots." If a frame is not applicable to a given situation, control will move to another frame.

A frame is a partition of knowledge; a slot describes its individual properties. The slot representation is a declarative statement for asserting attributes of a frame. The slot can have default values or subslots, which represent a further breakdown of attributes. Default values declare a constant value to be used for a particular slot during the reasoning process unless contradictory information is introduced.

Slots also allow for procedural attachments. Procedures can be attached to slots to drive the reasoning or problem-solving inference engine for that slot. The procedure is a set of instructions that, when executed, produces consistent results with the facts for a particular slot. Both declarative and procedural representations make up slots. Declarative representations are less efficient, but easier to maintain and understand. Procedural representations are more efficient, but harder to maintain and understand.

An example of the Dow Jones Industrial Index in frame structure is illustrated by the following:

DOW JONES INDUSTRIAL INDEX Frame

Superclass	New York Stock Exchange
Member	Financial market indexes
Use	Market indicator and financial analysis tool

Composition

        Type   Industrial stocks

        Number 30 Companies

Movement   Nonpredictable due to market forces of buying and selling

Measurement If needed, "Use Dow Jones Algorithm" to calculate the Index, Default: 0

This frame describes an object that is a financial market index and used as a financial analysis tool that identifies specific, nonpredictable movements in the stock market. Notice that the composition slot of this frame is broken down further into subslots of type and number of companies. That is, 30 stocks which are classified as industrial are used to define the Dow Jones Industrial Index. The value slot illustrates any default settings and procedural attachments. According to this frame, the value of the Dow Jones Industrial Index will default to zero unless the exact calculative value is needed within a specific contextual environment. If the value is needed in a particular context, the slot will execute the "Use Dow Jones Algorithm" procedure to determine the actual value for that situation.

The next frame is one level of hierarchy above the previous frame and illustrates how the New York Stock Exchange (NYSE) is related to, or different from, members of higher, lower, and similar classes. As in this example, the Dow Jones Industrial Index is one example of a financial analysis tool that is used for investments and for equity and debt financing. This was derived by noting that the Dow Jones Industrial Index is a measurement tool for the NYSE and the NYSE is a superclass of the Dow Jones Industrial Index.

NEW YORK STOCK EXCHANGE Frame

Superclass   Investment vehicles

Member   Stock exchanges

Use   Equity and debt financing source for corporations and the government; also an investment vehicle for individuals and corporations

Composition

      Type   Financial investment instruments

      Number Variable

Movement   The economy

Measurement Financial market indexes

Frames are arranged in a hierarchical manner such that frames can inherit relationships from other frames. Frame inheritance is not easy to visualize. Figure 3.7 is an example of a frame representation hierarchical model. Notice that frames are grouped into levels or classes and that a pseudo-hierarchical structure/relationship exists with each frame, each describing a different contextual situation. The relationship is pseudo-hierarchical because, just like semantic networks, various frames can have relationships. For example, commodities might also use the *Standard & Poor's* 500 as a variable in its calculations to

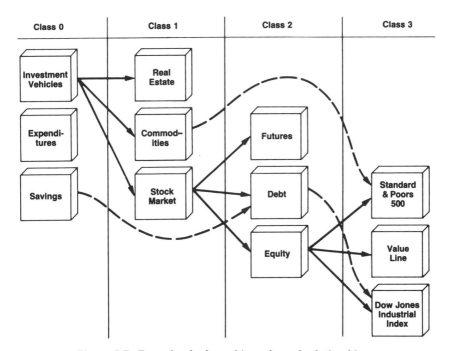

Figure 3.7. Example of a frame hierarchy and relationships.

know what prices to set; otherwise, debt might have a direct relationship with savings capacity in the investment industry.

The primary *advantage* of frame representation is that the more concise and compact the knowledge base, the shorter the amount of time required for searching for specific information. Frames allow for layers of abstraction to separate out low-level details from high-level abstracts.

Frames are best used in

Domains of Context Dependence. Domains which can be represented by a set of processes where one process input is dependent on the outcome(s) of one or more other processes. For example, in a chess match a player's move is dependent upon the prior moves of the match.

Domains Where Representation and Control Are Not Separable. For example, the instructions "turn right, turn left, turn right" without the street name representation would not lead you to your intended destination.

Domains of Concise Unified Data. Domains where the knowledge can be described in a well-defined environment; that is, the tenets of the domain are succinctly defined. Two excellent examples are textbook knowledge in the domains of physics and chemistry, as compared to economics where several tenets exist.

PRODUCTION RULES

Production rules are conditional *If–Then* and *If–Then–Else* descriptions of a given situation or context of a problem. The *If* clause describes an object, situation, or position. If the *If* clause is true, the *Then* clause of the production rule is activated. If the production rule contains an *Else* clause and the *If* clause is false, the *Else* clause of the production rule is activated. The *If* clause is called the premise; the *Then* and *Else* clauses are called the action. It is not necessary to have an *Else* clause. Production rules are of the format

IF [premise(s)] THEN [action(s)] ELSE [action(s)]

A rule is said to be activated when all of the conditions in the premise of a rule are satisfied by the current situation. The production rule is said to be fired (a terminology used in production systems) or executed when the action is performed. The following is a production rule representation that would describe the Dow Jones Industrial Index.

IF   the item is a financial market index, *AND*
          is used for financial analysis, *AND*
          is composed of 30 stocks, *AND*
          these 30 stocks can all be categorized in the industrial industry, *AND*
          its movement is nonpredictable due to the market forces of buying and selling,
THEN the item is the Dow Jones Industrial Index.

Production rules provide a more formal representation structure for O–A–V or A–V semantic networks. The premise(s) and action(s) can be either in O–A–V or A–V form. Table 3.1 takes the production rule representation of the Dow Jones Industrial Index and portrays it using O–A–V triplets.

Notice that the relationships within the premise of a production rule are described by conjunctive *AND*s. There is no inheritance with production rules. Just because a stock is in the industrial industry that does not imply that it is used as an indicator for investment vehicles. Although production rule systems must state all implications, they are

Table 3.1. O–A–V Production Rule Representation of the Dow Jones Industrial Index

	OBJECT	ATTRIBUTE	VALUE
	Item	Financial Market Index	True
	Item	Usage	Financial Analysis Tool
Premise	Item	Number of Stocks	30
	Stock	Category	Industrial
	Item	Movement	Non-predictable
Action	Item	Dow Jones Industrial Index	True

not as difficult to use as are semantic network, frame, and predicate calculus models.

Several different production systems, also known as rule-based systems, exist. Their general structure consists of three parts:

1. A rule base composed of a set of production rules
2. A context data structure
3. An inference engine which controls the system's activity

Since production rules have already been discussed, we will proceed directly to the second part of a rule-based system. The context data structure describes a specific problem area in the knowledge base. Each context contains information regarding the specific problem only. During a consultation session with the expert system, the inference engine instantiates (or calls) all relevant contexts to the system. More than one context is usually used to solve a problem. Figure 3.8 is an illustration of an automotive context tree.

The inference engine is responsible for controlling the activity of the production system through its operative cycle of matching, conflict resolution, and action. Matching is testing the conditions of various production rules against the current context environment to find those rules that can be activated. Conflict resolution invokes an ordering strategy to resolve which production rule to execute first in case several production rules have been activated. Action is the execution of the production rule, and the cycle repeats itself.

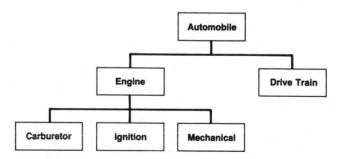

Figure 3.8. An example of an automotive context tree. (Courtesy of Texas Instrument PC manual.)

Rule-based systems have several *advantages*:

1. *Modular.* Individual production rules can be added, deleted, or changed independently of their relationship to other rules. This is because rules communicate solely through the context data structure.
2. *Uniform.* An homogeneous representation of knowledge is imposed to allow for ease of understanding by another person.
3. *Natural.* Production rules are structured similarly to the way people think about solving a problem. Given a situation, production rules best express "what to do next" statements. They also most frequently replicate the reasoning statements used in human problem-solving tasks.

Rule-based systems have two primary *disadvantages*:

1. *Rigid.* Uniformity can introduce a rigid structure that makes it difficult to follow the flow of control in problem solving. Rule-based systems do not reason at multiple levels. There is no subroutine hierarchy, making it difficult to conceptually point out high-level abstraction and low-level detail.
2. *Inefficient.* Production rules introduce inefficiency in execution. Every action must go through the match-action cycle in the context data structure, making it difficult to efficiently execute predetermined situational sequences or abstract the reasoning sequence to take larger steps (match–action cycles).

According to Barr and Feigenbaum (1981), production rules are best used in

Domains of Diffused Knowledge. These are domains consisting of many facts, such as clinical medicine.

Domains Where Representations and Control Are Separable. These are domains of knowledge that are easily separated from the manner in which they are used, such as biological classification taxonomy.

Domains of Independent Actions. These are domains whose processes are represented as a set of independent actions, such as a medical patient monitory system.

PREDICATE CALCULUS

Predicate calculus, or logic programming, relies on the truth and rules of inferences, such as "modus ponens," to represent symbols and their relationships to each other. For example, *If A, Then B*, and *A exists*, allow us to conclude *B*. This provides a simple way of determining the truth or falsity of a statement. Predicate calculus is actually an extension of propositional logic. It can be used not only to determine the truth or falsity of a statement, but also represent statements about specific objects or individuals.

Logic is one of the oldest formal mathematical and philosophical representation models of knowledge and thought. It is also one of the most developed problem-solving paradigms with a complete and concise vocabulary and syntax. The form of logic most often used is first-order predicate logic, which is an extension of predicate calculus.

First-order predicate logic works with variables, predicates, sentential connectives, qualifiers, and functions. Variables are placeholders to represent objects, things, and statements in question. Predicates describe a relationship or make a statement about the variable under consideration. Predicates can be thought of as verbs and can be applied to any number of arguments (variables). For example, *IS-A* uses one argument and *IS-LESS-THAN* uses two arguments. Sentential connectives are used to make complex sentences. The five most commonly used sentential connectives are

and	$\wedge$ or &
or	$\vee$
not	$\neg$
implies	$\rightarrow$ or $\supset$
equivalent	$\equiv$

Sentential connectives add more complexity because the truth or falsity of a complex statement is a breakdown of its individual statements analyzed by rules stored in a truth table (summarized in Table 3.2). Qualifiers work with variables in *ALL* objects and must be represented by the variable or *THERE EXIST* with at least one object which the variable can represent. The notion of a function is similar to that of a predicate, except that a function returns objects that are

Table 3.2. Truth Tables for Predicate Logic

x	y	x∧y	x∨y	x→y	¬x	x≡y
T	T	T	T	T	F	T
T	F	F	T	F	F	F
F	T	F	T	T	T	F
F	F	F	F	T	T	T

Example: x ≡ 3 is a number = T

y ≡ 4 is a car   = F

x∧y = F   x∨y = T

related to their arguments. For example, *Father-Of* (*X*,*Y*) will return a name, not a true/false value. The following illustrates how predicate calculus would represent the Dow Jones Industrial Index:

IS-A(X,DJII) ≡ *Composition Number* (*X*, 30 stocks) ∧

Composition Type (*X*, Industrial) ∧

Movement (*X*, Market forces) ∧

Used-As (*X*, Market indicator) ∨

Used-As (*X*, Financial analysis tool) ∧

Member-Of (*X*, Financial market index) ∧

Value (*X*, Dow Jones algorithm)

This can be interpreted to mean: there exists an object *X* that can be called the Dow Jones Industrial Index if, and only if, *X* is composed of 30 stocks of industrial type; its movement is due to market forces; *X* is used as a financial analysis tool; *X* is a member of the financial market indexes group; and *X*'s value can be calculated using the Dow Jones algorithm. Notice that *X* is a variable. *Value* is called a function because it returns an object (a numerical number) to represent the value. The others are predicates because they all return true or false to represent the value.

Predicate calculus has two major *advantages*:

1. *Preciseness.* Logic is a precise, standard method of determining the meaning of an expression. There is no gray area for interpretation.

2. *Modularity.* Statements can be added, deleted, or modified without having to consider the impact on the other statements, similarly to the modularity of production rules. Statements can be made without having to worry about the context in which they will be used.

The primary *disadvantage* of predicate calculus is that as the number of facts in the knowledge base increases, the number of ways to combine the facts to make inferences explodes exponentially. Reasoning with predicate calculus is done by using rules of inference, proof by refutation, or resolution theorem proving. Unfortunately, the resolution method of theorem proving is too indiscriminate, and the search process cannot be sufficiently constrained. The problem may be easily represented in predicate calculus form, but the problem-solving process (theorem proving) may become opaque and obscure. Reasoning using rules of inference and proof by refutation entails the solving of the problem by proving that the goal state is reachable from the initial state. The proof is the series of steps connecting the goal state to the initial state. If the goal state can be reached, then the problem cannot be refuted and is therefore solvable. Predicate calculus is best used in domains of concise unified theories such as physics and chemistry.

HYBRIDS

Since each representation model has its own limitations or a lack of functionality that other representation models do offer, a combination of the models is commonly used. The knowledge is commonly represented by frames and production rules, with the logic of predicate calculus imbedded to help express relationships. Hybrid usages are illustrated in the development tools KEE, SRL +, and ART.

In summary, Table 3.3 illustrates the differences between the various knowledge representation models, depending on the application characteristics and the areas of its domain, control strategy, and data structure.

WORKING MEMORY

Working memory is only invoked when the expert system is in operation. It is considered part of the knowledge base because it holds the

Table 3.3. Knowledge Representation Model Characteristics

MODEL	DOMAIN	DATA	DATA & CONTROL STRATEGY	STRUCTURE
Semantic Net	Context Dependent	General	Mixed	Hierarchical
Frame	Context Dependent	Unified, Concise	Mixed	Hierarchical
Rule	Context Independent	Diffused	Separable	Uniform
Predicate Calculus	Context Independent	Unified, Concise	Separable	Uniform

instances or dynamics of knowledge. Knowledge that is static, unchanging, factual, or definitive is represented in the knowledge base. Knowledge that is dynamic and changes from case to case (from each working session with the expert system) will be stored in working memory.

The University of California at Irvine is the name associated with *School-1* in Figure 3.3, representing an O–A–V triplet of *School-1*(object)–*Name*(attribute)–*UC IRVINE*(value). UC Irvine is an example of dynamic knowledge such that under another scenario, the graduate student may be attending Harvard. If the school name is Harvard, the O–A–V triplet changes to *School-1*(object)–*Name*(attribute)–*Harvard*(value). Working memory is the area where dynamic information is kept to fulfill values of various attributes relative to a particular session. During each session, the acquisition (or calling) of values from a particular context is called instantiation.

Each knowledge representation model uses working memory in its own fashion. Frame instantiation in working memory is called slot filling. In production systems, working memory is the context data structure. Predicate calculus uses working memory for theorem proving or proof by refutation.

4
Problem Representation and Problem-Solving Strategies

Three components are needed for a problem-solving system to work. The first component is the database to house the basic knowledge and data. The second component comprises the operators or rules that manipulate the database, commonly known as the knowledge base. These rules or operators are defined by the knowledge representation model, as discussed in the previous chapter, and include frames, production rules, semantic networks, and predicate calculus. The third component of a problem-solving system (to be discussed in this chapter) is the inference engine and control strategy of deciding what rules to apply next and where to apply them.

The inference engine must have some way of traversing, searching, solving, or reasoning through the knowledge base to logically deduce, infer, or prove why a problem occurred. It must know where to start solving a problem and be able to resolve any conflicts that might arise during the problem-solving process. The technique used by the computer to reason or search for an answer will depend on the type of application and the knowledge representation model. In essence, the inference engine attempts to emulate the way human experts would approach the same class of problems. For example, deciding which computer hardware configuration to purchase for home use is an example of a *forward reasoning* technique. Here, a salesperson will start at the beginning and ask a series of questions to determine the level of utilization for each software package (e.g., spreadsheet, word processing, games, financials).

Based on these responses, the salesperson will then recommend a personal computer configuration best suited to the customer's needs. In contrast, *backward reasoning* is a process of determining plausible causes of a problem and selecting the cause most likely to have led to the problem. Medicine is an ideal example of backward reasoning. "Why is this patient running a fever of 104°?" The physician evaluates the symptoms to then determine the cause of the fever.

The first section of this chapter discusses how different types of problems are represented and how computers represent a problem in a two-dimensional plane. The second section covers problem solving. It discusses the various search techniques used to find the answers. The last section covers reasoning, that is, the various strategies used to make inferences or assist with problem solving.

PROBLEM REPRESENTATION

In describing the problem representation used by expert systems, two models are most prevalent: state-space representation and problem reduction representation.

State-Space Representation

State-space representation involves

1. *States.* These are snapshots of varying conditions in an environment at one moment in time. All states are unique.
2. *Operators.* These act on a state to transform it into another state.

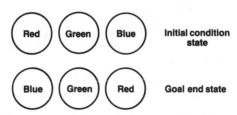

Figure 4.1. State-space representation of the initial state and goal end state for the red, green, and blue balls.

A state-space represents the set of all attainable states for a given problem. For example, in Figure 4.1 three balls are on a table in the order red, green, and blue from left to right. The goal is to reverse the order such that it becomes blue, green, and red. The only operator available is the ability to switch two adjacent balls simultaneously. One possible solution path is

1. First, execute the operator and switch the red and green balls. This results in a new state of green, red, and blue.

2. Next, switch the red and blue balls. Now the order is green, blue, and red.

3. The last step is to switch the green and blue balls to reach the goal state order of blue, green, and red.

Figure 4.2 illustrates the state-space representation for this problem. Notice that there is another path which would also arrive at the desired goal. State-space representation models identify all the alternatives to a problem to assure thorough analysis. They also can grow rapidly. Consider the addition of a yellow ball to the original problem. Four balls are now on a table in the order red, green, blue, and yellow from left to right. The end goal is to reverse the balls such that the order is yellow, blue, green and red from left to right. Applying the same operator rule, several paths exist to reach the goal state, as illustrated in Figure 4.3. The size of the state space has also increased fourfold in this example.

In more abstract terms, a state-space representation is a triplet of I–O–G. I is the set of one or more initial states. O is the set of operators

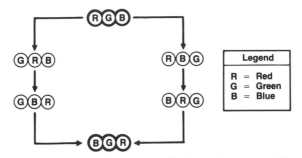

Figure 4.2. State-space solution space for the red, green, and blue balls.

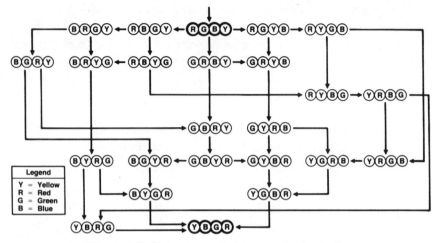

Figure 4.3. State-space solution space for four balls.

that can be used to initiate movement from one state to the next. G is the set of goal states. A solution path is the finite sequence of operator steps O applied to get from set I to set G. In these examples there are one initial state, one goal state, and one operator (switching two adjacent balls). A state space can also be easily represented as a directed graph, as illustrated in Figures 4.2 and 4.3. State-space representation is a common representation form used in project management to determine minimal cost, minimal distance, or critical paths in a project.

Problem Reduction Representation

Problem reduction representation starts with a problem statement. From there the statement is broken apart into subproblems. Repeatedly, the subproblems are broken down until a solution is immediate, in other words, until no further subdivision is necessary. The concept is simple: reduce the problem down to workable subproblems. Problem reduction representation consists of

1. The initial problem statement
2. A set of operators that transform the problem into a set of subproblems
3. Primitive problem statements that are solvable immediately (this is the lowest level of the problem)

For example, imagine the initial problem statement "Investment in a financial security." How does one invest in a security? This problem can be divided into three subproblems: (1) establish an account with a broker, (2) determine the type of security order, and (3) determine the type of security position. Subproblem (1), establishing an account with a broker, can be divided into two or more subproblems, such as: (a) selecting a broker, and (b) determining the type of brokerage account to open. The type of brokerage account can be a cash account or a margin account. Subproblem (2) can be broken down into either (a) buying the security long, or (b) selling the security short. Subproblems (a) and (b) can be broken down further into sub-subproblems of (i) time, and (ii) price limits for the order. Divisions of sub-subproblem (ii) include placing a market price order, limit price order, stop price order, or discretionary price order. Figure 4.4 illustrates the full problem reduction representation of the "Invest in a financial security" statement.

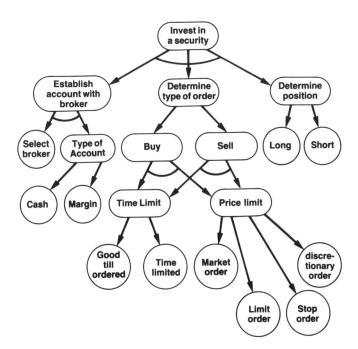

Figure 4.4. Problem reduction representation of the "Invest in a financial security" statement.

The best illustrations of problem reduction representations are *AND/OR* graphs with some additional definitions:

1. Primitive problem statements are considered terminal nodes.
2. Each node is a set or a single problem statement.
3. A node with several branches and a connecting arc between the branches is an *AND* branch, and all nodes must be solvable. An *AND* node is a node which is attached to an *AND* branch.
4. A node with several branches and no connecting arc between each branch is an *OR* branch (where the problem is solved by any branch node). An *OR* node is a node which is attached to an *OR* branch.
5. Nodes can be shared.

A node is considered solvable if it is terminal, if all *AND* nodes are solvable, or if one *OR* node is solvable. Figure 4.5 illustrates an *AND/OR* tree. Node *Z* is the initial problem statement. Nodes *E,K,L,G,H,I,M*, and *N* are primitive problems or terminal nodes. Nodes *B* and *F* are *AND* nodes. Nodes *A* and *J* are *OR* nodes. Review Figure 4.4 again. Notice the various *AND/OR* nodes used to express the problem.

State-space representations and problem reduction representations are interchangeable. Problems usually fit better into one representa-

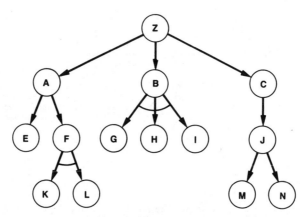

Figure 4.5. AND/OR tree representation.

tion model than the other. The perception of the problem remains the
same in either case.

PROBLEM SOLVING

Once the problem is described in a representation model, the computer
needs a strategy (using the constructs of the model) to solve the problem. Searching is the key to problem solving. It is by far the most
widely used problem solving technique. The trick is to match the technique with the application type. Searching involves choosing a path
through the knowledge base to find a solution. If the path is unsuccessful, alternative paths are tried in search of a solution.

The method of solving the problem is similar to that of solving a
maze: an expert starts with a given situation and tests alternatives
until a solution to the problem is found. In computer terms, alternatives are defined as paths or a series of steps/actions taken to traverse
through the domain (i.e., the knowledge base). Examples of search
techniques used in expert systems are depth first, breadth first, best
first, hill climbing, and branch and bound.

Table 4.1. The Three Layers of Problem Solving

Level One: Search Models

Blind Searches	Heuristic Searches
Exhaustive	Hill Climbing
Breath-first	Best-first
Depth-first	Branch-and-bound
	A*
	Generate-and-test

Level Two: Control Strategies

Forward Reasoning
Backward Reasoning
Bi-directional
Means-end Analysis
Least-Commitment Principle

Level Three: Additional Reasoning Strategies

Abstraction
Assumptions
Certainty Factors
Constraints
Disjunctive Facts
Guessing

The goal in problem solving is to find the best search technique which locates a solution path efficiently and effectively by limiting the number of data items (paths) examined. Problem solving can be divided into three layers:

1. *General Search Methods.* These are the foundation for any problem-solving technique.
2. *Control Strategies.* These guide the direction and execution of the search, that is, "reason."
3. *Additional Reasoning Techniques.* These assist with modeling and searching for the solution path.

Following is a discussion of these layers, as listed in Table 4.1.

Level 1: General Search Methods

Searches can be divided into two categories: blind searches and heuristic searches. Blind searches are referred to as "weak" searches, weak in the sense that they employ no intelligent decision making in the search. Blind searches are situations where the solution path is arbitrary; that is, no contextual or domain-specific information is needed to reach the goal. Blind searches can be very costly if a large state space has to be explored. Exhaustive, breadth-first and depth-first searches are examples of blind searches.

Heuristic searches are referred to as "strong" searches. Heuristic searches involve the analysis of domain-specific information which is not built into the state-space or operator definitions and can often reduce the size of the state space for searching. Contextual information is used to (1) decide which path (node) to search next, (2) determine what successor(s) to generate next, instead of looking at all of them, and/or (3) prune the state space such that some paths will be marked *NOT* to search due to some heuristic criterion which states that these paths will not satisfy the goal. Best-first, branch-and-bound, hill-climbing, A*, and generate-and-test are examples of heuristic searches. Sometimes the heuristic rules may not be effective enough to assist in reducing the state-space; in this case, the search becomes a blind search.

Blind Searches

Exhaustive

This is a search technique where every possible path through a decision tree or network is analyzed; it is time consuming and costly. This method may be unrealistic or impossible for some problems, due primarily to their size. However, this technique may be the appropriate method in applications where exactness is required and time is not of the essence.

Breadth-First

Breadth-first searching involves examining the first step (state) in all paths available from that state. If the answer has not been found, the next step of all paths available—derived from the first step of all paths—will then be explored. The available paths can be likened to a tree with branches; from each branch stems more branches, and so on. Figure 4.6 illustrates a breadth-first search. In this example, the initial

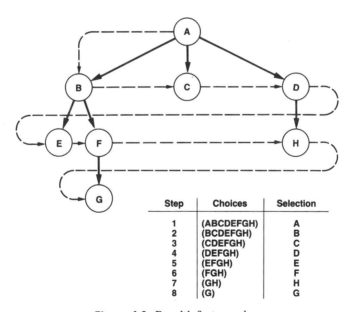

Step	Choices	Selection
1	(ABCDEFGH)	A
2	(BCDEFGH)	B
3	(CDEFGH)	C
4	(DEFGH)	D
5	(EFGH)	E
6	(FGH)	F
7	(GH)	H
8	(G)	G

Figure 4.6. Breadth-first search.

node is *A* and the goal node is *G*. A terminal node is not necessarily a goal node; it could be a dead-end node. Each node is evaluated for its contextual meaning. Breadth-first searches are good when the number of paths emanating from one node is not too large. However, they may be inappropriate and wasteful when all paths lead to the destination node at more or less the same depth.

Depth-First

A depth-first search is initiated downward along a given path until an answer is found or a dead end is reached. If a dead end is reached, the search will backtrack to the first alternative branch and try it. Iteratively, if a path fails, it will backtrack to the first alternative path and repeat the procedure. Depth-first is often used in conjunction with a backward-chaining reasoning strategy. Figure 4.7 is an illustration of a depth-first search. The initial node is *A*, and the goal node is *H*. Depth-first is best used when short paths exist and there are no lengthy subbranches.

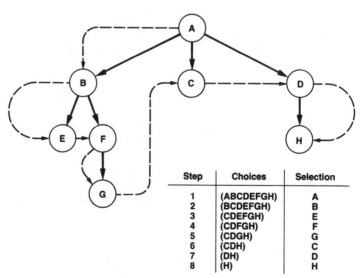

Step	Choices	Selection
1	(ABCDEFGH)	A
2	(BCDEFGH)	B
3	(CDEFGH)	E
4	(CDFGH)	F
5	(CDGH)	G
6	(CDH)	C
7	(DH)	D
8	(H)	H

Figure 4.7. Depth-first search.

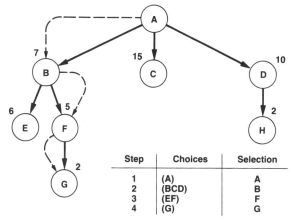

Step	Choices	Selection
1	(A)	A
2	(BCD)	B
3	(EF)	F
4	(G)	G

Figure 4.8. Hill-climbing search. The number is the distance to the goal.

Heuristic Searches

Hill-Climbing

Hill-climbing is similar to the blind search of depth-first, but the path selection is not arbitrarily sequential: it is based on an estimate of the closeness to the goal. If a particular search were unsuccessful, a path that was declined earlier would be reevaluated using additional rules to determine a goal's proximity before trying a new path not yet evaluated. Hill-climbing, illustrated in Figure 4.8, is an excellent choice when an intrinsic measuring tool can be applied to determine the distance from the goal. The initial node is *A*, and the goal node is *G*.

Best-First

In best-first searching an heuristic function is applied to determine which next state will be most likely to lead to a solution. The selection of the next state is the next best open node, no matter where it is located on the tree. "Best-first search works like a team of cooperating mountaineers seeking out the highest point in a mountain range: they maintain radio contact, move the highest subteam forward at all times, and divide subteams into subteams at path junctions" (Winston, 1979, p. 99). A best-first search is illustrated in Figure 4.9. The initial node is *A*, and the goal node is *H*. To determine the next best step, the entire

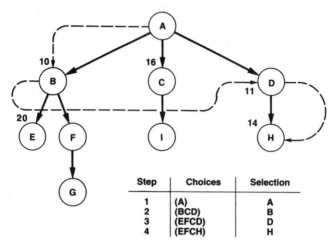

Step	Choices	Selection
1	(A)	A
2	(BCD)	B
3	(EFCD)	D
4	(EFCH)	H

Figure 4.9. Best-first search. The number is the distance from the node to the goal.

state space needs to be sorted based on some heuristic evaluation function.

Branch-and-Bound

In this search, at each step an evaluation is made of the shortest path of all uncompleted paths. Upon successful evaluation the shortest path is then extended to the next level, thereby generating more paths. The cycle repeats itself and all paths are reevaluated. Searching is complete when the shortest incomplete path is longer than the shortest completed path. The branch-and-bound technique requires an ordered state-space for searching. The search is greatly enhanced if the sorting order takes into consideration the distance already traveled and the distance remaining to the goal.

Figure 4.10 is an example of the branch-and-bound search. The initial node is *A*, and the goal node is *H*. The optimal path for Figure 4.10 is *A–D–H*. The number next to the node is the cumulative distance to the goal. The search stops when all incomplete paths are longer than the completed path. In Step 3, node *B* was selected to expand to make sure completed path *C* has the shortest distance. In Step 4, we discover that the distance is higher with *E* and *F*, so we do not have to expand anymore, but node *D* still needs to be investigated. Node *E* is a completed path, but its distance is still greater than *C*'s. In Step 5 node *H*

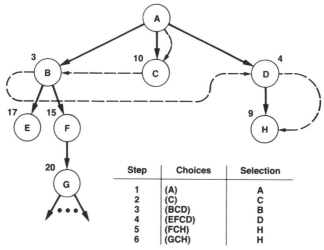

Step	Choices	Selection
1	(A)	A
2	(C)	C
3	(BCD)	B
4	(EFCD)	D
5	(FCH)	H
6	(GCH)	H

Figure 4.10 Branch-and bound search.

creates a completed path whose distance is less than completed path C. However, F is expanded so that all incomplete paths are longer. In Step 6, we stop because all incomplete paths have been expanded longer than the completed path $A-D-H$.

A* Algorithm

In this search technique an estimation of the closeness to the goal is added to each path before continuing to use the branch-and-bound methodology. The close approximation function replaces the shortest path evaluation. Using the distance accumulated so far and estimating future distances, A* will also prune branches that are too expensive to traverse to reach the goal state.

Generate-and-Test

Generate-and-test, also called hypothesize-and-test, is another method to search through the domain. The procedure is explained in the following steps:

1. Add a specification criterion (e.g., a known symptom).

2. Try a path that satisfies the specification (test the hypothesis).

3. Determine whether or not the path is plausible; "prune" that

path if it is not plausible—that is, do not follow that particular path of solutions. This will "prune" an entire level of possible solutions.

4. Move to the next path.
5. When complete, check to see if all specifications have been mentioned. If not, add the next specification criterion and reiterate the above steps by returning to Step 1. If all specifications (hypotheses) have been resolved, then the process is complete.

Generate-and-test is a weak method of reasoning when pruning rules do not reduce the solution space early on, requiring that virtually all possible solutions be evaluated. It can be iterative, tedious, and inefficient. But tremendous speed enhancements can be gained if the pruning rules are powerful enough to eliminate numerous paths through the domain at an early stage, making this method a simple straightforward searching technique.

When a specification criterion is added, the inference engine determines the smallest number of causes, represented by descriptions in the knowledge base, that explain all known manifestations of the application. The following is an example of the generate-and-test (hypothesize-and-test) methodology used in the KES development tool by Software Architecture & Engineering, Inc.

Cause of Problem:
    Water Main Turned Off or Pipes Frozen
        [Description: Nature of Problem = No Water Supply],
    Air Chamber Failure
        [Description: Nature of Problem = Noise]
            [Location = Pipe;
            Noise Type = Banging;
            Occurrence = Immediately After Water is Turned Off].

Level 2: Control Strategies

Search Strategies

Once the search method is selected, different situations require different reasoning strategies (control strategies) for deciding what to do

Table 4.2. Control Strategies That Are Commonly Applied in Various Application Areas

CONTROL STRATEGY	APPLICATION
Forward Chaining	1. Forecasting, projecting 2. Predicting 3. Designing 4. Planning
Backward Chaining	1. Diagnostic 2. Monitoring 3. Controlling
Means-End	1. Synthesizing 2. Normative Forecasting
Least-Commitment	1. Applications with Non-effective pruning rules 2. Applications with Large, factorable solution space

next—that is, deciding which operation to apply and where to apply it (Table 4.2).

Forward Chaining

The application of operators in a data-driven search starts with the initial given conditions and searches forward through the knowledge base towards a solution. This search is commonly known as forward-chaining, bottom-up processing, or antecedent reasoning; it is best used in "what-if" scenarios. The system begins with a fact and proceeds to search for a rule whose premise is verified by that fact. The conclusion is then added to working memory in pursuit of the solution. Figures 4.6 and 4.7 are illustrations of forward chaining.

Backward Chaining

The antithesis of the forward-chaining strategy is backward chaining. Backward chaining is a goal-directed search that starts at the end solution (goal state) and works backward towards the initial conditions. This is also known as top-down processing or consequent reasoning. The task is to see whether the necessary and sufficient antecedents that satisfy the goal exist in the domain by applying inverse operations. The process begins with a goal-state hypothesis. Next the system seeks to find a rule whose premise supports the hypothesis and then attempts to verify the premise by searching the knowledge base for a relevant fact. If no fact is found, the system searches for a rule that can be used to infer the fact. This process of searching and verifying the supporting facts continues until the original hypothesis is verified or disproved. Using Figure 4.6, a backward-chaining technique (breadth-first) would examine the nodes in the following order: *G,H,F,E,D,C,B,A.*

Bidirectional

Bidirectional reasoning involves going both forward and backward through the domain during a session. To begin a session, the inference engine begins at one end and proceeds either forward or backward. As the inference engine traverses through the knowledge base, at each decision node it has the choice of proceeding forward or backward, hence the term "bidirectional." The decision of whether to proceed forward or backward is made using an heuristic algorithm.

Means-End

Means-end analysis is actually the simultaneous application of forward and backward chaining. The inference engine proceeds from both ends and simultaneously performs forward and backward chaining until the paths meet to form a continuous trail from the initial state to the goal state. Means-end is an iterative process of subdividing the difference between the goal state and the current state until the difference is eliminated. At the conclusion of the iteration process a path has been formed between the initial state and the goal state, identifying the means by which to traverse the knowledge base. It is important to note that the selected operator to reduce the differences may not be applicable to the situation. Rather than select another operator, means-end will change the current object into an appropriate input for the selected operator. The result of means end is a recursive, goal-directed program that records its search history in an *AND/OR* graph.

Least Commitment

A different approach to solving a problem is to assume that no decision should be made until there is enough information. This requires the ability to know when there is enough information to make a decision, when to suspend solving a problem because not enough information is available, and when to combine the results and information from two different problems to solve an original problem. A "deadlock" will exist if all partially solved problems are waiting for more information. In this case, the expert system must make a guess. Sometimes the guess will allow the expert system to continue towards a solution; other times the guess will lead to conflict where a solution can never be reached. The least-commitment principle is of no assistance when there are many options and no compelling reasons for choices (e.g., equal probability weighting on all paths).

Level 3: Additional Reasoning Techniques

The key to an expert system and its ability to intelligently solve problems is the specificity of the knowledge domain. Problems in the real world are not necessarily easy to solve using general search methods. Most models are constructed under the assumption that the facts and relationships in the knowledge base are few, reliable, and static. Various techniques of assumptions, disjunctive facts, certainty factors, constraints, abstraction, fuzzy logic, blackboarding, and guessing assist in dealing with these anomalies of the real world and focus in on the problem.

When the knowledge base is reliable and static, **monotonic reasoning** is a straightforward, repetitive procedural technique. Used in conventional programming, monotonic reasoning simply states that once a fact is concluded (derived, calculated, defined) with a given set of inputs, that fact will not change for the duration of the program run. In other words, data input are consistent with data output. For example, when calculating a mortgage loan payment using a 13% interest rate, the interest rate does not change to 9% midway through the calculation.

Stating that an expert follows **nonmonotonic** reasoning simply implies that the expert makes and retracts assumptions throughout the session. The clarity and accuracy of the assumptions are key to the expert system because the assumptions will cut down on the number of initial solution paths. Unless proven otherwise, the expert system assumes all assumptions to be true (default values). During the search for a solution, if a contradiction occurs in an assumption, the expert system reasons that the assumption may no longer be valid, and additional solution paths will have to be traversed.

Also built into the system are certainty factors, disjunctive facts, and constraints. These are bits of information that aid in the efficiency of the search. Some solution paths may have a **certainty factor** associated with them. For example, past experience has shown that when a gas stove burner will not light, 90% of the time the pilot light has burned out. Thus, if the problem states that the gas stove burner did not light, the expert system will recommend that the user check the pilot light.

Certainty factors often fall into one of the following three categories:

1. *Certainty.* The proposition statement may be either true (a value of 1) or false (a value of 0). A value of zero will automatically halt the continuance of solving the problem along this solution path and will look for a different path.

2. *Confidence.* The proposition may range from -1 to $+1$. These factors do not imply absolute truth or falseness, but rather imply the strength or weakness of the proposition. A zero implies no tendency toward true or false, but maintains neutrality. A value of 1 would be the same as an absolute truth; a value of -1 would be an absolute falseness.

3. *Probability.* The proposition may have a probability of occurrence that ranges from 0 to 100. A value of 100 implies the maximum probability that the proposition will be true or occur. A value of 75 may imply a 75% chance of the proposition occurring and a 25% chance of it not occurring.

Disjunctive facts are relationships that seem to have no relationship, but are related in some way. The incorporation of these facts into the knowledge base can greatly reduce the search time by allowing the search to automatically jump from one state space to another state space that is not normally connected. These "personal" relationships, known to the expert, are not necessarily associated with general thinking.

Constraints are relationships that qualify or limit the number of plausible state spaces. Constraints may limit the number of paths that need to be traversed; they can also be relaxed to widen the search if no solution is found.

Another technique used to assist in the efficiency of the search is **abstraction.** The goal of the abstraction technique is to quickly and efficiently find a solution path. The computer should not get lost examining the details, but should abstract the information to a higher level to see if it is relevant. This abstraction can be done through forward or backward chaining. For example, to plan a trip from Los Angeles to San Francisco, the first phase is to look at the main highways that exist between the two cities. This abstraction from city-to-city detail (there is no need to examine every California city's street map) to major highways leads to finding a solution more quickly by reducing the number of alternative search paths. Although the knowledge base may also contain the street maps of all cities in the United States, as well as highways, the expert will abstract only to the level needed to solve the problem (i.e., within a state). In this example there is no need to abstract to all of the highways in the United States in order to drive from Los Angeles to San Francisco.

The reasoning technique to be used by the expert system depends on the domain. If the domain/knowledge base is small with relatively static data and reliable knowledge, then monotonic reasoning is appropriate and an exhaustive search is feasible. If the data become unreliable or incomplete, certainty factors must be added to the data structure to positively or negatively confirm a hypothesis. **Fuzzy logic** (see Glossary) can also be applied so that a statement can be interpreted by a set of probability values.

A large, factorable solution space can use the generate-and-test reasoning method, but the question of diminishing returns exists, depending on the pruning rules and how effective the method is for early pruning so that the entire database need not be traversed.

If no pruning rules can be applied for early pruning, the abstraction and ordering should be considered for large databases. The expert system will start at an initial condition, go through the abstracted paths, work through the details, and hopefully find a solution without backtracking. The difficulty lies in ensuring that no path is taken before all of the required information is available for deciding whether or not the path leads toward a solution.

If the database cannot be abstracted in fixed hierarchical sets and the number of details per abstraction level varies, the best approach toward a solution is top-down refinement. Abstraction for each problem is composed to fit the structure of the problem. A critical value is assigned to indicate the level of detail associated with the abstraction. The search starts from the most abstract knowledge and works toward the specific knowledge using a fixed partial ordering. The problem with top-down refinement is the lack of feedback about whether or not the expert system is close to a solution.

A different and extremely powerful problem-solving technique is called **blackboarding**. Blackboarding began during the development of the HEARSAY-II speech understanding system in the 1970s and is a highly specialized application of opportunistic reasoning. To backtrack, all of the previously mentioned techniques reason to solve a problem proceeding either forward (from the initial state to the goal state) or backward (from the goal state to the initial state) throughout the knowledge base. Opportunistic reasoning is a hybrid of the two, where pieces of knowledge are applied either backward or forward at the most "opportune" time.

In blackboarding, the knowledge required to solve a problem is segmented into separate and independent knowledge bases. At any given time the problem-solving knowledge is maintained in a global knowledge base called the blackboard. Knowledge in the independent knowledge bases effects changes in the blackboard knowledge. The independent knowledge bases communicate and effect changes in the blackboard opportunistically.

Here is a simple example of blackboarding. Consider the task of constructing a personal computer from scratch. Imagine a group of technicians in a room, each possessing one or more pieces of electronic equipment. The sum of these pieces equals the components of a completed personal computer. Each of the technicians is analogous to an independent knowledge base mentioned earlier. To begin the blackboarding process, volunteers put their most "promising" pieces on the table (from here on, it will be called the blackboard). Then each technician will analyze his piece(s) to see if any of them fit into the blackboard. With each piece contributed, new information about the status of the personal computer is available to each technician. This process continues until the construction of the personal computer is complete—in other words, until the goal state is reached. There is no exact construction procedure, only a general one which is imposed by the initiation of the technicians.

What makes blackboarding so powerful is that no communication is necessary between the independent knowledge bases; information is transferred between the blackboard and each individual knowledge base. Each knowledge base is self-activating—knowing and acting only when its piece(s) will contribute to the solution. To further enhance the power of blackboarding, the blackboard can be segmented into partitions of domain knowledge. This allows the independent knowledge bases to simultaneously communicate with different partitions of the blackboard. This enables a problem to be solved more quickly, especially when numerous independent tasks and/or domains of knowledge exist.

When the expert system runs out of problem-solving techniques, it takes a guess. Usually, a guess, also known as plausible reasoning, is made to cope with incomplete knowledge, or when solutions are plentiful and any path will do, or when trying to limit the scope of the

Table 4.3. Problem-Solving Techniques Used with Various Types of Knowledge Bases

TECHNIQUE	APPLICATION
Exhaustive Search	1. Knowledge base is static. 2. Reliable knowledge.
Certainty Factor	1. Unreliable knowledge.
Fuzzy Logic	1. Unclear knowledge.
Generate-and-Test	1. Large, factorable solution space.
Abstraction	1. Large, factorable solution space. 2. Non-effective pruning rules for generate-and-test.
Top-Down Refinement	1. Large, factorable solution space. 2. Non-effective pruning rules for generate-and-test. 3. Variable amount of detail per abstraction level.
Guessing	1. Incomplete knowledge. 2. Large, factorable solution space. 3. Non-effective pruning rules.
Disjunctive Facts	1. No clear relationships for reasoning.
Constraints	1. Large, factorable solution space.
Blackboarding	1. Several independent solution spaces

domain and converge upon the solution rapidly. This leads to a dependence-directed backtracking line of reasoning where the system makes assumptions and will retract beliefs if they are inconclusive (non-monotonic). Just like the expert, the expert system will guess by (1) randomly selecting a path, or (2) selecting a path based on some heuristic information formalized into an evaluation function.

No application will have a perfect fit for deciding what type of data representation, search method, or line of reasoning to use to model the expert; however, it is important to attempt to find the "best fit" of all of these components (Table 4.3).

PART THREE

COMPONENTS OF AN EXPERT SYSTEM

Analogous to the human body and intelligence are the computer hardware and software that seek to mimic the human. The illustration "Components of an Expert System" shows the broad levels which comprise an expert system.

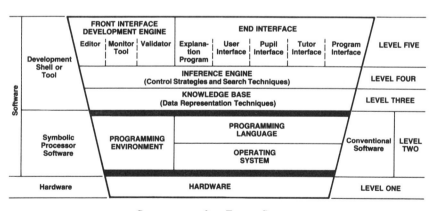

Components of an Expert System

Level 1—Hardware. The foundation of an expert system lies in the computer hardware. It provides the physical base for storage and also the venue for the operation of the software. Conventional and symbolic processing hardware systems are discussed in Chapter 5.

It is rare to hear or read debates on hardware when discussing the

91

topic of expert systems. Why? One answer may be that, historically, expert system development has been in the cozy, confined environs of well-funded research and development labs, with ample opportunity to acquire the finest, and most expensive, state-of-the-art equipment. But today that situation is rapidly changing. Expert systems have emerged into the real world where funding is limited and expert system development may not be the primary focus of the organization. Their use is often a support function for organizational operations, competing with other support functions for scarce resources.

It is now necessary to address the hardware used for expert systems. Most organizations currently have some form of computing hardware in operation, having invested large sums of money in their acquisition. Many have more than one computer system, oftentimes highly integrated. Enter expert systems. The organization must carefully consider whether or not existing computing hardware can additionally manage a proposed expert system; if not, then what type of equipment is necessary? There are conventional computing machines and there are specialized computing machines. The list of considerations goes on.

Beginning with computer hardware, Chapter 5 discusses hardware considerations and architectural differences between specialized symbolic processing machines and conventional machines, and it takes a look at today's leading symbolic processing machines. Chapter 5 also speculates on the direction of hardware in the future.

Level 2—Software. The intelligence of an expert system lies in the software, the second component of expert systems. The primary level of software can be either an operating system, with a programming language overlaid (as with conventional machines), or a dynamic programming environment (as with symbolic processing machines). This level provides the most basic functions for operating the hardware: functions such as device inputs and outputs, memory management, and sorting routines. This level of software is discussed in Chapter 6.

Level 3—Knowledge Base. The knowledge base contains the information and expertise for an application. The more complete the knowledge in the knowledge base, the more powerful the expert system. The importance of this level, then, is not only the completeness of the knowledge, but the method by which the knowledge is represented. Chapter 3 discusses knowledge representation techniques.

Level 4—Inference Engine. The inference engine is the workhorse of the expert system which massages the knowledge base. Within the inference engine resides a control strategy, which, as the name indicates, controls in some orderly fashion the inferencing processes of the expert system. Also included are search strategies, which provide one or more methods by which the inference engine can traverse the knowledge base. The strategies and techniques of an inference engine are discussed in Chapter 4.

Level 5—Interface. The highest level of the expert system is that which interfaces someone or something with the expert system. This interface is at both the front and end of the development process. The front interface is characteristically with the knowledge engineer or the expert. He interfaces through the development engine using an editor, monitor, and validator to construct, maintain, and debug the expert system. The end interface is that which communicates with the user after the expert system has been constructed. There are various ways to interface with the expert system, including interfacing to external programs, equipment (e.g., sensors, monitors), and devices (e.g., printers, plotters) for input and output.

Chapter 6 discusses three broad categories of software:

1. Programming language or environment
2. Development tool or shell
3. Prepackaged expert system

Building an expert system using a programming language or environment is the most involved way to build an expert system. The knowledge engineer must build from scratch all components of the expert system, knowledge base, inference engine, front interface, end interface, and development engine.

The second category of software is the expert system development tool. Here, the knowledge base has been predefined in the methods by which the knowledge will be represented in the expert system; only the knowledge itself is missing. The inference engine is also provided to the knowledge engineer. Control and search strategies are also predefined in development tools. The development engine may or may not be provided, however. In cases where the development engine is not provided by the tool, the knowledge engineer constructs and edits the knowledge base through an external text editor. After the knowledge base has been constructed, the knowledge engineer runs a parser or compiler on the file to validate the syntax of the file. Any incorrectness or incompleteness is edited through the external text editor, and the parser is run again. This process is continued until a clear parsed or compiled file is created.

In cases where the development engine is provided, the parser, compiler, and editor are incorporated. Also with development tools are "hooks" or interfaces that can communicate outside of the expert system—the other part of Level 5. User interfaces may or may not be provided. When not provided, these interfaces must be constructed by the knowledge engineer.

The third category of software is the prepackaged expert system. This category not only provides all levels of software, but also the knowledge and expertise within the knowledge base. Because expert systems are relatively new, there are only a few completed and commercially available expert systems, most of which were developed internally, for in-house use and not for commercial use. With the advent of microcomputer software, companies are forming for the purpose of developing expert systems to be sold on the commercial market.

5
Hardware

If an organization is interested in expanding into expert systems, what type of hardware is required? This can be a particularly perplexing question considering the vast range of hardware currently available for expert systems. Mainframes, minicomputers, microcomputers, and specialized symbolic processors will all run some form of expert system software.

Hardware can be divided into two general categories: (1) dedicated AI machines, referred to as symbolic processors or LISP machines and (2) conventional computing machines. The critical question then becomes "Do I need a symbolic processing machine or will a conventional computing machine suffice?"

HARDWARE CONSIDERATIONS

Many factors need to be considered prior to answering this question. As with any computer-based application, a systems analyst or competent knowledge engineer will clearly state that the selection of appropriate hardware is inexorably linked to issues such as the application size and complexity, software used, and user demands. When considering entering the specialized field of expert systems, these broad issues can be distilled into more specific questions:

- What is the objective/goal/intended use of the expert system?

- Will the computer system have multiple users?
- How large (estimated) will the knowledge base be?
- How many (estimated) production rules, frames, or semantic networks will be needed to model the expert?
- Will the expert system be expanded over time, and by how much?
- Will the expert system need to interface with other software packages?
- Will the computer system be required to run other, more conventional software packages such as word processing and database management?
- Will the expert system operate primarily for research and development, for manufacturing, or for some other use?
- Is there excess capacity on the existing in-house hardware?
- If there is excess capacity on the existing hardware, would the additional usage, attributed to the expert system, burden the computer system?
- Is there a potential for expanding the existing hardware?
- What categories of expert system software are available to run on the hardware under consideration?
- Would the available commercial expert system software suffice for the purpose of building, running, and maintaining an expert system?
- Will the expert system interface directly with other equipment, such as measurement devices?
- How quickly must the expert system run? Must it run immediately, or will delays be tolerated?
- Will down time be allowed, and if so, for how long?

Although this list is by no means complete, such questions must be carefully detailed prior to purchasing any expert system hardware. It is absolutely essential that the knowledge engineer or systems analyst, responsible for recommending the architecture, develop a working checklist of these or similar relevant questions. Answers to these questions form an important base of the *Expert System Project Study* prepared by the knowledge engineer (see Chapter 7). By proactively investigating alternative hardware and software combinations, the possibility of debilitating roadblocks arising later is substantially reduced.

Cost

Unquestionably, cost is an important consideration. There may not be sufficient internal resources to purchase expensive symbolic processing hardware, which ranges anywhere from $25,000 to $75,000 (per workstation) for hardware alone. When development costs are factored in, an expert system based on specialized symbolic processing hardware becomes even more expensive. This may force an organization to either "make do" with its existing hardware or arrange for alternative financing (such as leasing) to acquire. Since computing speed and hardware cost are directly related, it may not be economically feasible for many organizations, particularly those with restricted resources, to purchase symbolic processing machines unless high computational speed is of highest priority. On the other hand, conventional computing hardware can also involve substantial investment. Although microcomputers capable of running viable expert systems may cost only a couple of thousand dollars, minicomputers run upwards of $50,000 and mainframes run from $100,000.

Hardware cost, of course, should not be analyzed separately from total system cost. There are clear and distinct tradeoffs between hardware costs, software costs, and development costs; it is the combination of all three cost categories that must be understood. A more detailed discussion of total expert system costs is also found in Chapter 7.

Vendor Support

Vendor support, customer service, and ongoing maintenance are always relevant considerations. As an organization becomes dependent on its expert systems, the cost of down time can range from minor frustration to huge economic losses, and in some cases, to life-threatening disasters (e.g., medical, navigation). Down-time implications should always be explicitly discussed by all involved—the knowledge engineer, systems analyst, domain experts, end users, and management.

Vendor support is particularly crucial when dealing with symbolic processing machines. The inherent technology of these machines differs substantially from conventional hardware technology, and additional training of the organization's computer group is essential. Virtually every vendor currently offering symbolic processing hardware provides high quality assistance in equipment installation, maintenance support, and training classes. For conventional machines, however, the quality of vendor support runs the gamut from extremely professional to marginal, at best. Past experiences with implementing expert systems suggest that the hardware vendors' familiarity with expert system concepts and existing software greatly contributes to the success of an expert system implementation.

Upgradability of Hardware

The issue of hardware expansion and upgradability, always important as an organization's needs grow, is particularly relevant to expert systems. An initial system is inevitably a prototype, later maturing into a larger, more complete expert system environment. As the knowledge base is expanded, the software is integrated with other systems, and additional input and output devices are added. Once a working expert system is in place, the base hardware must have expansion capability to at least provide continuous and constant service/capacity levels. Implementing a new, more powerful, computer system midstream can be prohibitively expensive in terms of physically removing the old computer hardware, installing the new computer hardware, migrating the existing software to the new hardware, the nonproductive hours due to down time of the expert system, and the possibility that management's commitment may turn elsewhere. Especially relevant in the area of symbolic processing is the occurrence of rapid technological advancements, which tend to be quickly incorporated into the hardware. An organization should select a proper hardware architecture and vendor that allow the expert system to grow, taking advantage of new technologies without disrupting operations.

Processing Power

Expert systems typically consume substantially more machine cycles when compared with conventional programs. This is due to the extensive operations of pattern matching, searching and researching, and backtracking often required to tackle complex problems. Also, expert systems characteristically require extensive virtual memory capabilities and an efficient memory management environment in order to produce solutions to enigmatic problems in a reasonable amount of time. Speed, or processing power, becomes an important selection criterion, especially for more complex expert systems.

Software

As with any computer hardware decision, a major consideration is software compatibility. Software, such as AI programming languages and expert system development tools, is a key consideration. In addition, the technology of all types of expert system software is rapidly changing as AI advances. Rapid innovations in development tools, knowledge acquisition tools, and natural languages demand that forward thinking take place with hardware purchases. Will the hardware purchase of today support the state-of-the-art software of tomorrow?

It is also important to identify whether any other applications are intended to be applied to the hardware; integrated applications such as CAM (computer-aided manufacturing), CAD (computer-aided design), and CAE (computer-aided engineering) systems need to be detailed, as does the potential for networking expert systems with test equipment/ measuring devices, database management systems, word processing, and graphics programs. If the intention is to run traditional applications in addition to expert system applications, the choice of hardware might be immediately narrowed. This, again, stresses the importance of developing a checklist of relevant questions similar to those posed at the beginning of the chapter.

The ease of movement from development to implementation is also important. Integrating an expert system into the flow of normal organizational operations can be difficult. It requires careful and efficient coordination of time to physically install the equipment on location, provide training for the users, and compile complete documentation for both front interface users and end interface users. Proper installation of the system is vital, but is often overlooked during the initial stages of hardware consideration.

Also, developing an expert system on a specialized symbolic processing machine, then porting the system to a conventional computing machine, can yield unacceptable results—the internal architectures of the two types of machines are significantly different. It is analogous to developing a fuel-injection system on a rotary engine and then running it on a piston engine.

Table 5.1. Symbolic Processing Versus Conventional Computing Machines

SYMBOLIC PROCESSORS	CONVENTIONAL HARDWARE
1. Allows mixing of integer and floating point numbers	Doesn't allow mixing of data fields
2. Extensive virtual memory	Limited virtual memory
3. Extensive garbage collection	Limited garbage collection, which can lead to thrashing of the system
4. Incremental compilation	Entire programs must be recompiled and relinked after every program modification
5. Tagged memory architecture	Conventional architecture (i.e. 32-bit)
6. Not a multi-user system	Can be a multi-user system
7. Runs a combined, Lisp-optimized environment	Runs a separate operating system with a programming language overlayed
8. Dedicated Lisp processor	Conventional processor
9. High performance mass storage devices only	Employs various storage devices such as tape, floppy, and direct-access disk drives

As stated earlier, hardware design for expert systems falls into two categories: symbolic processing machines and conventional computing machines. Table 5.1 lists major differences between symbolic processing and conventional computing machines.

SYMBOLIC PROCESSING MACHINES

What is a "dedicated AI machine"? A dedicated AI machine is a computer system that is optimized for symbolic processing.What is "symbolic processing"? Symbolic processing is a method of computing that provides a richer set of representations of information than conventional numeric computing. This includes computation with symbols, relationships, and graphical objects as well as numbers, characters, and bits. Symbolic processing machines can be programmed to represent and store concepts, draw inferences, and make deductions. These systems use advanced problem-solving techniques, such as heuristic reasoning, to solve nonmathematical problems and problems containing incomplete or inconsistent information. As a result, complex tasks which involve a high degree of expert judgment such as medical diagnosis and oil exploration, can be executed more efficiently using symbolic processing techniques.

Symbolic processing machines are characteristically single-user systems. However, these systems are often networked together in order to share resources and processing power (Figure 5.1). Symbolic processors make complex real-world problems easier to represent. A symbolic processing system is more than just hardware; it is a dynamic development environment. For comparison, conventional computing environments demand a lot of redundant operations, and users often perceive the system as "hard to learn" and "easy to forget" (upon completion of a program, the values of the variables are lost). They are structured with an operating system and a programming language overlaid. On the other hand, symbolic processing environments are intelligent and dynamic. They have a LISP-optimized operating environment, which allows the environment to be customized to take advantage of the powerful AI features of the LISP language.

Symbolic processors also perform sophisticated functions such as memory allocation and elaborate system maintenance, also known as garbage collection or memory management. Garbage collection is a set of processes for recovering areas of address space in memory that are

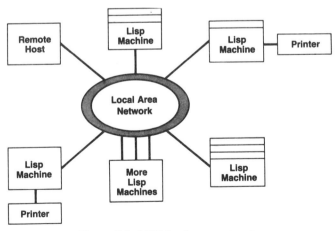

Figure 5.1. LISP local area network.

no longer in use. Once the memory is recovered, it can be reused to represent new objects. In conventional architecture, memory management is performed by the operating system. When an operation is initiated, it is allocated a fixed amount of space by the operating systems, and for some systems proceeds to impose memory management on the space given. With symbolic processors, all of the operations share the same virtual address space. Garbage collection can be done parallel to processing (real time) or not parallel to processing (stop-and-copy or stop-and-collect).

Symbolic processors provide extensive virtual memory capacity, which is required for efficient expert system processing. Virtual memory is a collection of pages of information, some of which reside in main memory and some of which reside on disk. Since programs can be run only when in main memory, hardware automatically swaps pages in and out of main memory to allow larger programs to be run faster and more efficiently. This swapping is transparent to the user.

There are many advantages to using a symbolic processing machine. One very important advantage is that the entire concept of expert systems is based on symbolic manipulation. Also, because symbols are processed dynamically (they can be broken apart or combined to form new symbols), there are certain memory allocation/deallocation requirements that do not occur with conventional programming languages. This process is so dynamic that the operating system does not know at compilation time just how large the data structures will be, or what they will look like when the program is finished. Symbolic processing machines afford the adaptability needed.

Tagged memory architecture is a unique structure of symbolic processors whereby the LISP-oriented environment attaches an extra word to each data word in order to easily identify the nature of the data. For example, by examining the tag field the processor can determine whether a word is an integer or a floating point number. Normally, the data types are tagged in the software. This architecture is critical in the following three areas:

Run-Time Storage Management (Garbage Collection). This is perhaps the most important facet of any LISP system. LISP programs generate objects for various purposes—such as program compilation—many of which are only temporary. Garbage collection makes these memory locations available for reuse.

Exception Handling. Tagged architecture enables compiled, production-level code to quickly detect and handle soft (characteristically nonfatal) errors during run time.

Object-Oriented Programming (Symbolic Processing). Utilization of symbols, relationships, and graphical objects in conjunction with numerical and character data allows a more exact and efficient representation of real-world situations. The tagged memory architecture provides a more efficient methodology by which to identify and manipulate different types of data.

Other advantages of symbolic processors also stem from the architecture, which offers the capacity for large physical memory, efficient symbolic manipulation, stack computations, and function calling. These machines provide the needed data-type memory tagging for quicker data identification. The high-speed processing afforded by these symbolic processors significantly increases the productivity of users and system developers.

Another important feature of a symbolic processing environment is incremental compilation. Incremental compilation speeds the program development process, allowing the programmer to thoroughly test small functions without waiting for lengthy recompiling and relinking. Symbolic processors also provide the ability to dynamically link and load program segments at execution time. This is a major departure from the traditional programming process of coding, compiling, executing, and debugging entire programs at a time. With symbolic processors, a programmer can design segments of a program, code, compile, and test, while the entire program is being formed. Validated segments may then be linked into the developing program, while problem segments can be eliminated without it being necessary to recompile the entire program.

The overall advantages of symbolic processing machines can be summarized in one word: **SPEED**.

Note, however, that symbolic processing machines are not solely limited to expert system applications. They run a spectrum of software applications, such as

1. Expert systems

2. Robotics (e.g., the automation of industrial production lines)

3. CAD/CAE design (e.g., the design of such complicated objects as VLSI circuits)

4. Software languages (e.g., LISP, PROLOG, PASCAL, and FORTRAN)

5. Sophisticated graphics

6. Financial applications (e.g., spreadsheets)

7. Communications (e.g., networking)

8. Training and simulation

9. Mathematics and physics research

10. Film and video animation

11. Speech recognition and understanding

12. Pattern recognition and image understanding (e.g., object digitization)

There are several symbolic processor manufacturers in the market today. The four leading companies are: (1) Symbolics with its Symbolics 3600 Series, (2) Lisp Machine, Inc. (LMI) with its Lambda Series, (3) Xerox with its 1100 Series, and (4) Texas Instruments with its Explorer System. Symbolics currently leads the symbolic processing hardware industry with a 58% market share, with LMI, Texas Instruments, and Xerox sharing the remaining 34% market share (Davis, 1986). It is important to consider not only the particulars of each company's hardware, but also the software available with the hardware.

Symbolics, Inc.

Symbolics was founded in 1980 by many of the original researchers of MIT's Artificial Intelligence Laboratory LISP Machine project. The Symbolics 3600 Series is designated by many in the field as the premier symbolic processing computer system line. Four systems comprise the series: the Symbolics 3670, 3675, 3640, and 3645. They feature an MC68000 front-end processor for controlling low- and medium- speed I/O (input/output) devices and are used for system diagnosis. For high performance, the 3600 Series uses an I/O board that handles 10-Mbit/s Ethernet local area networks (LANs), disk drives, and a high-performance graphics console.

Symbolics designed these machines around a tagged memory archi-

tecture. Usually, memory tagging is done in the software, which results in as many words in memory identifying the data type as there are
words of data. Because of this duplication, Symbolics performs data
tagging in the hardware (Figure 5.2). By appending 4 bits onto the
32-bit word to form "memory tags," the same data that were previously
put into memory serially, are placed into memory in parallel. This
forms a 36-bit architecture. As a result, all of the overhead of the extra
instructions disappears, and there is nearly an order of magnitude
increase in performance. This increase in speed is accomplished by
performing data-type checking in parallel with the instruction execution (called run-time data-type checking).

Because of the recursive nature of LISP, efficient processing requires a stack-oriented machine. Although not a pure stack machine,
the 3600 Series is stack-oriented and designed to make function calls
and returns as fast as possible. Most instructions, but not all, use the
stack to get operands and store results. The processor contains multiple stacks and buffers used for fast storage of temporary data. Stacks
are used to pass arguments. The processor controls the stack pointers
and buffer manipulation. A given computation is associated with a
particular stack group.

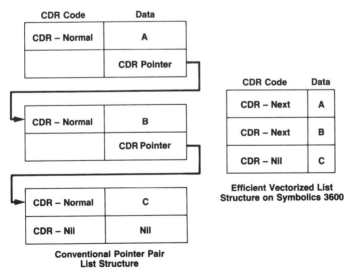

Figure 5.2. LISP (CDR) coding comparison between conventional computer implementation and Symbolics tagged architecture (Symbolics technical summary).

Each stack group contains three stacks for control, binding, and data. The control stack, containing the control environment, local environment, and caller list, is formatted into frames that correspond to function calls. A frame consists of a fixed header followed by arguments and local variable slots. Binding is the process by which a variable is temporarily given a value (a special variable). The binding stack contains special variables and previous values of those variables to be restored later. The data stack, which helps reduce garbage collection overhead, contains dynamic LISP objects, such as temporary arrays and lists.

Garbage collection on the Symbolics computers is incremental, run in the background only when necessary. Symbolics computers also feature a unique Ephemeral-Object Garbage Collector system (also called the Ephemeral GC) that significantly improves the interactive response of the system when garbage collection is in progress. Some compute-bound (CPU-intensive) programs that allocate large amounts of storage run faster with the Ephemeral GC. This is because pages of memory typically contain fewer unreferenced objects (less garbage), and the garbage collector's overhead is outweighed by reducing paging.

This feature is based on a strategy that classifies certain objects as ephemeral, meaning that they are likely to become garbage soon after their creation. When the Ephemeral GC is operating, the garbage collector concentrates on these objects. Objects are classified as ephemeral if they are created in designated areas of memory while the Ephemeral GC is working.

The advantage of the Ephemeral GC is that the garbage collector has to deal with only a small fraction of the total number of objects and the total storage area of the system. This greatly decreases paging as well as the time it takes to complete a full garbage collection. It also reduces the amount of address space that has to be committed to the garbage collector's use and frees it up for other operations.

The Symbolics LISP environment supports the ZETALISP Flavors system. Flavors represents generic objects. For example, a generic *ship* with its description could be a flavor. An aircraft carrier with the addition of its unique, nongeneric descriptors would be an instance of the flavor *ship*. The process of going from the generic to the specific is called instantiation. Such instantiated flavors are manipulated by sending messages that request specific operations. Since the proce-

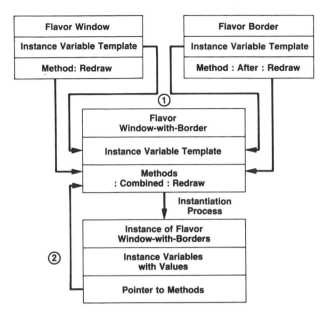

Figure 5.3. Flavors (abstract type) can be combined to produce new flavors, as illustrated at point 1. A flavor instance can be a pointer to request specific operations, as shown at point 2 (Symbolics technical summary).

dures are already contained within the object, it responds by performing the operation requested. Complex, dependent relationships can be declared among flavors and can be modified as needed (Figure 5.3)

Symbolics machines support a variety of languages: SYMBOLICS-LISP, SYMBOLICS PROLOG, ANSI STANDARD FORTRAN 77, PASCAL, ADA, COMMON LISP, ZETALISP and MACSYMA. Applications include: communications, expert system development tools, financial tools, image processing, natural language systems, software development, and text processing.

Lisp Machine, Inc. (LMI)

In 1983, LMI introduced the Lambda Series. The Lambda Series has seven units that integrate expert system concepts with traditional numerical processing. The machines are based on the MC68010/UNIX processor and LISP processor. Thus the machines support both LISP and UNIX programs, and their execution can take place concurrently or independently. This is a major deviation from designs that furnish

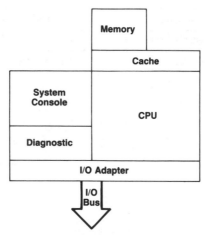

Figure 5.4. Traditional bus design. The CPU is the center of the system. Any other processors are subsidiary.

a more traditional environment that is based within a single processor. The Lambda processors are combined in a NuBus architecture that was developed at MIT's Laboratory for Computer Science. This produces an open-ended, modular and expandable LISP machine with multiprocessor capabilities. The top-of-the-line Lambda machine can support four independent concurrent LISP processors.

Traditional bus architectures are designed around a single CPU (Figure 5.4). The NuBus architecture is designed around a core of multiple processors to focus on a shared control system (Figure 5.5).

Lambda's specialized garbage collection algorithm not only runs in parallel with the program execution, but it can actually speed up the performance of many LISP programs by improving the locality of reference—keeping the program's working memory within a tight range of addresses. This minimizes disk access, thus improving virtual memory performance.

Xerox Corporation

Xerox manufactures the 1100 Series of AI machines. This series includes numerous configurations of the 1108 and 1132 AI workstations. These machines are fully compatible with Xerox's Ethernet network architecture. The systems operate under an INTERLISP-D environment: an interpreted, extensible, versatile, and flexible language. Be-

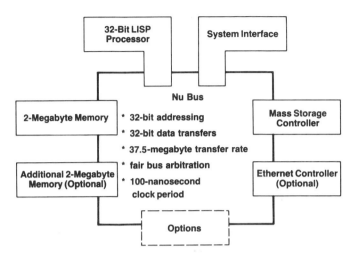

Figure 5.5. NuBus architecture.

cause it is interpreted, it provides rapid turnaround time and quick results during the development stage. Its versatility allows for extensive program modifications to take place while programs evolve and change. Features such as late binding and dynamic linking allow the programmer to defer aspects of the design until their specifications have stabilized.

Within the INTERLISP-D environment operates the Programmer's Assistant. The Programmer's Assistant works to free the programmer from mundane detail, thereby allowing concentration on higher-level design issues. Features include an error analysis capability, an input monitoring function, a spelling corrector, and sophisticated file/record management capabilities. The Masterscope facility also operates in the INTERLISP-D environment and can analyze a program, display the structure, answer questions, and assist in modification. It interfaces with the file package and editor, reanalyzing a program whenever a program is modified. Xerox supports QUINTUS PROLOG and LOOPS (a tool for research and expert system development).

Xerox provides a customized programming environment called NoteCards. NoteCards is a powerful integrated set of tools for manipulating idea-sized units of text, images, sketches, maps, and other electronic information stored in a NoteFile database. NoteCards is designed to move information from chaos to order; it is based on a

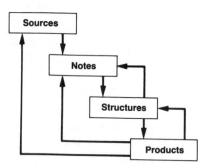

Figure 5.6. Xerox NoteCards information flow.

model that characterizes information movement as an iterative progression from sources to notes to structures to products (Figure 5.6). In most applications, the organization of ideas is expressed by a hierarchical partitioning of the collection of note cards, as well as by the semantic network inherent in the user-defined arcs between related note cards. It was developed jointly by Xerox Special Information Systems (XSIS) and Xerox Palo Alto Research Center (PARC).

The 1186/1185 machines offer an IBM PC emulation coprocessor option which enables the user to work on both AI and IBM PC (MS DOS) applications. This feature is an important link in bridging the gap between symbolic processors and conventional hardware.

Texas Instruments, Inc.

Texas Instruments began its AI research and development program in 1978 and has since grown into one of the world's largest corporate AI research laboratories. In October 1984, Texas Instruments announced its entry into the symbolic processing field with the Explorer Symbolic Processing System.

The Texas Instruments Explorer Symbolic Processing System is an advanced single-user workstation optimized for fast LISP language execution, large memory capacity, and high-quality graphics. As a member of the Texas Instruments Nu Generation family, the Explorer system provides a base for building high-performance multiprocessor configurations using NuBus technology (Figure 5.5). This is a flexible bus structure based on a master–slave concept. For each interaction, a device takes control of the NuBus interface, thus becoming a *master*, and addresses another device that becomes a *slave* for that interaction. The slave device, after decoding its address, acts on the command provided by the master. A simple handshake protocol between the master and the slave allows devices of different speeds to use the NuBus interface. The NuBus interface features a memory-mapped event mechanism rather than a hard-wired interrupt scheme. Interrupts are implemented as write operations and require no unique signals or protocols. This means that any device can interrupt any other device on the NuBus by writing into an area of the address space that is monitored by the other device. The NuBus features processor-independent architecture and multiprocessor support, which allows the addition of general-purpose or application-specific processors to existing configurations.

An additional bus, called the local bus, is a high speed 32-bit private bus that gives the processor direct access to main memory and graphics memory, thereby leaving the NuBus available for system-wide operations. Use of the local bus is completely transparent to the user and to the software.

Built with high-density 32-bit technology, the Explorer processor is microprogrammed for high-speed symbolic processing. Among other features, the processor includes tagged architecture for typed data, bit-field hardware to manipulate complex data structures, multi-branching to facilitate the complex control associated with symbolic processing, hardware-assisted memory management for garbage collection, and a large stack cache. The data typing is identified in the software by four trailing parity bits on each memory word. Explorer systems can also be configured for Ethernet LANs whereby the machines on the network can provide file and print server functions for shared resources among the users (Figure 5.1).

Garbage collection can be turned on or off and can be operated in both real-time and stop-and-collect modes. The real-time mode (also called the automatic incremental mode) occurs in parallel with program execution. It is automatically initiated when a user-specified threshold of available space has been crossed. The stop-and-collect mode occurs at a specified point in the program or whenever the garbage collector is turned on in this mode. At this point, and during the collection process, program execution is suspended.

Texas Instruments is now coupling symbolic and conventional processing on the Explorer system. There is a multiprocessor version that

combines both symbolic and numeric processing in the same chassis—
the Explorer LX system. The Explorer LX is designed for applications
requiring both knowledge-based programs written in LISP and compu-
tation-intensive programs written in conventional languages such as
C, FORTRAN, or PASCAL.

Linking these environments provides increased power and flexibility for development and delivery of AI applications integrated with
conventional computing. Because of its dual environment, the Explorer LX is excellent for process control, simulation and modeling
applications, and other applications that benefit from coupling a high-
performance LISP processor with a high-performance 68020-based
processor.

One of the Explorer LX system's unique features is shared physical
memory. It uses the global address structure of the NuBus architecture
to provide shared data access between LISP and UNIX applications
without having to move the data. It allows LISP applications to
"watch the execution" of UNIX-based applications and also modify
memory of the UNIX application. The user interface includes multiple
window capabilities, which facilitates multitasking. For example,
if a FORTRAN program is executing a simulation program, a LISP-
based expert system can monitor the process to determine if the simulation is proceeding within acceptable limits. If not, it can modify
the parameters to instruct changes to be made. This unique shared
memory feature is beyond the capability of other LISP/UNIX LAN
solutions.

The Explorer system is written entirely in LISP and operates under
a customized COMMON LISP environment providing extensions that
encompass the full ZETALISP environment (Figure 5.7).

The Explorer supports ZETALISP Flavors, an object-oriented programming system (Figure 5.3). What makes the Flavors system so powerful is that expert systems deal with objects, which are active entities
representing real-world objects. An object encompasses data and the
operations that can be performed on those data. Programs communicate with objects by sending messages to them, and the implementation of objects is hidden from programs that use them. Therefore,
programs using objects need only to be concerned with the performance of operations, not on how the operations are actually coded.
This technique substantially reduces the complexity of large systems
and makes them easier to use and maintain.

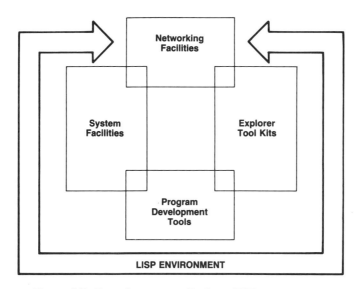

Figure 5.7. Texas Instruments Explorer LISP environment.

Flavors was discussed earlier for the Symbolics machines, but because it is somewhat difficult to conceptualize, Flavors will be discussed again, but from a TI orientation. A *flavor* is an abstract object that describes a whole class of similar objects. Thus, a flavor forms a conceptual model, and a specific object is an *instance* of the flavor. It is possible to create any number of instances of a flavor. The flavor has *instance variables*, which specify attributes of the conceptual model. Each instance holds its own set of values for the instance variables. The flavor can establish default initial values for instance variables or can supply them explicitly when instantiating a flavor. A flavor also has attached *methods*, which are functions that define generic operations for any instance of that flavor. Methods refers to any of the instance variables of that flavor. To operate on a specific object, the system creates an instance of the flavor and sends it messages naming the desired operations. The object reads each message and returns the result.

The Explorer system includes a large number of predefined flavors, which can be instantiated and used in program development. For example, the window system is based on flavors; instances of different types of existing window flavors can be created. Custom flavors can also be defined. The Flavors system provides many features to aid in this process. One of the most powerful features of the Flavors system is the ability to combine existing flavors to form a new flavor. The new flavor inherits all of the instance variables and methods belonging to the component flavors.

In recognition of future needs for the coexistence and integration of symbolic processors with conventional architectures and environments, future plans for the Texas Instruments symbolic processors include

- Integrating and networking the Explorer with conventional computing machines
- Networking and communicating with other symbolic processing machines
- Increasing performance
- Providing temporal garbage collection

CONVENTIONAL COMPUTING MACHINES

"Conventional" computing machines are the traditional, general computing systems, both large and small, that have the ability to run both AI programming languages (such as LISP and PROLOG) and general programming languages (such as BASIC, C, and FORTRAN). Conventional machines address problems that can be translated into alphabetics (strings), numbers, and numerical relationships.

Many development tools, AI languages, and prepackaged expert systems are already available for conventional computing machines. Since these systems were not originally designed for fast symbolic processing, they are not nearly as efficient in expert system processing as symbolic processors. They do, however, offer the flexibility of performing both traditional computing (e.g., data processing, spreadsheets, and word processing) and symbolic processing on the same machine. Thus users are not locked into symbolic processing architecture.

In recent years, expert systems have been developed to run on the entire spectrum of conventional hardware: from microcomputers, such as the IBM and Apple, to mainframes, such as IBM, Sperry Univac, and Xerox, to supercomputers, such as the Cray-1 and Control Data

Corporation (CDC) Cyber. Although expert systems can be designed to run on virtually any hardware system, the availability of appropriate software may become a limiting factor.

Supercomputers have generally been used in advanced research and development for extremely specialized AI problems that demand high machine speed (in exchange for the high cost); otherwise, most AI research and development has traditionally been accomplished on mainframes which offer substantial computer power at a lesser cost. Recently, minicomputers have offered close to the same speed, memory, and flexibility. More and more expert systems are being developed on minicomputers and supermicrocomputers which offer, besides speed, memory and flexibility, predictably high performance per single user, use of all computing facilities, and sufficient resources for general utilities and AI tools. They also have sophisticated expansion peripherals such as high-resolution screens, graphics packages, editors, and debuggers.

But take note of microcomputers. With the onslaught of development tools designed for microcomputers, they are very attractive as a system for small applications, or for prototyping larger applications. Their entry cost is extremely low, and development time can be relatively short. IBM's RT PC, for example, provides a high-performance workstation to meet the requirements of the engineering/scientific, academic, and CAD/CAM communities. The IBM RT PC operates under the Advanced Interactive Executive (AIX) operating system. It is a 32-bit machine based on reduced instruction set computer (RISC) architecture. It also has a 40-bit virtual memory management chip that provides a large amount of addressable storage, ideal for sizeable expert system applications. Extensive information regarding microcomputer architectures is readily found in other reference books.

In summary, the selection of hardware for expert system development must be closely matched to software compatibility and application usage. Experience has shown that scrimping on hardware will inevitably result in higher total development costs. One does not buy a Volkswagen to race at Monte Carlo. By the time modifications are made to the Volkswagen, its cost will be higher than that of buying a high-performance race car in the beginning. To race in a local road rally, however, the Volkswagen may be appropriate.

We leave the question "Is a symbolic processing machine the preferred choice, or will a conventional computer suffice?" unanswered.

This chapter serves to heighten the awareness of the reader that special hardware systems do exist; they are expensive, but provide for sophisticated and specialized requirements of expert system applications. Due to this specialized application area, many of the prominent symbolic processing hardware vendors are attempting to broaden their products' usefulness in two ways. They are (1) making their equipment compatible with industry standards such as the UNIX operating system and the IBM microcomputing architectures, and (2) introducing new lower-cost models of their symbolic processors to serve as delivery vehicles for products developed on their more powerful machines. Thus the distinguishing gaps between conventional computing and symbolic processing machines are quickly closing.

6

Software

If computing hardware can be considered the physical "body" of expert systems, then expert system software can certainly be compared to the driving "intelligence"—the brain that directs and controls problem analysis and decision making. Hardware and software decisions must be made as a "unitas multiplex"; they are separate entities, but closely united in compatibility. Decisions regarding either expert system software or hardware cannot be made in isolation of each other. The price of hardware, software, training, support, and ongoing maintenance are all major concerns when developing an expert system.

DATA VERSUS KNOWLEDGE PROCESSING

Just as hardware may be classified either as conventional or symbolic processing architecture, software may be either of a conventional data processing nature or of a specialized AI knowledge processing nature. There are three essential differences between data processing and knowledge processing software.

I. Conventional software represents and manipulates data; knowledge-based systems represent and manipulate knowledge.

This distinction is not very useful unless the difference between data and knowledge is recognized. The dividing line is fuzzy. For our purpose, we define data to be static information about the domain; knowledge refers to the dynamic relationships about the data in the

117

domain. Knowledge is thus related data, sufficiently tied to the real world for intelligent action.

For example, suppose the natural gas pipeline to a nearby copper smelter flows at a rate of 12,000 ft^3 per minute. That is a piece of data—an isolated bit of information. It has no useful meaning until it is compared with other data on flow rates and to an interpretation of what an abnormally high rate might signify. As supervisor of a natural gas pumping station, you have watched the previously mentioned pipeline for a year; the flow rate has never exceeded 11,000 ft^3 per minute, even with the smelter going full blast. Now, you have related that single piece of data to all other like data. The smelter manager reports that the gas pressure has risen. The piece of data is now related to the real world; new knowledge can be inferred by correctly combining just a few facts. Swiftly, you close the cutoff valve, dispatch the emergency crew, call out the nearest fire department, and hope to hear "all clear" sirens instead of an explosion.

Conventional computer systems are not stupid. Anything that can perform differential calculus in seconds should not be called stupid. Conventional computers are simply ignorant. They do not know how to interrelate data to produce knowledge, because we have not been able to tell them how to do it—until recently.

II. Conventional software primarily uses algorithms; knowledge-based software uses both algorithms and heuristics.

Think of algorithms as equations and heuristics as rules of thumb. Consider the following examples:

1. The number of gallons of gasoline purchased, multiplied by the price per gallon, equals the total price paid—every time. Put the same numbers in, get the same number out. This is an algorithm; conventional data processing software can calculate it flawlessly, several thousand times a second.

2. An heuristic may look like this: Suppose it is the first cold day of winter; snow is falling as you walk to your car after work. The car will not start. When the tow truck arrives, the driver pulls up nose-to-nose with your car, pops open his hood, and walks toward you with jumper cables in his hand. He has not discussed the problem with you or examined your car, but still he is prepared to first try a jump start. Why? Heuristic knowledge. He knows from experience that there's a high 94% probability a jump start will get you on the road again. Of course, something else could be wrong with the car. You could, instead, stubbornly insist that the tow truck driver begin first with basic auto repair principles, making a thorough, methodical examination of your car's various systems. But you will probably get home late, cold and hungry, angrily clutching a substantial repair bill. Without the frequent use of heuristics, everyday life would be unbearable.

Expert systems use algorithms whenever they are available, to make knowledge precise. They also use heuristics where knowledge cannot be made precise and certain—or where it is not economical to be precise. Because heuristics "play the odds," most expert systems usually assign certainty factors to draw inferences using heuristic knowledge. The expert system would thus report your gasoline bill, in the example above, "with a certainty of 1.0," but give its recommendation to try a jump start first "with a certainty of 0.94."

III. Conventional software uses repetitive processes; knowledge-based software uses inferential processes.

The hallmark of conventional software is the completely reliable and accurate repetition of the same routine throughout a particular job. If your board of directors has declared a dividend of $0.25 per share, and you, as chief accountant, have dividend checks to prepare for one million stockholders, you want the precise algorithm applied repeatedly, to the penny. It is not up to the computer to decide that paying $0.20 a share will save earnings to plow back into the long-term growth of the company, or that paying $0.30 a share will impress Wall Street's security analysts. It is the responsibility of the board of directors to make such determinations, based on hundreds of factors—only a few of which can be neatly reduced to equations. However, a simple expert system might assist the board of directors to make the dividend decision process more effective—not faster, but better. This is because expert systems can draw inferences; that is, they can take many facts and relate them in a logical manner, thereby producing new facts and recommendations.

To accomplish this, expert system software is constructed to carry out *symbolic reasoning* to accommodate the specialized requirements of AI and expert systems. The process is called *symbolic* because both facts and their relationships are put into the computer; they are reported by the computer not as numbers, but largely as human words, having been manipulated according to strict rules of logic. It is called *reasoning* because that is the word we use for the process of drawing inferences or conclusions from facts known or assumed.

Since expert systems evolved from an AI foundation, the natural inclination is to use symbolic programming languages developed especially for AI to emulate human thought processes. Current expert system software falls into three categories:

1. General-purpose AI languages (such as LISP and PROLOG)
2. Development tools (such as PERSONAL CONSULTANT and GURU)
3. Prepackaged commercial expert systems (such as LENDING ADVISOR)

SOFTWARE CONSIDERATIONS

When considering the appropriate type of expert system software, numerous questions (parallel to those addressed in Chapter 5) should be carefully addressed. As with most system-related tasks, the degree of initial planning and designing has a direct and immediate effect on the system's final success. Listed here are a few of the more important questions for the knowledge engineer to consider:

- What categories of software listed previously are available on the existing in-house hardware, or any proposed future hardware?
- How is the knowledge initially acquired (i.e., manually or automatically)?
- What type of data representation best represents the domain knowledge (e.g., rules, examples, etc.)?
- Is there a time constraint for the implementation of the expert system?
- Is the expert system intended to interface with external programs?
- What is the estimated size of the knowledge base?
- How is the knowledge to be maintained on the expert system?
- How is the knowledge accessed inside the expert system?
- How difficult will it be to model the expert?

- What reasoning method is best suited to reach the goal state of the problem (e.g., forward chaining, backward chaining)?
- How is the knowledge modified in light of new experience and information (i.e., manually or automatically)?
- Is there a financial constraint?
- Are there any existing prepackaged expert systems whose application is similar in nature?

GENERAL-PURPOSE AI LANGUAGES

Every expert system is developed using some type of programming language, although most employ a general-purpose AI language. The most common AI languages for expert systems are LISP and PROLOG. Several expert systems have been designed in general-purpose non-AI languages (such as PASCAL, FORTRAN, and C), primarily for ease of maintenance since there are more of these programmers available than AI programmers.

The *advantage* of developing a system using an AI language is that it provides the base for symbolic processing. Flexibility and speed (efficient processing) are now in the knowledge engineer's hands. The *disadvantage* is that it requires another level of "expertise," that is, an individual who is proficient in AI language programming. A simple conditional statement, for example, may take five or more lines of program code to accurately express the desired relationship. Developing an expert system in-house at this level can be very costly. A well-known example is Schlumberger's DIPMETER ADVISOR (for analyzing oil well logging data), estimated to have totaled some $21 million in development costs.

LISP

Most expert systems throughout the United States are programmed in LISP (LISt Processing). Developed in the 1950s by John McCarthy while at MIT, LISP deals with symbols. A symbol can be composed of any combination of characters on a terminal keyboard, but symbols are mainly alphanumeric. The data structure is represented by lists of strings of "atoms" (such as numbers, symbols, or words) enclosed by parentheses. Mathematical functions, predicate logic, logical connectives, and list manipulations can be applied to these lists. LISP is a highly interactive, flexible, and recursive language. The major advantage of LISP is its nesting nature, which lends itself to many problem-solving techniques, such as searching. Figure 6.1 illustrates a LISP statement.

Several limitations were evident with early versions of LISP: problems such as (1) large memory requirements, (2) extensive CPU demands, and (3) limited applicational use. Due to recent innovations in hardware design, LISP has been given renewed power. Today, it is a mature, sophisticated language that has taken on a variety of dialects in conformance to the demands of different hardware systems, thus optimizing machine performance and language constructs.

One of the primary reasons LISP is so popular is because a symbolic program is naturally represented in LISP data structures. Programs and data have the same form and thus can be treated somewhat interchangeably, allowing LISP users to write programs capable of running and modifying other programs. This permits an expert system program to make changes to lines of its own code while running.

LISP programs seem to "learn" because of this self-modifying ability. For example, an expert system program incorporating a collection of rules that tell it how to react under certain conditions might discard some of those rules if it concludes that they are not being used. The expert system could then generate replacement rules. In practice, however, self-modifying programs are prone to disastrous results (such as "runaway" processing), so most AI programming employs higher-level concepts built on top of LISP (e.g., development tools) which force additional discipline on program behavior.

Other specialized features of LISP include (1) powerful debugging facilities, (2) the availability of both a compiler and an interpreter for

```
(DE HIRING (ATTITUDE REFERENCE EDUCATION EXPERIENCE)
    (COND ((NULL ATTITUDE) NIL)
          ((EQUAL ATTITUDE 'POOR) NIL)
          ((EQUAL ATTITUDE 'GOOD)
           (COND ((EQUAL REFERENCE 'GOOD) 'HIRE)
                 ((EQUAL REFERENCE 'POOR)
                  (COND ((AND (EQUAL EDUCATION 'ADEQUATE)
                              (LGREATERP EXPERIENCE 1)
                   'HIRE)]
```

Figure 6.1. INTERLISP example of hiring problem stated in Chapter 9.

program development, (3) run-time checking, (4) garbage collection, (5) a macro facility that allows for easy extensions of the language, (6) the modeling of procedural knowledge (i.e., "how to do something" as opposed to "what something is"), and (7) the promotion of modularity by imposing no penalty for dividing a program into dozens, or even hundreds, of functions.

There are two main families of LISP. One, based on the MACLISP dialect, was developed on a Digital Equipment Corporation PDP-10 at MIT. Descendants of MACLISP include ZETALISP, COMMON LISP, and FRANZLISP. The other main family is the INTERLISP family, which also gained widespread use on the Digital Equipment Corporation PDP-10. Variations of INTERLISP include T-LISP, NLISP, LISP/VM, IQLISP, and GCLISP.

PROLOG

PROLOG, invented around 1970 by Alain Colmerauer and his associates at the University of Marseille, France, represents the major competition to LISP in the AI community. PROLOG stands for PROgramming in LOGic; it is used much more widely outside the United States, particularly in Japan and western Europe. The basis of PROLOG is the notion of logic programming in which computation can be viewed as controlled, logical inferences. PROLOG is a language suitable for applications requiring the simulation of intelligence—applications in such areas as expert systems, deductive databases, language processing, robotic control, planning systems, and design applications.

It is not an algorithmic language such as COBOL or PASCAL, but is based on the concepts of formal logic (predicate calculus). It dispenses with the notions of "go to," "do for," and "do while," and instead incorporates the mechanisms required by intelligent programs—advanced pattern matching, generalized record structuring, list manipulation, assertional database, and depth-first search strategy based on backtracking. PROLOG is a pattern-matching system that allows the user to specify variables. PROLOG backtracks to try to match the requested patterns, and continues to backtrack until the problem is solved.

PROLOG uses symbolic representations of the objects and relationships between those objects to specify known facts and relationships about a problem, thus creating "clauses." Clauses, or implications, make up the program, with the conclusions being stated first. Programming in PROLOG is very different from programming in a conventional language. Instead of asking "What is the algorithm that will solve my problem?" the programmer asks, "What formal facts and relationships occur in the problem?" and "What rules are associated with these facts and relationships?"

PROLOG allows these facts, rules, and relationships to be expressed naturally, thus producing clear and concise programs. An example of PROLOG is illustrated in Figure 6.2. PROLOG is designed to automate searches through a tree-structured domain by doing a depth-first search with backtracking. It seems to be a natural candidate for parallel processing systems. PROLOG's power lies in its ability to infer facts from other facts. The user can give the computer nonnumeric information and have it deduce additional nonnumeric information.

Another *advantage* of PROLOG is its compactness. A three-page listing of LISP can be condensed to one page of PROLOG. This can be accomplished because control is implicit—it is already provided by the system—whereas in LISP a control system must be written to run on the application. All the user has to do in PROLOG is declare statements, either high-level, as in the application, or low-level, such as in the system software.

One *disadvantage* of PROLOG is the frequent need for an awkward mix of procedural and nonprocedural styles. PROLOG is usually not able to express negative conclusions or embedded conditionals. For example, it cannot say "X is not a share of stock if X pays interest coupon payments." Nor is PROLOG able to express a definition that contains more than one "if" statement, such as "X is a safe investment if X always increases in value if X is invested."

PROLOG, like LISP, has its language derivations, such as PROLOG-2, MPROLOG, LM-PROLOG, C-PROLOG, QUINTUS PROLOG, and TURBO PROLOG.

```
Hire (Attitude, References, Education, Experience) : -
    Attitude = good, References = good.
Hire (Attitude, References, Education, Experience) : -
    Attitude = good, References = poor, Education = adequate,
    Experience > 1.
```

Figure 6.2. PROLOG example of hiring problem stated in Chapter 9.

EXPERT SYSTEM DEVELOPMENT TOOLS ("SHELLS")

During the past several years, the industry has seen a tremendous influx of development tools explicitly designed to assist the knowledge engineer in building expert systems. Several companies have introduced tools with various functions, standards, and features. Expert system tools are "off-the-shelf" skeleton expert systems. Also known as "shells," they are comprised of

- A predefined inference engine that knows how to use the knowledge base to reach conclusions

They may also contain

- A knowledge base development engine (editor) for constructing and editing the knowledge base
- Knowledge integrity checks to weed out contradictory facts, rules, redundant or missing information, and syntactical errors— otherwise known as a validator
- A spelling checker to make sure words are typed correctly
- An on-line logic reasoning base for explaining how and why a conclusion was reached
- Performance monitoring tools for testing and debugging the expert system during development; this enables the knowledge engineer to set trace and break point conditions (for debugging purposes) based on the knowledge base versus a location counter in the program
- A graphics/windowing package for ease of interactive use to illustrate information and relationships, allowing knowledge engineers to switch from one environment to another without losing context
- Integration with traditional software tools such as word processors, spreadsheets,and communication programs

Future development tools may include:

- Simulation kits (offering the knowledge engineer the ability to test all aspects of an expert system)

- Text generation and explanation packages (which provide the ability to input data from textbooks for knowledge acquisition).
- Sound generation and voice recognition packages (used for knowledge acquisition and end user interfaces)
- Sophisticated natural language front ends (to simulate carrying on a conversation with a human expert directly)

An *advantage* of starting with a development tool is that the knowledge engineering acquisition tools and utilities have already been built. The knowledge engineer is able to build an expert system without having to create the reasoning and data structure components from scratch. "You supply the knowledge, we supply the intelligence," claims a typical promotional brochure. Many systems offer a complete interactive development engine for entering knowledge into the system.

Development tools can drastically reduce the time spent creating the prototype, allowing for more time to test and debug the prototype. Another reason in favor of purchasing a development tool is to exploit an existing rule language and inference engine. This structure imposes a control on the natural language of the system, usually LISP or PRO-LOG, which are infamous for their "runaway" characteristics. In addition, a development tool usually provides numerous peripheral utilities that have been developed to support a large system. This gives the knowledge engineer more power for manipulating the knowledge base and inference engine.

The primary *disadvantage* of a development tool is that it will generally embody only one reasoning methodology and knowledge representation technique, while sophisticated applications often require a combination of techniques. By limiting the constructs of the predefined inference engine, it is not always possible to accurately model the expert in some applications. More and more software development tools, however, are providing hybrid combinations of identifiable reasoning techniques to attain closer adaptations of the expert system to the actual application. For example, KES (by Software Architecture & Engineering), PICON (by LMI), 1ST CLASS (by Programs In Motion), and GURU (by Micro Data Base Systems) use forward chaining, backward chaining, or bidirectional.

The functions of development tools, the associated hardware for the tools, and the usefulness of the application all vary tremendously.

Most development tools available today are rule based. The knowledge engineer is thus restricted to constructing the knowledge base as a series of *If–Then*, or *If–Then–Else* statements.

Another possible *disadvantage* of development tools is cost. For microcomputer systems, the low cost of recent development tools has all but eliminated this as a major consideration. Minicomputer and mainframe development tools, while also rapidly declining in cost, still require a substantial investment.

Some of the well-known tools available for symbolic processors, minicomputers, and mainframes are PERSONAL CONSULTANT PLUS, KES, S.1, KEE, SRL +, ART, REVEAL, RULEMASTER, LOOPS, KNOWLEDGE CRAFT, EMYCIN, HEARSAY-III, EXSYS, and TIMM.

Over the past couple years, expert systems have entered the microcomputer world, thanks to advancements such as faster 32- and 16-bit microcomputer processors, inexpensive memory enhancements, better LISP programming environments, and the general proliferation of microcomputers throughout all industries. Many development tools are available for a variety of microcomputers (although predominantly for the IBM PCs): PERSONAL CONSULTANT PLUS, EXSYS, GURU, KES II, 1ST CLASS, INSIGHT 2 +, ADVISOR, EXPERT-EASE, EXPERT EDGE, M.1, and EXPERT CHOICE. Most packages are quite new, while a few were developed in the 1970s. For a more in-depth glance at development tools on the market today, see Appendix C.

Micro-based systems allow an organization to spend as little as a few thousand dollars to get a fairly complete expert system (including both hardware and software). Some micro-based development tools cost as little as $100. The key to micro-based expert systems is that they are excellent sources for (1) educating and training users in the building of expert systems, and (2) developing systems for simple to semi-complex problems with a limited number of rules (e.g., excellent for prototyping systems). Larger, more complex problems will, however, inevitably require the power of the larger machines. There is no average number of rules established for micro-based expert systems. Viable micro-based systems have been developed with numbers of rules ranging from 50 to 4000.

In terms of functionality, PERSONAL CONSULTANT PLUS, TIMM, and EXSYS are just three out of the many tools which embody English-based command editors for the creation of the knowledge base.

KDS and TIMM are two examples of tools that are menu driven and require no programming background. As previously mentioned, the majority of these tools are rule-based systems using the *If–Then* or *If–Then–Else* data representations. EXPERT-EASE, KDS, 1ST CLASS, and RULEMASTER are representative of example-based systems where the rules in the knowledge base are derived, via inductive logic, from inputted examples.

Some researchers are cautious, believing that "true" micro-based expert systems have yet to arrive. Mickey Williamson in *PC Products* magazine states,

> Recently, programs incorporating some of the concepts of artificial intelligence have filtered down to the personal computer area, giving birth to such things as natural language systems and expert system shells. For the most part, however, these programs are basically prototypes of software that has yet to be developed, the first step on the road to true micro-based experts. (Williamson, Dec. 1985, pp. 43–76)

There are vast differences in the quality and sophistication of the available development tools. A good knowledge engineer must be familiar with the available products and be able to judge their quality and usefulness for specific applications. What are some of the considerations when comparing development tools?

The Power and Capacity of the Tool. Many rule-based development tools, particularly micro-based, come with an imposed limit on the number of rules allowed by the tool. Although many have high limits, approaching the limit imposes a significant problem on the knowledge engineer and possibly the quality of the expert system.

The Editing Capabilities of the Knowledge Base. This is a primary concern to the knowledge engineer and is generally transparent to the user. The speed and ease of editing can greatly enhance, or impair, the productivity of the knowledge engineer.

Hardware Requirements for the Tool. Many tools require different amounts of memory, disk space, and graphics capabilities.

Software Requirements for the Tool. Several tools require additional software to run. For example, the LISP-based micro-based tools PER-

SONAL CONSULTANT from Texas Instruments and KES from Software Architecture & Engineering require that the system have IQLISP resident. (PERSONAL CONSULTANT PLUS and KES's C-based versions have no additional software requirements.)

Cost. With this new industry breaking into the commercial market, it is important for the organization and knowledge engineer to be aware that cost is not a *primary* factor for software selection (particularly for micro-based tools). Currently, software cost is not indicative of the software's power or capabilities.

Training and Support. Just as expert system software is different from conventional software, the expert system industry is different from the traditional computing industry. Training and support from the vendor is vitally important and can have a major impact upon productivity in the system's early development stages. For example, some micro-based companies have full customer support groups, available via the telephone during normal business hours. Other micro-based companies provide customer support only on a call-back basis. This means that the knowledge engineer places a call and explains his situation, and the vendor then has a software engineer return the call. One such company's reasoning is that "until the software is saturated into the market, and demand exists for full-time support, there is no reason to expend the funds for full-time support."

Compiled Versus Interpreted Code. Interpreted code is program code that converts to object code when the expert system is run. Development time is fast because there is no additional time required for compilation, but the run-time execution is slowed due to conversion. Compiled code is the opposite. Development time is slowed due to compilation requirements, but the object code executed at run time reduces the execution time. This difference is apt to be a factor only in those applications where the execution time of the expert system is absolutely critical, or if the system is so large and complex that execution delays adversely frustrate the user.

The Reasoning Strategies. The prevalent reasoning strategies are forward and backward chaining. These techniques are preferred for certain types of applications and do not apply well to other types of applications. For example, forward chaining begins with premises and attempts to solve for the solutions. Good areas of application are forecasting and prediction. Backward chaining is the opposite: it begins with solutions and attempts to solve for the premises. An excellent application for backward chaining is diagnosis.

The Search Technique. What is the most efficient and effective way to traverse through the knowledge base? The most effective way is one that will always consider every piece of data—an exhaustive search. Unfortunately, exhaustive searches are not very efficient. There are many efficient ways of searching, including depth-first and breadth-first. The question then is "Do I want the most effective or the most efficient search technique?" If time is critical, then efficient may be the answer; if accuracy is critical, then effective may be the answer.

Table 6.1 presents a list matching the available development tools and AI languages with the hardware vendors (categorized by microcomputers and mini-/mainframe computers).

PREPACKAGED COMMERCIAL EXPERT SYSTEMS

The last category of software is the prepackaged or "canned" expert system. The packaged commercial expert systems come complete with an expert's knowledge and problem-solving heuristics already embodied in the system. No development or knowledge acquisition time is required, providing immediate run-time capabilities upon installation. Most of the existing expert systems were developed by large corporations since they had the resource bases to hurdle the high costs historically associated with developing in-house systems. Recently, however, demands by small- to medium-size companies, who want the benefits of expert systems but cannot afford a full-time development staff, have created a fertile, untapped market for prepackaged systems. Venture capitalists have recently backed several start-up companies seeking to find a niche in this market, and several commercial prepackaged expert systems are now available.

Many of the prepackaged expert systems are in the financial service, insurance underwriting, and medical industries. Companies like Applied Expert Systems (APEX), Arthur Andersen, Arthur D. Little,

Table 6.1. Available Software Packages

PACKAGE	TOOL (T) OR LAN- GUAGE (L)	HARDWARE VENDOR	SOFTWARE VENDOR
MicroComputers			
1ST CLASS	T	IBM	Programs In Motion, Inc.
ADS/PC	T	IBM	Aion Corporation
ADVISOR	T	Apple Atari Commodore	Texas Instruments
ARITY EXPERT SYSTEM	T	IBM	Arity Corporation
ART	T	IBM	Inference Corporation
DOCUMENT MODELER	T	Apple	The Model Office Company
ESP ADVISOR	T	IBM	Expert Systems International
EXPERLISP	L	Apple	Expertelligence
EXPEROPS5	L	Apple	Expertelligence
EXPERT-2 in MMSFORTH	T	IBM	Miller Microcomputer Services
EXPERT CHOICE	T	IBM	Decision Support Software, Inc.
EXPERTEACH-II	T	IBM	Intelligence Ware, Inc.
EXPERT-EASE	T	IBM DEC Victor	Human Edge Software Corp.
EXPERT EDGE	T	IBM	Human Edge Software Corp.
EXSYS	T	IBM	Exsys, Inc.
GCLISP	L	IBM	Gold Hill Computers
GURU	T	IBM DEC	Micro Data Base Systems, Inc.
IN-ATE	T	Apple	Automated Reasoning Corporation
INSIGHT 2 +	T	DEC IBM Victor	Level Five Research, Inc.
IQLISP	L	IBM Texas In- struments	Integral Quality

Table 6.1 (continued)

PACKAGE	TOOL (T) OR LAN-GUAGE (L)	HARDWARE VENDOR	SOFTWARE VENDOR
MicroComputers (cont.)			
KDS Development System	T	IBM	KDS Corporation
KEE	T	IBM	Intellicorp
KES II	T	IBM	Software A & E
M.1	T	IBM	Teknowledge
MACSMARTS	T	Apple	Cognitive Technology Corporation
MPROLOG	L	IBM	Logicware
MULISP	L	IBM	Microsoft
ODS/SALES CONS	T	Apple	Organizational Software, Inc.
OPS5+	L	Apple IBM	Artelligence
PCSCHEME	T	IBM Texas In-struments	Texas Instruments
PERSONAL CON-SULTANT PLUS	T	IBM Texas In-struments	Texas Instruments
PRODIGY	T	IBM	Artelligence, Inc.
REVEAL	T	IBM	McDonnell Douglas
SKIPPER	T	IBM	RCA
TIMM-PC	T	IBM	General Research Corporation
TURBO PROLOG	L	IBM	Borland International
WIZDOM	T	IBM	Software Intelligence Laboratory
Xi	T	IBM	Portable Software, Inc.
XSYS	T	IBM	California Intelligence, Inc.

Table 6.1 (continued)

PACKAGE	TOOL (T) OR LAN- GUAGE (L)	HARDWARE VENDOR	SOFTWARE VENDOR
Mini/Mainframe Computers			
ADS/MVS	T	IBM	Aion Corporation
ART	T	DEC Lisp Machine Sun Micro- system Symbolics Texas In- struments	Inference Corporation
ESP ADVISOR	T	DEC	Expert Systems International
EXSYS	T	DEC	Exsys, Inc.
FRANZLISP	L	Amdahl Apollo AT&T DEC Integrated Solutions Masscomp Silicon Graphics	Franz, Inc.
IN-ATE	T	DEC Lisp Machine Symbolics Texas In- struments	Automated Reasoning Corporation
INSIGHT 2+	T	DEC	Level Five Research
KEE	T	Apollo DEC IBM Hewlett- Packard Lisp Machine Sun Micro- systems Symbolics Texas In- struments Xerox	Intellicorp

Table 6.1 (continued)

PACKAGE	TOOL (T) OR LAN- GUAGE (L)	HARDWARE VENDOR	SOFTWARE VENDOR
Mini/Mainframe Computers (cont.)			
KES	T	Apollo Control Data DEC Sun Micro- systems Tektronix	Software Architecture & Engineering, Inc.
KNOWLEDGE CRAFT	T	DEC Hewlett- Packard Lisp Machine Texas In- struments Symbolics	The Carnegie Group, Inc.
OPS5	L	DEC Xerox Symbolics	Carnegie-Mellon University DEC
PICON	T	Lisp Machine	Lisp Machine, Inc.
PERSONAL CONSULTANT	T	Texas In- struments IBM	Texas Instruments
QUINTUS PROLOG	L	Apollo DEC Sun Micro- systems Xerox	Quintus
REVEAL	T	DEC IBM Prime	Infotym
RULEMASTER	T	Apollo AT&T Burroughs Celerity DEC Gould Hewlett- Packard IBM Masscomp	Radian Corporation

Table 6.1 (continued)

PACKAGE	TOOL (T) OR LAN-GUAGE (L)	HARDWARE VENDOR	SOFTWARE VENDOR
Mini/Mainframe Computers (cont.)			
RULEMASTER (cont.)		Perkin-Elmer Pyramid Sun Micro-systems Tektronix Texas In-struments	
S.1	T	Amdahl Apollo AT&T DEC Gould Hewlett-Packard IBM Motorola NCR Sun Micro-systems Symbolics Tektronix Xerox	Teknowledge
SRL+	T	DEC Lisp Machine Perq Symbolics	The Carnegie Group, Inc.
TI PROLOG	L	Texas In-struments	Texas Instruments
TIMM	T	Amdahl DEC IBM Prime Zenith	General Research Corporation

Brattle Research, Jeffrey Perrone, Level Five Research, Management Decision Systems, Palladian, and Syntelligence offer prepackaged expert systems and services for developing expert systems. Appendix A houses a list of companies that market expert system software and offer consulting and training.

An example of a prepackaged expert system is COCOMO 1, offered by Level Five Research. COCOMO 1 is a software costing assistant which estimates resource requirements such as manpower for large-scale software development projects. It was developed using INSIGHT 2 +, also from Level Five Research. The costing function is based on the COCOMO model developed by Dr. Barry Boehm at TRW. Results of a COCOMO 1 run include schedules regarding: effects of the development process given modifications in any phase; estimated completion time of each phase and the entire project; projected resource requirements by phase; programmer productivity; and an audit trail to show costing assumptions of the user.

In the face of deregulation and changing economic conditions, a new wave of competition is forcing financial services institutions to reexamine their traditional conservative business practices. Banks are contending with problem commercial loan portfolios, thinner margins, and mounting competition from within the industry and from nontraditional institutions that offer similar financial services. Likewise, heavy commercial underwriting losses and archaic business practices are challenging insurance companies to find better ways of analyzing and controlling the selection of insurance risks. Financial services institutions are meeting these competitive challenges in two ways: by increasing revenues through new products and services, and by controlling costs and losses to increase profits. Many prepackaged expert systems focusing on financial service applications are coming to the market in response to this need. Syntelligence, for example, offers two prepackaged expert systems—the UNDERWRITING ADVISOR and the LENDING ADVISOR (see Chapter 2).

In evaluating packaged commercial expert systems, several questions should be asked:

1. Who is the expert whose knowledge is embodied in the program, and what is the expert's track record? Is the expert really an expert; that is, does the expert stand "head and shoulders" above the average in his field?

2. Does the commercial expert system actually fit the application? Remember, an expert system is suited primarily to limited domain problems and is not easily transported to different domains. Therefore, the domain of the existing problem must be similar to the original domain in the expert system.

3. Is the expert system well constructed, with proper regard to appropriate data structures, search techniques, reasoning strategies, and user friendliness?

4. Is the knowledge base relatively complete, embodying most of the available knowledge in the domain?

5. Does the system have sufficient flexibility to allow for modification to adapt it to the specific application?

6. Does the system allow interaction or networking with conventional programs such as spreadsheets and measurement devices as needed by the application?

Unfortunately, many newly introduced commercial systems do not satisfy the basic requirements for a competent expert system and are often little more than a first-cut prototype. In fact, some systems, promoted as "advanced" expert systems, are nothing more than repackaged decision support systems under a new "high-tech" label. The prepackaged expert system industry, as it currently stands, is clearly one of caveat emptor, in spite of the determined attempts of some conscientious vendors to market professionally designed and well-tested systems. Disappointments will likely be many, but a competent knowledge engineer can reduce such disappointments by carefully screening the previous questions.

It is definitely easier to start with a prepackaged expert system, but undoubtedly the knowledge base will need to be modified or customized to reflect the particular corporate environment and philosophy. Imagine, for example, what an industry would be like if all of the companies in an industry bought the same prepackaged expert system on corporate strategy and strategic planning. Several experts argue that prepackaged expert systems will not be as prominent as originally anticipated. For many problems, prepackaged expert systems are simply too limited in their domain applications. But perhaps the most limiting factor revolves around the availability of true experts. Real expertise is a valuable commodity and is usually carefully guarded within existing organizations. Well-developed expert systems often never escape organizational walls.

In this chapter we have addressed the differences between conventional and expert system software and the three categories of expert system software: general AI languages, development tools, and prepackaged expert systems. Tradeoffs exist with respect to (1) initial cost, (2) development time, (3) development cost, and (4) degree of

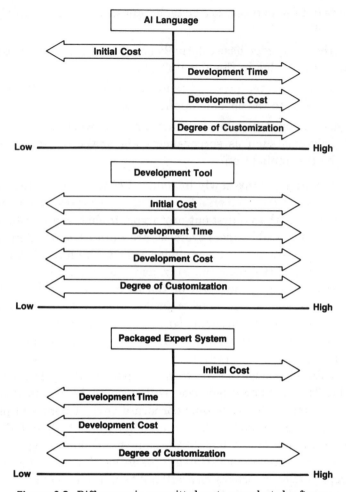

Figure 6.3. Differences in committed costs per selected software.

customization for all three categories of expert system software. Figure 6.3 graphically emphasizes four differences of these software categories. Prepackaged expert system software tends to have a high initial cost, but a much shorter development cycle. AI languages have a low initial cost, but a much longer development cycle. Development tools are lower in initial cost than prepackaged expert systems, and have a shorter development cycle than AI languages. Each of these software categories has its own advantages and disadvantages; it is up to the knowledge engineer to match the proper software category to the type of application, time constraints, and budget constraints.

PART FOUR

CONSTRUCTION OF AN EXPERT SYSTEM

Building an expert system is vastly different from coding a program. It is an entirely new area of computing. The first chapter addresses a new area of expertise: *knowledge engineering*. A knowledge engineer differs from a programmer in that the knowledge engineer must not only be technically adept with expert system software, but must also possess superior psychological, communicative, and management skills. A programmer, given an application with known inputs and outputs, must provide the means to transform the inputs into outputs. A knowledge engineer is typically given a person—someone who is an expert at a specific task in a specific area. The primary task of the knowledge engineer is to identify critical inputs and outputs, discern the inner process by which the expert transforms these inputs into outputs, establish this knowledge in the appropriate computer system, and finally, encourage the successful integration of the expert system into the organization.

The second chapter of Part Four emphasizes one of the most difficult steps for the knowledge engineer in the knowledge engineering process: *knowledge acquisition*. Knowledge acquisition can be defined as the process of extracting and documenting expertise (primarily from human experts, but often from archival sources), which then serves as the basis for building the knowledge base and inference engine. Knowledge acquisition is a critical responsibility of the knowledge engineer, playing a vital role in what Dr. Edward A. Feigenbaum of Stanford University calls the "Knowledge Principle." The Knowledge

Principle says that the competence of an expert system is a function of its knowledge, not of its inference procedures.

Chapter 9 details the *construction* of an expert system; it begins by identifying the necessary steps for constructing a simple expert system and follows each step from start to finish. The construction process of one expert system application is repeated five times, each time employing a different expert system development tool. This chapter concludes by noting various differences of the tools, and implications of these differences.

7

Knowledge Engineering

Expert systems are not immaculate creations: they require complex and lengthy development and maintenance. Many companies, excited by the potential of expert systems, have prematurely jumped into expert system development, concluding with disappointing results and costly overruns. A key to efficient and effective expert system development is proper knowledge engineering. Knowledge engineering is the process of synthesizing knowledge into a computer system so that problems are electronically solved through symbolic manipulation and reasoning of the knowledge base.

Knowledge engineering is a science that entails the task of building an expert system by (as identified in Chapter 1, Figure 1.4)

Stage 1: Identification and Definition of the Problem

1. Recognizing the dimensions of knowledge
2. Identifying and evaluating an application

Stage 2: Development of the Prototype

3. Formulating the application into an organized problem
4. Collecting preliminary knowledge (knowledge discovery)
5. Articulating this knowledge into an organized form
6. Building a prototype expert system

Stage 3: Construction of the Expert System

   7. Acquiring detailed knowledge

   8. Building the rules and inferences to manipulate the data

   9. Organizing and refining knowledge for effective implementation

  10. Automating this information into the system chosen

Stage 4: Testing and Evaluation of the Expert System

  11. Evaluating the expert system

Stage 5: Integration and Implementation of the Expert System

  12. Integrating the expert system into the environment and coordinating user training

  13. Documenting the expert system

Stage 6: Maintenance of the Expert System

  14. Supporting domain expansion or heuristic improvements

STAGE 1: IDENTIFICATION AND DEFINITION OF THE PROBLEM

Dimensions of Knowledge

Proficiency in knowledge engineering is synonomous with understanding the dimensions of knowledge; that is, what types of knowledge can an expert system effectively capture? Several different taxonomies of knowledge have been proposed. Knowledge can be categorized along dimensions of definitional versus empirical, imperative versus declarative, heuristic versus algorithmic, theoretic versus pragmatic, general versus specific, descriptive versus prescriptive, and certain versus uncertain.

    A useful taxonomy is provided by Hayes-Roth (1984), who describes knowledge along three dimensions: scope, purpose, and validity (as

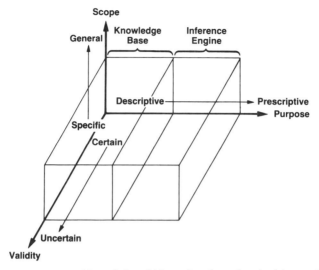

Figure 7.1. Dimensions of knowledge. [Adapted and reprinted with permission from Hayes-Roth, "The Knowledge-Based Expert Systems: A Tutorial," *IEEE Computer*, Sept. 1984 (© 1984 IEEE).]

illustrated in Figure 7.1). One axis is the scope of knowledge, ranging from general, common statements to very specific, focused statements. The purpose of knowledge, another axis, ranges from descriptive (factual) statements to prescriptive (procedural) statements. Descriptive statements usually describe or classify physical objects. Prescriptive statements describe rules, orders, or directions to follow rather than observable physical attributes. On the third axis is the validity of knowledge. Validity ranges from 100% certain to 100% uncertain. Based on this description, knowledge can be classified into eight categories. Given is an example of knowledge within each category.

General, Descriptive, Certain

Stars are a point of light in the sky.

General, Prescriptive, Certain

To conclude $p(x)$, show that $-p(x)$ is impossible.

General, Descriptive, Uncertain

Family life events are observable.

General, Prescriptive, Uncertain

If A then C; if C or B then D; if D exists, then conclude A.

Specific, Descriptive, Certain

$2 + 2 = 4$ Base 10.

Specific, Prescriptive, Certain

If the chemical composition is H_2O, then it is water.

Specific, Descriptive, Uncertain

A person has two hands. This statement is uncertain because not every person has two hands. A person may have lost a hand in an accident or may not have been born with two (as a result of a birth defect).

Specific, Prescriptive, Uncertain

The prefix title to the name Kyle is Mr.

Using this taxonomy, the knowledge base of an expert system almost exclusively encompasses specific, descriptive knowledge along the validity axis of Figure 7.1. This area is a bounded set of knowledge that the expert system can best represent. Specific, descriptive knowledge along the validity axis is best incorporated into the inference engine and problem-solving strategies, although it can also be found in the knowledge base (e.g., incorporated in frame inheritance).

Current applications of specific, descriptive, and certain knowledge are

- Definitions and taxonomies
- Discrete descriptions
- Simple constraints and invariants
- Empirical associations
- Perceptual structures
- Deductive methods
- Simple inductive methods
- Simple physical models
- Simple search heuristics

Expert systems have difficulty working with other categories of knowledge, such as in the general, prescriptive plane of Figure 7.1.

General Problem-Solving Knowledge

Expert systems cannot yet emulate the general problem-solving behavior of humans because humans are able to solve problems in a multidomain environment. Multidomain relationships and interactions are difficult to model accurately.

Naïve Physics

This is the common, nonverbal understanding of the basic laws of physics (even demonstrated in young children). For example, the law of gravity and physical properties states, "If I knock my mother's crystal vase off the living room table onto the hardwood floor, it will drop and shatter." The fact that I can simulate the image/effect before it happens warns me that knocking the vase is not a viable action. Expert systems do not have the ability to effectively simulate possible effects.

Metaknowledge

Metaknowledge is knowledge about knowledge. Expert systems currently do not have the ability to reason with metaknowledge. For example, knowing that I can speak the language, ask for assistance, or read street signs, illustrates metaknowledge when I am planning a vacation to another country.

Metaknowledge Representation

It is not clear how one should represent metaknowledge. How does one express the relationship between the ability to read signs and planning a trip? In order to determine if I was successful in executing the trip, I need to know whether or not I was on course.

First Principle

Expert systems do not have a core set of principles that represent general rules for solving a multitude of problems. This is the ability to recognize solutions based on previous examples of problems. This ability is not necessary in expert systems if the experts are able to provide more specialized rules that work well within the domain.

Analogy

Expert systems cannot yet solve problems by using analogy. Many forecasts by experts, for example, are based on their intuitive understanding of analogous events in history, either in the same or completely different domains.

Within the broad scope of knowledge domains are many specific types of knowledge that can be classified into areas of "domains." For example, statements such as "A whale is a mammal" and "Los Angeles is a city in California" fall into the same specific, descriptive category of knowledge, yet into different domains. "A whale is a mammal" has no relevancy when talking about U.S. cities and locations, yet it is an important statement in the sphere of oceanographic sciences.

Proper domain identification is important because of the need to focus on facts relevant to solving the problem and limit the number of potential statements in the knowledge base. The knowledge base is divided into two categories of (1) domain-independent knowledge, and (2) domain-dependent knowledge. No expert, or expert system, solves a problem completely in one domain, but rather uses a variety of knowledge.

Domain-independent knowledge is the underlying foundation of general information used by the expert, although it is not directly related to the specific problem. For example, the principles of integral calculus and differential calculus are part of the domain-independent knowledge incorporated into the well-known medical expert system MYCIN. Or, in our example of the whale, U.S. cities and their locations are part of domain-independent knowledge when analyzing the migratory path of the gray whale (Figure 7.2).

Domain-dependent knowledge takes the domain-independent knowledge one step further and enhances or "customizes" it according to the particulars of the problem. For example, MYCIN contains domain-dependent knowledge about relationships between specimen cultures, smears, infections, drugs, and symptoms for infectious blood diseases.

Expert systems work best where, within the knowledge base, the domain-dependent knowledge is a significant percentage, and the domain-independent knowledge is less significant. Most viable expert systems have the primary scope of the knowledge base in domain-dependent (specific) knowledge.

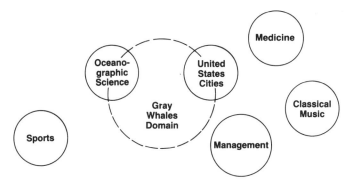

Figure 7.2. Different domains and relationships used to study the migratory path of gray whales.

Problem Identification and Evaluation

A knowledge engineer will inevitably ask the question, "Which of my problems and applications fit expert systems?" The identification and evaluation phase focuses on this question and encompasses:

1. Identification of the problem task
2. Identification of the problem domain
3. Identification of the scope of the problem
4. Identification of application appropriateness
5. Assessment of organizational benefits and costs
6. Identification of potential source(s) of expertise
7. Identification of the users
8. Evaluation of modeling feasibility
9. Evaluation of project effort (duration, time, cost, etc.)
10. Assessment of utility
11. Identification of appropriate hardware and software

The knowledge engineer formally addresses each of these issues in an *Expert System Project Study*. This document should be circulated among top management, potential experts, information systems and user departments, and any other groups or individuals that have a stake in the expert system project. This will serve to gain valuable feedback as well as to "gear the organization up" for expert system integration. When examining the viability of expert systems, several issues in the areas of domain type, data type, economic considerations, and source of expertise need to be addressed. Expert systems are viable when

1. The problem is well-defined, not too large and not too small. A problem that takes only a few minutes to solve or where well-known solutions exist but are not cost/benefit justifiable is not viable. Problems that are too large realistically require a large, complicated solution space. Ill-defined problems only lead to a chaotic system (similar to conventional systems engineering).

2. The domain is reliable, relatively stable, available, and complete. The scope and size of the knowledge base must be clearly definable. Dynamic, incomplete knowledge can lead to faulty recommendations. If the domain knowledge exists but is not easily accessible (e.g., proprietary or top secret data), then the application may not be viable from an "availability" viewpoint.

3. The domain is representable; that is, it can be modeled in a computer knowledge data structure. A large percentage of the domain knowledge must be incorporated into the knowledge base. The state-space representation should also be contained. A large solution space is pragmatically infeasible for an expert system.

4. The data required to be inputted to the expert system for analysis are reliable, available, and complete. Similar to domain knowledge, the expert system must have a well-defined scope of data input. Other issues of how the data are acquired: Can there be missing data? How much data needs to be inputted? Are the data acquired over various periods of time? These questions also need to be considered.

5. The thought process of the expert is not "common sense." If the expert insists it is common sense, then he probably does not have a sufficiently clear understanding of his own thought process to articulate it during knowledge acquisition. Intuition is not easy to capture; avoid applications where reasoning is by first principles, analogy, learning, or via metaknowledge. The best methodologies to model are heuristic, judgmental, or experimental—specific, descriptive knowledge.

6. One overall control strategy is capable of solving a majority of the domain's problems. Knowledge engineering complexities arise when the inference engine must constantly change its "thought process" in order to solve the problem.

7. Users exist. What benefit is derived from an expert system that no one uses? The vocabularly used to converse with the user should be limited, concise, and related to the domain. This will help alleviate ambiguous questions or answers. The flow of the conversation should be "natural." The recommendation from the expert system must have value to the user.

8. The source of expertise is recognized as an authority on the subject matter and is readily available. If several experts with recognized authority exist, the best expert to select for knowledge acquisition is one that is articulate, is introspective, has the patience and ability to explain problem solving, and is committed to the project.

9. The knowledge is symbolic and not data intensive. If the application is data intensive or numerical, or has a set of standard procedures to solve the problem, then it is probably better to approach it as a conventional programming problem.

10. The application is bottlenecked by existing methods, and only a few good experts exist. Expert systems provide substantial economic benefits under these conditions.

11. Management commitment is sufficient to support the application selected and to allocate the appropriate amount of time and resources to the development of the system. As with any new project, the expert system must be in line with the direction and focus of the organization, or chartered as a separate research and development project.

12. If multiple experts exist, then typical domain problems can be solved with a general consensus among the experts; otherwise, it is not a viable application. If no agreement exists among experts, then the solution may only represent nontraceable opinions or guesses. Under these conditions, an expert system may not be worth implementing.

13. The organizational culture is sufficiently attuned to accepting and integrating new technologies and innovations. Expert systems, like any new innovation, need to be successfully integrated into an organization's day-to-day operations.

STAGE 2: DEVELOPMENT OF THE PROTOTYPE

At the end of Stage 1, the knowledge engineer should have completed a preliminary *Expert System Project Study*. In Stage 2, prototype development, further knowledge is collected to formulate the application into a well-organized problem and convert it into a prototype expert system.

Knowledge Discovery

Discerning and collecting information for the knowledge base is undoubtedly the most difficult, frustrating, and time-consuming process undertaken by the knowledge engineer. There are two primary sources of data for the knowledge engineer to investigate, as discussed previously:

1. Domain-independent facts such as broad, usually public archival information
2. Domain-dependent facts such as domain specific, often proprietary, archival information and heuristic, judgmental, and logical information from the expert

Domain-independent knowledge is the basic foundation for the knowledge base; it is found in books, journals, pamphlets, and articles. This provides the "meat" of the knowledge base for the application and allows the knowledge engineer to begin formalizing the structure and outline of the application. Domain-dependent knowledge often comes from the organization itself and can consist of proprietary documents and manuals that are a result of internal research and development. This information begins to customize the model and tie the foundation data together. Additional domain-dependent knowledge comes from the expert. The expert primarily offers situational information, and little raw data. This situational information includes relationships of problems, tendencies, where to begin troubleshooting, what to look for in certain situations, and procedural rules. These are "what-if" and "if-this, do-that" types of information that add the human interpretive (heuristic) aspect to the expert system.

The process of extracting information from the expert is called *Knowledge acquisition* and is discussed in depth in Chapter 8. Briefly, to extract information from the expert, the knowledge engineer follows three basic steps. (1) The knowledge engineer must familiarize himself with the specifics of the application. The first step is called *knowledge discovery*. Specifics such as the jargon (he must be able to interpret exactly what the expert is saying) and procedure (he must be able to visualize and understand what the expert is doing) must be understood. (2) The knowledge engineer interviews the expert about the application, the expert's job, problem-solving techniques, and sources of additional information about the application in case of discrepancies. (3) The knowledge engineer must analyze, code, and validate knowledge. In many technical and complex applications it is not uncommon for an expert to omit knowledge (which may be unimportant or may be crucial) regarding a particular procedure or to say one thing and perform another. It is up to the knowledge engineer to spot these discrepancies and identify and validate correct information. In cases of discrepancies where the expert cannot provide a satisfactory answer, a second or third expert can be consulted.

Prototype Development

Once sufficient information has been gathered and the knowledge engineer has a good understanding of the application and problem-solving structure, a prototype can be constructed. Prototyping is usually accomplished using a development tool, oftentimes a microcomputer version. If a development tool is not employed, then the inference engine, development engine, and knowledge base must be built from scratch. When prototyping, the knowledge engineer considers the following items (this information is usually documented in *The Knowledge Handbook* described in more detail in Chapter 8):

- Any hypotheses and procedural rules that relate to the problem.
- A descriptive, perhaps visual, model of the expert system; this model should be as detailed as possible, showing the problem-solving process and the front and end interfaces and should also contain the goals of the expert system.
- All of the characteristics of the data that have been collected.
  — The amount of data
  — The certainty of the data
  — Any unknown data

— The temporal sequence of the data and whether it affects the viability of the data
— The reliability of the data
— The consistency and completeness of the data
— The relationships of the data
— The methods of maintaining current data

STAGE 3: CONSTRUCTION OF THE EXPERT SYSTEM

Stage 3 is an elaboration and completion of the prototype model from Stage 2. It is in this phase that all rules and inferences of the expert system are built; this involves acquiring the detailed knowledge of the domain, the "personal" and "private" knowledge of the expert. Do not be surprised if the prototype is totally scrapped and the expert system is rebuilt from scratch. The first attempt at emulating the expert's domain may not be the best; structrual representations, control strategies, and databases are constantly in flux as new knowledge is acquired. One well-known expert system developer uses this rule of thumb: define the first 100 rules, then toss them out and start again.

Stage 3 is also where some organizations may evaluate the prototype, and decide whether or not to embark on a full expert system development program. At this point the full cost of system development needs to be made explicit; in all likelihood, hardware, software, and development time will differ substantially from the prototype model.

Cost of Expert Systems

The cost of expert systems can be divided into three interrelated categories:

1. cost of hardware
2. cost of software
3. cost of development (labor and time)

For clarity, the cost of software includes any language, development tool, or prepackaged system that is needed to develop the application. There are tradeoffs, of course, between all three cost segments.

For example, for expert system applications on mainframe computers the cost difference between purchasing an AI language, which runs about $18,000 for LISP or PROLOG, and a development tool, which usually runs over $50,000 (for example Teknowledge's S.1 costs about $60,000), can be quite substantial. But the additional cost of developing a tool from an AI language may easily exceed $50,000, depending on the programming skills of the organization. Development costs also include user training, the salaries of the knowledge engineer(s), the expert's time (either as an opportunity cost for internal experts or a real cost for external expertise), and the salaries of the expert system development and maintenance staff. In fact, staffing costs become a major consideration during this stage and may exceed the combined cost of hardware and software by a factor of ten. The staff for a successful expert system application will likely include

1. One or more senior knowledge engineers
2. One or more knowledge engineers, either novice or experienced
3. One or more knowledge paratechnicals (less training than knowledge engineers, but useful in some types of knowledge acquisition, coding, and documentation)
4. Technical management
5. Project leader (usually a senior knowledge engineer)
6. Programmers, if an AI language is selected, or if the expert system is to be networked with other systems or programs
7. And, of course, the expert(s)

The number of personnel within each category will vary with the application. A small application project, for example, will probably have a single person assuming role responsibilities from a number of categories, but large applications may have staffs of over 30 individuals—for projects lasting several years.

An important consideration in estimating the cost of development is the level of in-house knowledge engineering capabilities desired. Often an organization will not need, or even desire, permanent in-house knowledge engineering capabilities, but will contract out for the necessary services. The time delays for training in-house personnel, the complexity and size of the application, and the degree of top management's commitment to expert systems are all factors that will determine the level of knowledge engineering retained on the in-house staff.

A number of sources provide knowledge engineering services on a contract basis. The first, the primary source, is the company where the hardware and/or software (tools) were obtained. Another source is a private consulting company that specializes in expert system applications. A non-exhaustive list of expert system consultants is provided in Appendix B. A third source is the faculty of a local university's computer science, management, or information systems department. Developing in-house expertise can be accomplished by a combination of (1) working with external consultants, (2) training programs and assistance offered by vendor companies to clients, (3) short, intensive courses offered by private firms in specialty areas (such as the weeklong knowledge engineering course offered by Teknowledge), and (4) longer, more traditional courses offered by universities and colleges. These development and staffing costs, which usually become clearer after the prototype stage, must be factored into decisions regarding final project development.

The total cost of building an expert system from an AI language on a mainframe computer is estimated to exceed $1 million. This includes the necessary hardware, software, and development time. DIPMETER ADVISOR, as previously mentioned, cost upwards of $20 million. Using an expert system development tool may substantially reduce the cost of development. The costs for minicomputer development tools range from $25,000 to $40,000, while microcomputer versions range from $250 to $10,000, depending on the tool's size and functionality. Development costs are still the primary expense, however. A "canned" or prepackaged expert system designed for a specific application is estimated to cost a minimum of $100,000. Expert systems are expensive investments; in all, the more complex the application and amorphous the expert, the longer it will take to prototype the expert system, and the greater the total cost, regardless of the hardware and software used.

Software Type	*Cost*	
AI language	$6000–18,000	+ hardware + development
Microcomputer tool	$250–10,000	+ hardware + development
Mini-mainframe tool	$25,000–40,000	+ hardware + development
Prepackaged	$100,000	

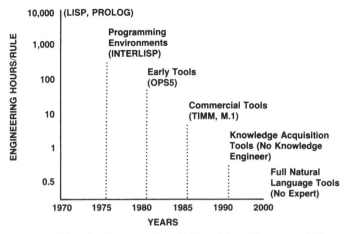

Figure 7.3. Declining development time. (Adapted from Harmon and King, 1985.)

Note, however, that the cost and time of developing an expert system are rapidly declining and will continue to decline for some time. The declining cost of expert systems appears to be following the classic learning curve model of exponential reduction and can be attributed primarily to improved development tools, improved hardware (new built-in features), and the diffusion of trained knowledge engineers into the industry. The decreasing cost and development time of an expert system can be seen in Figure 7.3.

Knowledge Engineering Project Management

Oftentimes, prototype development is somewhat haphazard with both the organization and the knowledge engineer learning as they go. By Stage 3, however, formal and careful management of the development effort is critical. As such, traditional project management techniques are completely appropriate. High technology should not equal high confusion. Reviewed briefly, the management of an expert system project requires

1. Identification of organization's needs (needs assessment)
2. Definition of the project's objectives
3. Determination of resources required
4. Identification and prioritization of project subtasks

5. Allocation of resources

6. Projection of estimated completion date (project schedule)

7. Establishment of control and feedback evaluation loops

8. Adjustment of resources and project timing

9. Implementation and integration of project into the organization

Several common problems can arise, any of which can cause serious delays in the project's schedule. Without proper project management, the expert system may never reach the integration and implementation stage. Delays in the project schedule will vary, depending on the severity of each problem. Problems most typically seen can be grouped into seven broad classes:

1. The initial project plan was inadequately researched (wrong application, wrong software, wrong hardware, etc.).

2. Inadequate time or slack resources were allocated for unplanned emergencies such as an unforeseen subtask, fire fighting, or changing organizational priorities.

3. Controls were not adequately in place to keep abreast of the project status.

4. Overly optimistic delivery or completion dates were made, resulting in understaffing and project quality degeneration.

5. The source of expertise is unavailable, or the "expert" turned out to be a "nonexpert."

6. Unrealistic evaluation and test scenario cases delayed organizational acceptance.

7. Knowledge discovery and acquisition was slower than planned (known as "knowledge acquisition bottleneck").

As an organization gains experience in expert system development, formal project management techniques, such as PERT and CPM, can be applied earlier in the overall process for new, or related, projects; then the likelihood of the aforementioned problems occurring will be reduced.

STAGE 4: TESTING AND EVALUATION OF THE EXPERT SYSTEM

This stage evaluates the performance of the expert system against a set of standards. Expert system evaluation is often nebulous since there are no universally accepted or unbiased formal specifications, or "gold standards," against which the system can be judged. Expert system evaluation is analogous to evaluating a financial portfolio. Several performance indexes exist (e.g., liquidity ratios, profitability measures, GNP, leading indicators, composite measures, industry performance levels), but no measure or group of values has been universally accepted as a standard to evaluate portfolio performance. A portfolio can be measured against several criteria for analysis, but the analysis will always be subject to personal interpretation. Prototype development standard setting is not overly useful either. If the formal evaluation specifications are written after the prototype is developed, a biased evaluation will most likely result.

How is an expert system to be evaluated objectively? Certainly, some attempt should be made to establish some type of measurable predevelopment standards. Many dimensions exist in evaluating the effectiveness or utility of an expert system in an organization—evaluations relating to

1. User acceptance
2. Performance of the system, completeness, and accuracy
3. Utility or value-added benefits
4. Effects on other systems
5. Liability and risk
6. Feedback to the knowledge engineers during development stages

Evaluations can be formal or informal. Formal evaluations are planned milestones with predefined test scenarios used to guide the project toward an accurate and complete system. The danger of formal evaluations is the lack of clear understanding of the evaluation objective and the potential of biasing the test scenario designs such that the evaluation objectives will always be achieved (i.e., a self-fulfilling prophecy). Informal evaluations, or general reviews, will often alleviate some of the "hardness" of formal evaluations, but may not have the potential of completely testing a system. Either way, system failures will often lead to important discoveries concerning incorrect domain or control representation. Strict evaluations too early in the development stage will probably lead to less misdirection and misrepresentation of the expert.

From the user's perspective, the system needs to have a smooth, efficient, and "natural" interface; the system must be simplistic in the amount of computer expertise needed. The expert system's advice must be useful, and an explanation and justification module needs to be present to explain its decisions in case any questions should arise during the working session. System response time is important; users of expert systems normally demand a "natural" conversation—pauses of several minutes will not be tolerated. The system must be quick enough to hold the user's attention. As previously mentioned, speed is a key concern when evaluating compiled versus interpreted development tools, symbolic processing machines versus conventional computing machines, and AI languages versus general-purpose languages.

A critical performance and validation check is to execute several test scenarios that the expert has already solved to see if the expert system produces the same answers (with the correct reasoning process). The evaluation is broken down into two areas: a static evaluation and a dynamic evaluation. The *static evaluation* is the testing of the knowledge base for consistency and completeness. Is the knowledge base sufficient in its representation of the domain? Is it too limited a domain? Does more knowledge need to be added for producing correct answer? It is virtually impossible to incorporate 100% of the domain knowledge in the knowledge base; on the other hand, a knowledge base with only 10% of the relevant knowledge would clearly be unacceptable. The knowledge base is the "intelligence" of the system—the more intelligent the better the decision; completeness of the knowledge base is foremost for a viable expert system. The *dynamic evaluation* is the testing of the reasoning process and advice given. Is the decision reliable and accurate? Asking for an audit trail of a decision, and comparing it against the expert's reasoning, is an important part of dynamic evaluation. The static and dynamic evaluations are best judged against the correctness of the advice from the expert system against the expert (or a panel of experts).

Questions arise as to what percentage of successful advice from the expert system is considered a "passing mark." The question is twofold. How accurate is the expert system in modeling the expert, and what is the competence level of the expert system against other experts in the industry? The percentage of successful expert system advice may be difficult to interpret, especially in the areas of interpretation and diagnosis where (1) advice is relatively subjective, and (2) there are significant biases against computer competence. This was the somewhat painful, albeit important, lesson learned when MYCIN was evaluated against a panel of medical experts. When a panel of medical experts evaluated MYCIN's advice, knowing that the advice came from an expert system, they only agreed with the advice 75% of the time; however, when MYCIN's advice was intermixed with diagnosis from other faculty members, residents, and medical personnel, the panel's approval of MYCIN's advice went up (the panel did not know which advice came from MYCIN and which advice came from human experts), exceeding any of the human experts in agreed-upon diagnosis. This improvement in diagnostic agreement clearly shows the bias many professionals hold against computer solutions and indicates the need to construct unbiased evaluations when testing expert systems.

Currently, a target concensus of 90–95% is discussed in the literature. Of course, the more ill-defined the domain, the less one can expect a high degree of consensus. However, a well-designed expert system in a well-defined domain should be able to achieve a 90–95% level.

The question of competence or performance can be weighed against the utility or value-added benefits of an expert system. By establishing an expert system, how much time and money did the organization save? Did the expert system increase productivity? Was it effective? This evaluation is organizationally dependent, as each organization operates under a different utility function.

One aspect of the evaluation phase is the liability risk an organization can incur when using an expert system. Just how costly are expert system errors? All errors are not equal. What happens if a problem exists, but the expert system does not act? The liability risks associated with errors are highly dependent on the industry; an incorrect medical diagnostic recommendation, for example, may carry a higher liability risk than an error in financial analysis. As the focus of decision making shifts to computers, away from human experts, all sorts of liability questions arise.

Establishing reasonable milestones, hurdle points, and feedback evaluations during Stages 2 and 3 will greatly enhance the chances that the expert system development is proceeding in the right direction, thus minimizing postdevelopment disappointments. These evaluations should be included in the *Expert System Project Study*; this provides both a working project management system and a written audit of successful and unsuccessful evaluation methods for future expert systems.

Testing

A lengthy and time-consuming testing period follows prototype development. Everything is tested and verified—from the most insignificant piece of data, to certainty factors, to the particulars of the troubleshooting methodology. Experience indicates that a lengthy and detailed prototyping, evaluation, testing, and revision period is preferred to a lengthy predevelopment design period for several reasons: (1) human experts find it easier to evaluate a working system than to analyze a system on paper; (2) experts find it easier to give exceptions to rules given realistic problems—one often does not think of everything during even the most careful knowledge acquisition, and exceptions come as problems are encountered; and (3) seeing an expert system in actual operation keeps the people motivated.

An underlying psychological trait endemic to all types of complicated system developments is called the "Hawthorne Effect"—as an experimental change takes place in the workplace, people will tend to work harder in the short run and bias their evaluation either favorably or unfavorably. The fact that the organization is directing more attention than usual to a particular effort, such as an expert system, will alter the normal work behavior of all employees—experts, management, technicians, and even knowledge engineers.

STAGE 5: INTEGRATION AND IMPLEMENTATION OF THE EXPERT SYSTEM

The last phase of knowledge engineering involves releasing the expert system to the users for field use. This stage is very similar to that in conventional software engineering projects where the knowledge engineer must

1. Coordinate user training

2. Establish the field environment for the expert system—this may involve porting the expert system from a development system on a LISP machine to a conventional hardware system

3. Document the expert system—this includes the user's guide, formal functional specifications, the knowledge engineer's development guide, and software documentation

4. Promote organizational acceptance—the system should offer the organization productivity gains

STAGE 6: MAINTENANCE OF THE EXPERT SYSTEM

Maintenance of the expert system is usually done by people other than the knowledge engineers who initially developed the system. An expert system is never static. As the environment changes and new knowledge is discovered, an expert system's database, knowledge base, and inference engine must be updated to reflect the new order. The knowledge engineer will continue to add enhancements in the areas of domain expansion and heuristic improvements. In some respects, the maintenance knowledge engineer must be a better technician than the expert system's initial developer. The maintenance knowledge engineer must be able to carefully debug and improve code, develop more efficient end interfaces, skillfully network the expert system with other hardware and software, and further decipher the expert's thought process to locate problems or validate additions to the knowledge base.

8

Knowledge Acquisition

One of the most critical responsibilities of the knowledge engineer is "knowledge acquisition." Knowledge acquisition is defined as the process of identifying, extracting, documenting, and analyzing the information processing behavior of domain experts in order to define an expert system's knowledge base and inference engine. The knowledge acquisition process can be broken down into four broad phases:

1. Discovery of preliminary knowledge and problem range
2. Identifying sources of information
3. Acquiring detailed knowledge from sources
4. Analyzing, coding, and documenting knowledge

KNOWLEDGE DISCOVERY

Knowledge discovery involves initially identifying the range of problems the system must handle, the characteristics of the problem domain, the bounds of knowledge of the domain, the user expectations, and some typical reasoning scenarios to define broad rules and concepts. The knowledge engineer needs to do extensive preliminary archival research, as well as consult several experts for their conception of the domain, in order to grasp the fundamentals of the problem.

Background Research

Knowledge discovery is prerequisite to any attempt at accurate knowledge acquisition and involves documenting the unique vocabulary and associated concepts of a particular domain. Background knowledge is gained by extensive study of professional magazines, academic journals, novels, textbooks, instruction manuals, physical facilities, or any other appropriate sources. The acquisition of background knowledge gives the knowledge engineer credibility in future interactions with experts, saves time in acquiring and documenting domain vocabulary, and in some cases may provide sufficient insight into the problem domain to actually implement a preliminary prototype expert system. In such cases, the system can then be refined by later expert consultations.

Preliminary consultation with several experts and end users also helps the knowledge engineer acquire a broad understanding of the problem, what subproblems or subdomains are inherent in the overall problem, and how these subdomains interrelate with each other. During knowledge discovery, the knowledge engineer should not be biased by a single approach to the problem, usually the result of consulting a single expert during the initial phase. Consulting multiple experts, and simply discussing general ideas, will often highlight common points and provide high-level elements of the problem at hand. There is ample time later to extract the more detailed and personal knowledge of the selected expert.

Problem Domain

The application domain should be formally divided into subdomains where each subdomain represents a quasi-independent set of similar problems, databases, and expertise. This is known as the "divide-and-conquer" approach. As an example, consider the process of examining a signature on a paycheck to determine whether or not it is a forgery. The process may be divided into five basic subdomains (the subdomains are determined by initial archival research and preliminary consultation with qualified document examiners). The subdomains are (1) preliminary planning, (2) comparing known authentic handwriting against the questioned signature by side-by-side visual inspection of slope, pressure, and other characteristics, (3) comparing the types of material used to write the signatures (i.e., are the inks the same or different?), (4) comparing paper types, and (5) synthesizing the above analyses to draw conclusions regarding the authenticity of the questioned signature.

For each subdomain, the knowledge engineer attempts to establish the primary type of problem (e.g., diagnostic, synthesis, planning, etc.), the characteristics of the application, and the information needed for the task, all of which determine the appropriate control strategy(s) to be employed in the system.

Prototype Domain Selection

Because expert systems are extremely complicated and time-consuming projects, with time horizons often extending several years, organizations often lose interest in such systems before they are properly completed. Prototype development allows the knowledge engineer, and the developing organization, to gain both experience and confidence in the building process. Therefore, when selecting a domain (or subdomain) for prototype development, attention must be given to the ease and speed with which the prototype can be completed. In addition, since a successful prototype will serve to motivate the organization to invest additional resources, the knowledge engineer should select a prototype domain that is both relatively independent and organizationally useful so that the prototype system can provide "stand-alone" performance.

Two different strategies are currently employed when selecting a domain for prototyping. The first strategy is to select a small, relatively independent subdomain for a simple, yet complete, expert system. This always involves some form of detailed knowledge acquisition. The second strategy is to develop a less refined, but usable, version of an expert system in a larger domain using higher-order rules gained from preliminary knowledge discovery. Researchers differ in their opinions regarding which prototyping strategy is most successful; however, the prototyping strategy chosen should reflect the nature of the problem and the culture of the organization.

The Need for Documentation: *The Knowledge Handbook*

At the end of the knowledge discovery phase, the knowledge engineer should aim to document, by way of a handbook or manual,

1. The general problem description
2. Who the users are and their expectations of the system
3. A breakdown of the subproblems and subdomains for future knowledge acquisition; this is the birth of what is called a *comprehensive domain listing* (discussed later in this chapter)
4. A more detailed description of the domain or subdomain to be used for the prototype system and the reason why this should be the prototype
5. A bibliography of reference documents; detailed documents to be used in establishing the database and overview documents for background review by system development team members
6. A list of vocabulary, concepts, terms, phrases, and acronyms used in the domain
7. A list of experts for the prototype
8. Some reasonable performance standards for the system, based upon consultation with both experts and users
9. Descriptions of typical reasoning scenarios gained from the knowledge discovery phase

Lack of documentation is often cited as a major bottleneck, capable of sidetracking the most ambitious program. Since most systems take anywhere from several months to several years to complete and will typically include a number of experts, a host of supporting technicians, and oftentimes, different knowledge engineers, documentation of every step will prove to be critical. In addition, a well-documented prototype will provide an evidence trail that can be analyzed and improved upon for future system development.

The Knowledge Handbook should be considered coexistent with the *Expert Systems Project Study*, but not the same. The *Expert Systems Project Study*'s purpose is quite different; that is, it is written to manage the total expert system project, from beginning to end, and disseminate general background material to various stakeholders. *The Knowledge Handbook*, however, is a dynamic, ever-changing compendium of knowledge. It is often loose leaf so additions and deletions can be made as additional information is accumulated during more detailed knowledge acquisition.

KNOWLEDGE SOURCES

Selecting the Domain Expert

Are there really experts in the field? *Webster's New Collegiate Edition* defines an expert as "having, involving, or displaying special skill or knowledge derived from training or experience." Everyone likes to be considered an expert, but clearly there are experts and there are "EXPERTS." An expert system will be only as good as the expertise it is built on—quality of knowledge is key.

For some domains it is sufficient that only a minimal level of expertise be achieved by the system or subsystem; thus any number of technicians who have achieved this level through experience or training could be used. In other domains, such as medical diagnostics, it is absolutely essential that the "best" expertise is incorporated. In these cases, true expertise is typically rare and in high demand. Some prepackaged commercial systems, hastily developed in the current rush to the marketplace, have been built around questionable, or even nonexistent, "expertise." Any knowledge engineer or manager considering a turn-key expert system should carefully check the expertise embodied in such systems.

Credibility of the Domain Expert

Credibility of the expert is an often overlooked concern. The expert must be credible to

- The user community who will ultimately determine the initial acceptance and subsequent success of the expert system
- The system project team, which will need to work closely with the expert over a period of time; the initial expert will often become a "knowledge czar" since his knowledge and reasoning processes will provide the framework for the complete system
- The "expert" community; since other experts will often be called upon to refine the initial system, or become the source of expertise for other subdomains, the expert's credibility in the eyes of the professional "fraternity" is crucial to gaining future cooperation
- The organization's management, who provides initial system development resources and the inevitable follow-up financing,

and who will ultimately determine the level of organizational integration.

Motivating the Expert

Motivating experts is key for successful knowledge acquisition. Experts often view the development of expert systems as a threat to their position or status; the classic argument of "knowledge is power" is reversed—loss of knowledge is loss of power. Psychologically, as the knowledge engineer extracts more and more detailed information, the expert often sees the knowledge engineer, now infused with the expert's private knowledge, in direct competition for his job. A second, and perhaps more difficult issue, is the perceived threat that the expert system itself will replace the expert, which of course may be a partial objective of some systems. This fear is particularly evident in situations where the expert is internal to the organization developing the system. The response "once this system is built I lose my job" is common in these situations. A good knowledge engineer needs to allay such fears. Under such conditions a knowledge engineer needs to represent oneself in a nonthreatening, trustful, and intriguing manner. The final point in motivation is holding the expert's interest over time. True experts usually have high demands on their time, and their interest often lags once the initial novelty and excitement of expert systems wears off.

Motivating the domain expert, and the rest of the system development team, can be frustrating at best. Egos can collide and conflicts often escalate, leading to the ultimate collapse of the team. A thorough understanding of basic motivational concepts—Maslow's "hierarchy of needs," McClelland's "need to achieve," Herzberg's "motivation/hygiene theory," and "expectancy theory"—is prerequisite to establishing a positive work environment. Motivation theories play a central role in most good management textbooks.

Most experts, however, are highly trained specialists, oftentimes with advanced degrees and academic credentials. Motivating these professional employees requires a special appreciation of the experts' unique needs. Only recently have management researchers begun to understand the subtle differences in motivating professional employees—scientists, engineers, and technicians. Research suggests that professional employees can be classified as either *local* or *cosmo-*

politan with regard to their work motivations. A *local* employee is one whose primary loyalties are directly to the employing organization, while a *cosmopolitan* employee is an individual whose loyalty is primarily to the profession, or field of specialty. The cosmopolitan's loyalties span several organizations—the employer, professional societies, academic peers, and so forth. Ritti (1968) reports that

> Locals are more interested in application, working on technology that is applicable to the business aims of the company. The 'local' type is expected to pattern his behavior and to measure his success against internal or company standards; the 'cosmopolitan' is expected to measure his success against the standards of his entire profession or field of speciality.

Whereas the local type is motivated by opportunities for pay increases, challenging work, and career advancement, the cosmopolitan is motivated by such things as communication with the professional community, autonomy, professional prestige and reputation, and publishing journal articles. Research has consistently shown that engineers and computer specialists tend to be more local in nature, while scientists fall into the cosmopolitan category.

Falling into one class or another does not mean that a professional employee is more or less cooperative, but simply that their work motivations are very different. Since domain experts may be either locals or cosmopolitans, successful knowledge engineers will adjust work environments, reward systems, project schedules, and their own personal interactive management style, to accommodate the experts' individual motivation requirements.

KNOWLEDGE ACQUISITION

Objectives of Knowledge Acquisition

The objectives of knowledge acquisition can be separated into *preliminary knowledge* and *detailed knowledge*.

Preliminary Knowledge

The objective of *preliminary knowledge* acquisition, usually achieved during the initial interviews and consultations in knowledge discovery, are to

- Identify the basic, often called "primitive," terms and concepts
- Identify typical inputs and outputs for the system
- Identify typical solutions or classes of solutions
- Identify strategies for handling problems, capable, perhaps, of forming control strategies for initial implementation of the system

Detailed Knowledge

The objective of *detailed knowledge* acquisition is to gain the "private" knowledge of the domain expert, the knowledge that reflects years of training and experience. This includes

- Identifying relationships between various data and rules
- Identifying the hierarchy of rules, what rules are intermediate, and what rules lead directly to the conclusions
- Judging the relative validity and importance of data
- Judging the certainty of data and the relative probabilities regarding assumptions, strategies, and conclusions
- Identifying the basis for the expert's assumptions and "educated guesses"
- Judging the priorities and order of performing tasks
- Determining how conflicts between rules and conclusions are resolved
- Recognizing alternative paths and strategies for problem solving
- Determining shortcuts in reasoning and the conditions under which they are used
- Understanding tradeoffs and the implications of tradeoffs
- Detailing responses to both expected and unexpected outcomes
- Determining the "strength of belief" in different rules, outcomes, and data
- Understanding the input demands of different goals and subgoals

- Determining appropriate measures of performance in outcomes and of data in inputs

As detailed knowledge is acquired, it is added to *The Knowledge Handbook.*

KNOWLEDGE ACQUISITION TECHNIQUES

Five major classes of techniques can be employed to acquire knowledge from the domain expert: interviews, protocols, walkthroughs, questionnaires, and expert reports.

Interviews

Interviews are useful mainly during the discovery and acquisition of preliminary knowledge, to give a "first approximation" of the problem structure, rules and control strategy. Two types of interviews can be used: unstructured and open-ended.

Unstructured Interviews

Unstructured interviews are interviews in which the knowledge engineer allows the domain expert to introduce concepts, vocabulary, and ideas and set the overall direction of the interview. The knowledge engineer's role is essentially to record the expert's statements and encourage expansion on points that appear important. Unstructured interviews are useful in gaining a sense of the domain and the range of issues that need to be addressed. Experience has shown, however, that unstructured interviews can be extremely frustrating since the domain expert, with unchecked enthusiasm, will often perform a type of "data dump," discussing extremely detailed issues which range far beyond the exploratory objective of the interview. For relatively small, non-complex problems, unstructured interviews may provide a sufficiently exhaustive recording of knowledge to construct a working prototype. For larger, more complex problems, however, unstructured interviews should be considered primarily a knowledge discovery tool, unless the knowledge engineer, armed with sufficient background knowledge, can keep the expert on track.

Open-Ended Interviews

Open-ended interviews assume that the knowledge engineer has prior background knowledge. In open-ended interviews the knowledge engineer controls the direction of the interview by asking questions on certain aspects of the domain, leaving the expert free to respond and elaborate as necessary. Questions such as "What are the most important tasks associated with forgery detection?" or "How do you decide that the slope of one letter is different from another letter?" are examples of open-ended interview questions that could be posed to an expert documents examiner. Both of these questions assume that the knowledge engineer has sufficient background knowledge to ask useful and enlightening questions. This is important since experts will inevitably lose interest in the interviewing process if they perceive the knowledge engineer to be asking irrelevant or trivial questions. Since open-ended questions are essentially a form of specific and directed probes, the caveats discussed under "the use of Probes, Questions, or Prompts" in the Protocol Analysis section apply.

Other Types of Interviews

Other interviews, such as "group interviews" (which are useful since one person's response in a group setting will often trigger elaboration by other group members) or highly structured interviews (both questions and range of answers are specified), can be useful under proper conditions. In general, however, interviews are best regarded as tools for knowledge discovery or, at best, only preliminary attempts at detailed knowledge acquisition. Regardless of the type of interview, five conditions are necessary for a good interview session:

1. The knowledge engineer should have the "trust" of the expert.
2. The knowledge engineer should have some background understanding of the domain concepts and vocabulary.
3. The knowledge engineer should be sufficiently trained in interviewing techniques, style, and poise, to hold the interest of the expert during the interview sessions.
4. Interruptions of any form should be kept to a minimum.
5. Privacy should be maintained (even in group interviews group privacy is important).

In designing an interview session the knowledge engineer needs to consider the objectives of the process (knowledge discovery or more detailed knowledge acquisition), the size and complexity of the domain under investigation, the skill levels and personalities of the domain experts, the degree of background knowledge already obtained through other sources, and finally, the knowledge engineer's own level of training and understanding in the art of interviewing. In regards to the last point, a number of excellent books on interviewing are available, and many colleges and universities offer short courses in interviewing skills.

Protocol Analysis

Protocol analysis, particularly a set of techniques known as verbal protocol analysis, is by far the most common method by which the knowledge engineer acquires *detailed knowledge* from the expert. A protocol is a record or documentation of the expert's step-by-step information processing and decision-making behavior. Three types of protocols are available to the knowledge engineer: verbal protocols, motor protocols, and eye-movement protocols.

Verbal Protocols

The collection of verbal protocols is conceptually straightforward and is certainly one of the most practiced methods of acquiring detailed information from the expert. The expert is asked by the knowledge engineer to "think aloud" while performing the task or solving the problem under observation. Usually, a recording is made as the expert thinks aloud, describing every aspect of his information processing and decision-making behavior. This recording then becomes a record or protocol of the expert's ongoing behavior, with an utterance at time t taken to indicate knowledge or operation at time t. Because of this sequential recording of the expert's utterances, verbal protocols are also known as process-tracing techniques. Later, the recording is transcribed for further analysis and coding by the knowledge engineer.

While collecting verbal protocols appears relatively easy on the surface, many important issues need to be understood by the knowledge engineer before embarking on such an effort. Failure to understand these issues will ultimately lead to wasted time, or even an inability to successfully implement an expert system. Verbal protocol analysis can be divided into three stages: collection, analysis, and testing.

Collection of Protocols

Collection involves the actual verbalization and subsequent documentation of the task performed by the expert. Several rules for successful protocol collection can be suggested.

Timing of Protocols. Verbal protocols should be collected during the performance of the task (concurrent protocols) rather than after the task (retrospective protocols). If the expert is verbalizing information that is currently being attended to (in short-term memory), research has shown that the act of verbalizing does not affect the course or structure of the expert's thinking behavior. On the other hand, if the expert is required to verbalize after the task (in long-term memory), current knowledge is often mixed with past knowledge, thus making inferences difficult, if not impossible, to identify.

Clearly, one problem of concurrent protocols is that the expert's thought processes work much faster than the ability to verbalize. For this reason, the knowledge engineer needs to be aware of three problems associated with concurrent protocols.

1. The expert will often slow down the task he is performing during the verbalization. This is particularly true when the task becomes more complicated. Usually, however, only the speed of the task is affected, not its course or structure.

2. If the expert is asked to report information or do something not usually associated with the performance of the task (e.g., "Tell me every time during the operation that you think of your upcoming vacation" or "Write down *X*"), the reporting may modify the expert's normal performance of the task. The knowledge engineer needs to structure the verbal protocol session to minimize this type of interference.

3. The expert will typically utter about two words per second while verbalizing. This clearly indicates that verbal protocols can give only a partial trace of the process, particularly during complex or risky tasks. This does not invalidate the information collected, but simply points out that some details of the expert's behavior are probably absent. In order to gain a more complete record the knowledge engineer oftentimes needs to combine several verbal protocols, use probes and questions requesting more detail, or use other knowledge acquisition techniques concurrently with the verbal protocols.

Extent of Verbalization. A mistake often made is asking the expert to verbalize thoughts only of interest to the research. Research has shown that this request often interferes with the expert's performance of the task, leading to the possible omission of important information. Asking the expert to verbalize all his thoughts eliminates this problem. Later, during the analysis phase, the knowledge engineer can screen out nonrelevant information. Any utterances, even sighs and swearing, can indicate an important step in the expert's thought process.

Training the Expert in Protocol Analysis. Most experts will provide good verbalization with a minimum amount of instruction. For short tasks, often the instructions "think aloud" will be sufficient. For more complex or longer tasks, the expert should be given some preliminary instruction to motivate the verbalization process. Experts will usually omit information because the task has become sufficiently complicated that the expert falls silent as his attention is diverted solely into solving the problem or the task is so routine for the expert that it is performed automatically, thus resulting in either silence or broad "metacomments" (e.g., "and I solved this"). Some preliminary instructions in protocol analysis will motivate the expert to verbalize at all times. If silence does result during the task, the knowledge engineer, who should be present during the session, needs to encourage the expert to "keep talking."

The Use of Probes, Questions, or Prompts. As discussed previously, there is a variety of situations in which concurrent verbal protocols may omit information. The use of probes and questions may be used to fill in the omitted information. Current practice suggests that detailed knowledge acquisition via verbal protocols is probably best obtained through a two-step process. During the first step, the expert is asked to verbalize, with a minimum amount of interference from the knowledge engineer; an exception is the encouragement to "keep talking." During the second step, the same task is examined, with the expert providing additional verbalization. During these follow-up verbalization sessions, the knowledge engineer can probe the expert if there is evidence of incomplete information. Such probes should occur quickly since details are often available only in short-term memory, which may last just a few seconds. This is particularly true for situations where the expert is performing well-known or routine tasks.

If the nature of the problem prohibits analysis of the same task, additional information can be obtained soon after the task performance. When clear probes are used, and when reports are requested immediately after the last trial, informative verbal reports can usually be obtained. The knowledge engineer can later obtain more information by asking the expert to review the transcript or tape of his verbalization and provide additional information at appropriate places. There are several types of probes:

Specific and Directed Probes. Asking the expert "Did you look at information X?" is a question that is both specific (immediately related to the task) and directed (offering a limited choice or forcing an answer). Specific probes, when asked concurrently with the performance of the task, will often alter the structure of the task. In addition, directed probes will often influence the expert to offer only information he perceives the knowledge engineer to be looking for, which may or may not actually be related to the task. Specific and directed probes should be used cautiously during detailed knowledge acquisition; they are best used after several interference-free protocols have been collected, or when the expert needs to be reminded of the task when too much time has lapsed since the task performance.

General and Undirected Probes. Good examples of general and undirected probes are "What happened?" and "Keep talking." The evidence acquired during verbal protocols is stronger when the probes are more general and undirected and when the probe occurs soon after the performance of the task (i.e., when information is in short-term memory). In short, verbosity and lack of selectivity in the verbalization of the expert are an advantage, as is noninterference by the knowledge engineer, particularly during the initial phases of collecting protocols.

Motor Protocols

To obtain motor protocols, observations of the expert's physical performance of the task, such as walking, reaching, and pulling, are recorded. Documentation of physical activities can be done by observation, with the knowledge engineer describing the activities into a tape recording or through video taping. The degree of documentation of physical activities is related to the extent that such activities are important to the task.

Motor protocols are used primarily as a way of supplementing verbal protocols. Obviously, in tasks that involve either essential or numerous physical activities, motor protocols are critical. Even when verbal protocols seem sufficient, motor protocols can provide additional information. A clenched fist or smile may mean as much, or even more, than a verbal record in documenting the expert's information processing behavior. Like verbal protocols, motor protocols also need to be analyzed and coded, with the same attention to reliability questions.

Eye-Movement Protocols

An eye-movement protocol is a record of where the expert fixes his gaze; it is particularly useful in documenting the expert's information gathering and alternative evaluation processes. In some circumstances the knowledge engineer can record left, right, up, or down movements by simple observation of the expert's eyes. In other situations, sophisticated eye-movement cameras need to be employed. The usefulness of eye-movement protocols can be shown in an expert chess player's analysis of a board. The first 5 seconds of an expert examining attack and defense relationships among chess pieces is shown in Figure 8.1. Clearly, if the knowledge engineer were to rely solely on verbal protocols, important information regarding the expert's behavior would be omitted. The importance of eye-movement protocols can also be seen in the problem-solving behavior of radiologists, who tend to process information from X-rays (as verified by eye-movement cameras) very differently than their verbal protocols would indicate. Like motor protocols, eye-movement protocols are used to supplement verbal protocol analysis, usually when the task involves acquiring and updating information from some type of a display, such as in game playing, financial analysis, military fire control, and traffic control.

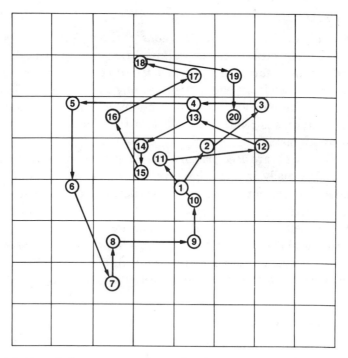

Figure 8.1. Record of eye movement for the first five seconds for middle game position. (Reported in Hayes, 1982.)

Other Knowledge Acquisition Techniques During Protocols

Many tasks require that the expert make subjective assessments of various activities or objects, such as "There is a probability that economic condition X will occur," "Trend A is similar to trend B," or "Stock Y has a high rating." Also, in some systems the expert's "strength of belief" or certainty in data, rules, or conclusions is important. Under these circumstances, verbal protocols may omit important information. If the knowledge engineer were to probe the expert during the verbalization as to "What 'probability' do you mean?" or "What exactly does 'similar' constitute?" or "How strongly do you believe that statement?" the knowledge engineer may be injecting sufficient interference to alter the expert's performance of the task. Likewise, clarification of these points after the task often leads to inaccurate information since the subtle nuances of these statements may be long forgotten. Another solution, particularly when the task involves a number of subjective assessments by the expert, is to provide the expert with some mechanism to scale the assessment in an unobtrusive way while the task is being performed. This can be done by pressure sensors that the expert can squeeze (more pressure is a stronger recording) or a spectrum the expert can point to. It is important that the expert be instructed in the use of these assessment devices and that the devices not alter the task in a significant manner.

Walkthroughs

Walkthroughs are a common method of knowledge acquisition. A *walkthrough* is the process of asking the domain expert to "walk" the knowledge engineer through the task under observation. Walkthroughs can take two forms. The first form is asking the domain expert to pretend he is accomplishing a given task and verbalize the various steps needed to accomplish the task. Even though the task is a "pretend task," the domain expert should work with any equipment, monitors, or manuals that are normally available during actual task performance. The knowledge engineer makes a record of the walkthrough. Since a walkthrough is not in "real time," there is more opportunity for the knowledge engineer to probe the expert for additional information when needed.

The second form of walkthrough, sometimes called a *teachthrough*, is when the domain expert acts as an instructor and the knowledge engineer acts as a student or apprentice. During the teachthrough session, the expert, rather than simply describing the steps, instructs the knowledge engineer in the skills and strategies needed to perform the task. The knowledge engineer, as any student, is encouraged to ask questions and challenge the expert when appropriate. Since the knowledge engineer is actively involved with the task, a second knowledge engineer or paratechnical is usually present to record the process.

Walkthroughs offer several advantages over interviews: they take place in the normal environment of the task, thus offering cues to the expert's memory; they represent an actual problem-solving exercise and, as such, are a type of protocol; and they are relatively unobtrusive since they do not take the expert from the workplace.

The disadvantages (over protocol analysis) are: the task is not in "real time," and thus the knowledge engineer may not be actually getting the details of normal problem solving; since the task performed is an artificial task set up by the knowledge engineer, knowledge about how one task interacts with other tasks (in other domains) may be unattainable; and, since the walkthrough is not under any time constraint, the expert may digress on irrelevant tangents, particularly if the knowledge engineer is asking questions during the session. A successful walkthrough session requires the knowledge engineer to carefully define the task to be examined.

Walkthroughs can be considered an intermediate tool of knowledge acquisition, allowing more detailed knowledge acquisition than interviews, but not replacing protocol analysis. Walkthroughs are particularly useful in giving first indications of how experts use "shortcuts" and "rules of thumb" and of the priority and subordination of certain rules. Walkthroughs can also point out areas of knowledge acquisition that need further research and sensitize the knowledge engineer to problem areas during a later protocol analysis. As with interviews, in relatively simple, noncomplex tasks walkthroughs may provide sufficient knowledge to implement an initial prototype system.

A variation on the walkthrough idea developed at the Naval Ocean Systems Center (NOSC) is called a *readthrough*. A "readthrough" is when the expert is asked to instruct the knowledge engineer in how to read and interpret the documents that are normally used for the task. Readthroughs are primarily useful when the task involves a number of manuals, files, or documentation that are either complex or poorly written and indexed. For example, a computer programmer or analyst, working with undecipherable, incomplete, or outdated hardware/software documentation, will oftentimes develop their own internal method of locating, assimilating, and using information for the task while ignoring the formal procedures established in the manuals. A readthrough allows the domain expert to define what kind of information is used, where it is located, and the priorities of use. Likely candidates for readthroughs, for example, are situations where the complexity of the manuals requires classes for teaching the users to use the materials.

Collectively, walkthroughs can provide insightful and useful information. Since the knowledge acquired by walkthroughs is more detailed and personal than during interviews, greater concern needs to be given regarding the quality of expertise being modeled during the session.

Questionnaires

Questionnaires, whether open-ended, short-answer, or forced-answer, are useful under certain conditions. *Open-ended questionnaires*, like open-ended interviews, are appropriate for knowledge discovery since high-level concepts are usually the result. The advantage of open-ended questionnaires is that the experts can work on the questionnaire when time is available and interest is high. Because of the simple physical limitations of writing, the problem of "data dumping" common with open-ended interviews is somewhat reduced. However, since the knowledge engineer is typically not present when the questionnaire is being completed, there is little control over the direction of the answers. Experience has shown that respondents typically head off on unimportant tangents and occasionally embark on philosophical discourses.

Short-answer questionnaires, because of their nature, are generally incapable of obtaining process or problem-solving explanations and are best used to elicit descriptive information, such as the colors, sizes, and shapes of objects. Of course, the construction of such questionnaires presumes that the knowledge engineer has completed sufficient knowledge discovery to write meaningful questions. Compared with direct probes or interviewing, the primary advantage of short-answer questionnaires is the unobtrusiveness of the instrument; many experts can be consulted, quickly, with little interference of the workplace.

Forced-answer questionnaires, that is, when the expert is presented with a specified list of answers, are primarily useful as a knowledge validation tool, when the expert is forced to recognize the truth of the statement or the reasonability of the answer set. For example, in the case of forgery detection the question "Should pencil pressure be examined first?" will help to validate the database and rule set. As such, this type of questionnaire is relatively useless for knowledge discovery or detailed knowledge acquisition. Experts, when confronted with a limited set of answers, will typically balk and actively fight categorization. The knowledge engineer needs to communicate carefully the purpose of the exercise to gain cooperation.

Expert Reports

An expert report is the expert's own written summary of problem-solving behavior. In the past, expert reports were a favored method of knowledge acquisition, although their use has diminished rapidly among more sophisticated and experienced builders of expert systems. Expert reports can take two forms. The first form is where the expert simply writes down how a given task is approached, strategies and rules for the problem solution, the data required for the task, and what the outputs are. The knowledge engineer must then interpret and analyze the expert report to obtain the necessary knowledge for the expert system. The second approach to expert reporting is when the expert is asked to formalize the decision-making process, via flowcharting or some other process documenting technique, thus saving the knowledge engineer this step.

Expert reports, while superficially attractive, suffer a number of problems:

1. They essentially require the expert to act as a knowledge engineer, without a knowledge engineer's training.

2. Expert reports tend to have a high degree of bias; the reports typically reflect the expert's opinion concerning how the task "should be done" rather than "how it really is done."

3. Experts will oftentimes describe new and untested ideas and strategies they have been contemplating, but still have not included in their decision-making behavior. The mixing of actual behavior and "ideal future" behavior is endemic.

4. Expert reports are time-consuming efforts, and the expert loses interest rapidly. The quality of information attained will rapidly decrease as the report progresses.

5. Experts must be proficient in flowcharting or other process documenting techniques.

Given these caveats, under certain conditions, such as the inaccessibility of an expert to the knowledge engineer (e.g., expert located in Katmandu, Nepal), expert reports may provide useful preliminary knowledge discovery and acquisition. It is surprising, however, that a number of suppliers of prepackaged application expert systems still use expert reporting techniques as the primary source of knowledge acquisition.

KNOWLEDGE ANALYSIS, CODING, AND DOCUMENTATION

This involves the formal procedure of analyzing any knowledge acquired and subsequently documenting the rules, networks, relationships, attributes, and such that are relevant to the problem domain. All sources of knowledge need to be formally analyzed, documented, and included in *The Knowledge Handbook.* Since protocols are the most complex, and detailed, methods of knowledge acquisition, they provide a good framework to examine the process of analysis and coding. Of course, knowledge gained from any knowledge acquisition method needs to be examined by a similar, detailed analysis. The examples and worksheets shown here are for illustrative purposes only; the exact procedure should be individually adapted to each expert system project, depending on the nature and complexity of the problem, the skills of the experts and knowledge engineers, and whether the project team is large or small.

Analysis typically involves a four step process.

Transcription

Obviously, a complete transcription of the verbal report should be made, including not only the expert's utterances, but also those of the knowledge engineer and any other distractions or interferences that may have occurred during the session. Any visual observations of actions (recorded by either the knowledge engineer or a paratechnical) should be inserted into the transcription (identified as an observation) for future analysis of meaning.

Phrase Indexing

A useful process is to break up the transcription into short phrases, each identified by an index number. Each phrase should correspond to the knowledge engineer's assessment of what constitutes a piece of knowledge, that is, a single task, assertion, or data collection process by the expert. By breaking the transcription into short phrases, it is easier to establish the type of process the expert went through at a particular time and measure how much information the expert had to perform the task.

Knowledge Coding

The knowledge is next analyzed according to the type of knowledge attended to, the operators used, the evaluation criteria used, and the reasoning underlying the choices and decisions. Whatever method is used—protocols, interviews, or walkthroughs—each piece of knowledge must be carefully analyzed and coded. It is useful to think of two general categories of knowledge during the coding phase: *descriptive knowledge* and *procedural knowledge* (adapted from NOSC).

Descriptive Knowledge. This knowledge relates to a particular object (physical or mental). Categories for descriptive knowledge include meanings, roles, associations, environments, resources, activities, and outcomes. Most descriptive knowledge is gathered by archival methods, although some is provided by experts. A further breakdown of descriptive knowledge is presented here:

Meanings

Definition

Axiom

Jargon, acronym

Assumption

Hypothesis, theory

Model

Analogy

Concept

Roles

Function

Attribute

System state

Constraint

Event

Operator/agent

Environments

Physical setting

Shape, size

Location, position

Time, duration, schedule

Regularity, periodicity

Resources

Data

Tool

Reference

Activities

Action

Action outcome

Action outcome, feedback

Object of action

Recipient of action

Associations	*Outcomes*
Relationship	Goal
Interaction	Measure of effectiveness
Hierarchy	Criterion of success
Network	Diagnosis
Solution	

Procedural Knowledge. This knowledge relates to the procedures employed in the problem solving process. Broad categories of procedural knowledge include problem definition, problem planning, data/resource gathering, solution process, solution evaluation, and solution reporting. Most procedural knowledge is gained from the expert, although background reading (e.g., manuals, training notes) may provide some valuable procedural knowledge. A further breakdown of procedural knowledge follows:

Problem Definition
System model adequacy evalution
Contexting/scoping/checking appropriateness of problem
Problem analysis/restatement/analogy

Problem Planning
Problem solution planning, ordering of steps
Stages/resources for problem solution
Prioritization, goal setting
Boundary/limit setting
Hypothesis generation
Estimation, approximation, assumption setting
Simplifying assumptions
Solution search technique (forward or backward chaining)

Data/Resource Gathering
Resource, knowledge location
Data gathering

Solution Process

Task enumeration/ordering/procedure

Tool using/measurement/dimensioning

Data reduction/evaluation

Missing data compensation

Probability setting

Inductive/deductive/problem solving

Heuristic rule, rule of thumb, mnemonic rule consideration

Rule reliability/applicability evaluation

Rule interrelationship, tradeoff

Rule invocation requirement determination

Rule invocation effect, outcome determination

State-changing action appropriateness/precondition determination

State-changing procedure

Changed-state recognition

Judgment making

Conclusion/solution/outcome determination

Solution Evaluation

Measure of effectiveness setting/use

Criterion setting (confidence level)

Criterion setting (certainty level)

Criterion setting (probability level)

Criterion-satisfaction determination

Solution Reporting

Judgment/conclusion justification

Presentation/justification of problem solution/outcome

Each piece of knowledge is indexed as to its category of knowledge, both broad and detailed; for example, *solution evaluation/criterion setting (probability)* would be the index for the phrase "There is a 75% chance of success." After this initial coding, each piece of knowledge needs to be further analyzed, documented in a form appropriate to the system's requirements, and included in *The Knowledge Handbook.*

Documenting

The knowledge engineer will inevitably use various forms and worksheets to assist in formulating data structures and documenting the knowledge acquired. This material should be included in *The Knowledge Handbook*, augmenting and replacing existing knowledge. There are at least four knowledge-related sections to any knowledge handbook: comprehensive domain listing, descriptive knowledge, procedural knowledge, and glossary. Each section is updated as new knowledge is acquired.

Comprehensive Domain Listing. This is a detailed list of subdomains, further divided into sub-subdomains, and so forth. Each category represents a distinct activity or task. Each task needs to be clearly described with

1. Goal of task (e.g., to arrest speeders)
2. The information needed to accomplish the task (e.g., speed of cars)
3. How this information is measured (e.g., scales, categories, etc.)
4. Sources of information (e.g., radar display, people, etc.)
5. Objects or instruments used in the task performance (e.g., police patrol cars)
6. Relationships between objects (e.g., compatibility, etc.)
7. Type of problem class (e.g., diagnostic, prediction, etc.)

The comprehensive domain listing may also contain flow diagrams or charts showing how the subdomains are related. These diagrams are cross-referenced to the various knowledge worksheets for computer entry of knowledge.

Descriptive Knowledge. This is the section that includes the worksheets and forms detailing descriptive knowledge. As descriptive knowledge is acquired it is added, as necessary, to the comprehensive domain listing and glossary. Descriptive knowledge worksheets typically ask for

1. A short description of the object (e.g., a police patrol car)
2. When the object is used (e.g., traffic control)
3. Object attributes (e.g., crew size, crew fatigue, gas tanks)
4. Object states (e.g., One/two, healthy/tired, empty/full)
5. Relationships among objects (e.g., crew in car)
6. Exceptions (e.g., car not used for off-road pursuit)
7. Detailed category for piece of knowledge [e.g., definition, function, or attribute (from list of descriptive knowledge)]

Procedural Knowledge. This is the section that contains the worksheets and forms detailing procedural knowledge, the heart of knowledge acquisition. Figure 8.2 shows a procedural knowledge worksheet detailing an actual heuristic production rule of an expert document examiner when examining a signature for possible forgery (in this case, to determine whether somebody has traced a signature on a paycheck).

This worksheet first identifies the relevant domains and subdomains for the piece of knowledge, asks if the expert has validated the correctness of the report (in this case, yes), and shows whether this piece of knowledge has been entered into the computer (in this case, no). This piece of knowledge represents a *solution process* in general and, specifically, an *heuristic rule*. The goal of this solution process is to determine if a signature is a tracing (i.e., if a forger has placed an unsigned check over a legitimate signature, and traced the signature). Objects needed for analysis are the questioned signature and a special microscope. The procedural rule says that if the signature does not have the normal changes in pressure (in up and down strokes) characteristic of normal handwriting and the signature is wobbly (has a tremor), which is characteristic of slower-than-normal handwriting strokes, then turn the document over and with the microscope check to see if any pencil lead or pen ink is stuck on the backside of the questioned signature (this debris would have come off the legitimate signature when pressure was placed on it during the tracing). The exception to this rule is when the questioned signature was made using a soft-tip pen (tracing pressure is

Worksheet for Procedural Knowledge

Domain: *Forgery Detection*

Subdomain: *Visual Inspection*

Sub-Subdomain: *Signature tracing detection*

Knowledge Acquirer Name: *Devon Scott*

Source of Knowledge: *Interview Nanette G. Galbraith; Galbraith*

Forensic Sciences, LTD. Sept, 1986

Has Expert Validated Knowledge? __X__ **Yes** _____ **No**

Is knowledge entered into Expert System? _____ **Yes** __X__ **No**

Knowledge Statement:

_____ **Problem Definition**	_____ **Problem Planning**
_____ **Data Gathering**	__X__ **Solution Process**
_____ **Solution Evaluation**	_____ **Solution Reporting**

Goal: *To determine if questioned signature is a tracing*

Objects Involved in task: *1) Questioned Document*

2) stereoscopic Zoom Microscope

Initial States of Objects: *1) Available   2) Available*

Procedure (100 words or less): *If the signature shows constant pressure*

and a tremor is present,

Then examine reverse side of document for evidence of debris

Exceptions (when procedure should not be used): *when soft-tip pen*

was used to write signature

Detailed Category for knowledge (from detailed list): *Heuristic Rule*

Figure 8.2. Capturing forgery detection knowledge.

not enough to make debris stick on the backside). This type of work-sheet would be used for fairly complex problems, where several knowl-edge engineers might be acquiring knowledge simultaneously and each piece of knowledge needs to be accurately detailed, recorded, and indexed.

A variety of forms can be developed for documenting procedural knowledge; the proper level of detail is dependent on the nature of the problem and the software. Figures 8.3 and 8.4 are additional worksheet examples from PERSONAL CONSULTANT by Texas Instruments and TIMM by General Research Corporation. These worksheets would be more appropriate for less complex applications or prototype development (such as the hiring model example described in Chapter 9).

```
Personal Consultant                              Concepts
Texas Instruments
                          MAPPING FORM
        Context name:
        _____

        Parent Context name:
        _____

        Child Context name:
        _____

        Initial value parameters:
        _____
        _____

        Goal parameters:
        _____
        _____

        Related rules:
        _____
        _____
        _____
        _____
        _____
        _____
        _____

        Related parameters:
        _____
        _____
        _____
        _____
```

Figure 8.3. Texas Instruments PERSONAL CONSULTANT mapping form.

```
TIMM
General Research Corporation

                EXPERT SYSTEM DEFINITION WORKSHEET
================================================================
Brief Description of the Problem to be Solved:


================================================================
Decision to Be Made:
================================================================
Possible Choices:      _____
                       _____
                       _____
                       _____
                       _____


================================================================

   FACTOR NAME      POSSIBLE FACTOR VALUES    PHRASE TYPE  ORDER TYPE

_____     _____   _____  _____
                     _____
                     _____
                     _____
_____     _____   _____  _____
                     _____
                     _____
                     _____
_____     _____   _____  _____
                     _____
                     _____
                     _____
_____     _____   _____  _____
                     _____
                     _____
                     _____

================================================================
Filename:                              Default Filetype = DAT
================================================================
System Name:
================================================================
System Developer:
================================================================
```

Figure 8.4. TIMM expert system definition worksheet.

Glossary. This is where the domain's special vocabulary terms, axioms, jargon, and acronyms are defined.

All knowledge contained in the *comprehensive domain listing, descriptive knowledge,* and *procedural knowledge* sections should be carefully cross-referenced and cross-indexed at all times.

Coding reliability is a particularly important issue in knowledge analysis. Although no hard or fast rules exist, some coders are more accurate in modeling the domain than others. Coder reliability is usually associated with familiarity and experience in coding, appropriate training in knowledge engineering techniques, and coder independence from the task performed by the expert. For example, having a former air traffic controller (acting as the knowledge engineer) code the protocol of another air traffic controller may bias the coding process. Reliability can also be established by having several coders code knowledge, then comparing the results. Reliability, and thus confidence that the code accurately reflects the expert's knowledge, can be established by simple statistical analysis. To ensure additional accuracy, the expert himself should review the record. The expert will identify any inferences that he feels are incorrect.

KNOWLEDGE ACQUISITION TOOLS

Matching a cooperative and motivated expert with a skilled knowledge engineer and extracting knowledge that embodies true expertise via protocols, interviews, or walkthroughs are fraught with numerous delays and frustrations—collectively known as the "knowledge acquisition bottleneck." The delays caused by the one-on-one human interaction between the knowledge engineer and the expert have long been recognized by AI researchers. As a result, a number of knowledge acquisition tools have been developed, or are currently in production, which are designed to ease the knowledge acquisition bottleneck. These tools enable the expert to interact with the computer directly, thus defining the knowledge base and control strategies while minimizing the intermediate step of interacting with the knowledge engineer. Essentially, these tools "interview" the domain expert and interpret from his responses the knowledge base and production rules to be incorporated into the expert system. Acquiring knowledge directly from the experts can take one of two forms: *induction by examples* and *knowledge elicitation tools*.

Induction by Examples

This first set of programs is based on the idea of the learning program, in which rules are logically induced by the solutions to examples provided by the domain expert. A number of ambitious projects using inductive techniques are currently underway, and several commercial systems based on these ideas have been introduced for smaller applications. These include 1ST CLASS, RULEMASTER, EXPERT-EASE, and WIZARD. More specific details of these systems are provided elsewhere in this book. Knowledge acquisition tools based on induction by example, while extremely powerful for smaller systems in the 20–200 rule range, are generally not considered suitable for larger expert systems. Several researchers believe that example-based systems would collapse under the complexities and conflicts inherent in larger systems, and that while rules can be generated for larger systems with example-based tools, many of the important subtleties would be lost. For relatively independent, smaller subdomains, however, example-based systems may provide an expedient and attractive solution if they can be acceptably integrated into the larger system.

Knowledge Elicitation Tools

Here the tool interacts directly with the domain expert to elicit and structure the knowledge base without induction. Several systems have recently been implemented: these include ROGET (named for the English thesaurist and developed by James Bennet at Stanford University), MORE (which resulted from the MUD drilling advisor), and ETS (Expert Transfer System), among others.

Knowledge elicitation tools have made tremendous progress in both sophistication and application in the last few years and may become the primary form of knowledge acquisition in the near future. Assuming that the domain expert will remain indispensable, Richard Hill (1985) states the goals of an ideal knowledge acquisition system:

- Direct interaction with the expert without intervention by a knowledge engineer through to completion of the system
- Applicability to unlimited, or at least a broad class of, problem domains
- Tutorial capabilities to eliminate the need for prior training of the expert
- Ability to analyze work in progress to detect inconsistencies and gaps in knowledge
- Ability to incorporate multiple sources of knowledge
- A human interface (i.e., a natural conversation) that will make using the system enjoyable and attractive

- Ability to interface easily with different expert system tools, as appropriate to the problem domain

While no current knowledge acquisition system satisfies all these goals, many researchers are currently developing systems with these objectives in mind. Present knowledge acquisition systems tend to be applicable primarily to classification-type problem domains. Knowledge acquisition tools are usually linked to a target expert system development tool or language (such as ROGET's interface with the target system development tool EMYCIN) and are primarily useful for prototype system development with the recognition that complete system development still requires substantial interaction between the knowledge engineer and the expert. In spite of these limitations, these systems still provide powerful tools for acquiring knowledge under appropriate constraints. The ETS provides a good state-of-the-art example of the power achieved by such systems.

The ETS was developed by the Boeing Computer Services Division of Boeing Corporation and represents one of the few nonacademic attempts at computerizing knowledge acquisition. The ETS assumes a classification-type problem domain and produces a knowledge base for Teknowledge's OPS5 and K-300 development languages.

The ETS is based on the personal construct theory developed by George Kelly; originally employed for psychotherapy, the techniques were translated to expert interviewing by the computer. The basic theory is that individuals predict events by having theories, testing hypotheses, and weighing experimental evidence. Based on these ideas, the ETS interviews the domain expert to obtain elements in the domain. The ETS then establishes relationships between these elements by presenting the expert with triads of elements and asking the expert to elicit two traits that distinguish the elements. These comparisons are called "constructs." The expert then classifies these constructs into larger groups, called "constellations," with similar characteristics. The expert also determines subordinate constructs by a process called "laddering."

Classification rules are internally established by analyzing the construct set by means of various statistical, clustering and multidimensional scaling techniques. Two types of rules are generated: conclusion rules and intermediate rules of the if–then–else nature required by the development language; each rule also has a certainty factor associated with it which represents "strength of belief." Additional interviewing of the expert by ETS serves to refine the knowledge base, alter rules, and expand the construct set.

The stated objective of ETS is to computerize the knowledge acquisition process to a point where prototype systems can be efficiently developed. Although the developers of ETS claim that some 200 prototype systems have been developed, with an average savings of two to five months (over manual interviewing techniques), experience has indicated that manual interviewing of the expert is still necessary for relatively complex systems. It is clear, however, that computerized knowledge acquisition tools are rapidly reaching the goals stated earlier, although it may be some time before they replace human knowledge engineers.

Machine Learning

While computerized knowledge acquisition tools, in theory, perform the role of the knowledge engineer, tools based on machine learning attempt to replace both the knowledge engineer and the expert. In the future, constructing expert systems may be primarily electronic.

Expert systems will scan on-line databases and digitize books, journals, and magazines. If a library, either public or institutional, has an on-line database library, the expert system may call that library and access relevant information. Data stored on another computer system could be electronically retrieved to create or update the data and knowledge base of the expert system, all without the intervention of the knowledge engineer or the expert.

Potential benefits of automated knowledge analysis are (1) automated methods may prove more competent than humans for acquiring and fine-tuning the databases and knowledge bases (especially as the amount of information grows and becomes more complex), thus producing systems with greater expertise, and (2) automated methods would significantly reduce the high cost of human resources and time involved in constructing the knowledge base. To maximize this process, the focus should be on acquiring the kinds of knowledge that are difficult to acquire manually (e.g., large databases), but for which automated methods are feasible.

While tremendous advances have been made in AI and machine learning, such systems still remain elusive, although some prototype systems will certainly be implemented before the turn of the century.

9

Building an Expert System: A Hiring Model

The purpose of this chapter is to provide examples of how to build a simple expert system. Five different commercial expert system development tools are employed for this purpose, developing the same expert system application five times, each time using a different tool. The examples are addressed to the student of expert systems in general and the knowledge engineer in particular, demonstrating the steps required to build an expert system.

The intent of these examples is twofold. First, they illustrate the critically important steps involved in building a successful expert system; second, the examples highlight differences between the development tools and briefly discuss their implications. Several points are illustrated in these examples which should be considered when purchasing a development tool. A more complete list of software considerations is given in Chapter 6.

For conciseness and comparability purposes, only rule-based and example-based development tools were selected. All of the following examples were developed on an IBM PC XT. The costs for the following development tools range from several hundred dollars to several thousand dollars.

The development tools chosen for this example are

Software	*Software Vendor*
1ST CLASS	Programs In Motion, Inc.
PERSONAL CONSULTANT	Texas Instruments, Inc.
EXSYS	Exsys, Inc.
GURU	Micro Data Base Systems, Inc.
KES	Software Architecture & Engineering, Inc.

STAGE 1: IDENTIFICATION AND DEFINITION OF THE PROBLEM

The first step in the development process is to identify the problem. The example used will be an employee hiring expert system where the expert system will assist the personnel officer in evaluating applicants for a specific job position. This is a common business problem representing a classification type problem (hire, don't hire) and is a good application for expert systems, even though the example has been scaled down to a simplistic level. Although this example requires little judgement and heuristics on the part of the expert system, and the expert system is clearly an overkill for this simple application, evaluating employment applications can be tedious and time consuming. An expert system can make this job much more time and cost efficient (more so than an elaborate decision tree).

STAGE 2: DEVELOPMENT OF THE PROTOTYPE

The development of the prototype entails the identification or discovery of the preliminary information for the knowledge base and the sources of this information, and the construction of the prototype expert system. For this example, the knowledge engineer will use this step purely as the information source and identification stage and defer the construction of the expert system to the next step. In virtually all real-life applications the construction of the prototype is an important stage and must not be overlooked.

The knowledge engineer begins the development process by identifying the information required by the expert (in this example, the personnel officer) to make the appropriate evaluation of the applicant. In actual practice the preliminary information would be extracted from the expert through some form of protocol analysis, interviewing, or some other knowledge acquisition technique, and/or by archival research. In this example, the personnel officer has identified four pertinent parameters of information regarding the applicant:

1. *Attitude.* The applicant's personality and outlook on life, such as work, ambition, communication, and dedication

2. *References.* The personal letters of recommendation on behalf of the applicant

3. *Education.* The level of formal education attained in a private or public educational system; for this position, an adequate education is a high school diploma

4. *Experience.* The time spent working in similar job areas

Next the expert, along with the knowledge engineer, identifies possible values for each of the four parameters; values may be qualitative or quantitative.

Parameter	Value	Type
Attitude	Good, poor	Qualitative
References	Good, poor	Qualitative
Education	Adequate, inadequate	Qualitative
Experience	$0, 1.0, 1.5, \ldots, n$ (years)	Quantitative

Information on these parameters comes from the applicant's written application and a personal interview by the personnel officer. Note that the information obtained from the application—references, experience, and education—is fairly objective. The applicant has either good or poor references, adequate or inadequate education, and a certain number of years experience. The quality of the references may be somewhat subjective, but for this example, we assume that the personnel officer will form unbiased opinions. In practice, however, "bias" may actually indicate a "rule-of-thumb" decision; the knowledge engineer needs to carefully investigate such issues. The information obtained from the personal interview (attitude) is fairly subjective.

At this point, the knowledge engineer identifies the minimal qualifications for hiring an applicant. This begins the process of extracting the decision procedures from the expert and formulating the reasoning strategy. Accurate knowledge acquisition is critical since the nature of the problem will determine the best-suited reasoning technique and data structure. This, in turn, will reduce the number of development tools under consideration. For this example, the knowledge engineer has chosen several development tools, all of which are either rule-based or example-based. The selected tools employ an internal production rule data structure. This allows a common ground on which to compare the tools, but at the same time identify important differences.

```
Personal Consultant                                    Concepts
Texas Instruments
                              MAPPING FORM

        Context name:
            HIRING
        _____

        Parent Context name:
            N/A
        _____

        Child Context name:
            N/A
        _____


        Initial value parameters:
            Attitude (good, poor),  References (good, poor),
        ____Education (adequate, inadequate),  Experience (years)
        _____

        Goal parameters:
            Decision (hire, dont hire)
        _____
        _____

        Related rules:
            1) if Attitude is good and References are poor and Education is
               adequate and the person has at least one year of Experience
               then hire.
        _____
            2) if Attitude is good and References are good
               then hire.
        _____
            3) if the first rule is not activated and second rule is not
               activated
               then dont hire.
        _____

        Related parameters:
        _____
        _____
        _____
        _____
```

Figure 9.1. Extracting knowledge for the hiring example from Chapter 9.

Suppose that the personnel officer has designated the following rules of thumb to hire an applicant:

- If the attitude is good but the references are poor, the applicant must also have adequate education and at least one year of experience in a similar job position.
- If both the attitude and references are good, nothing else is of any consequence.

Last, the knowledge engineer identifies the final parameter of the expert system—the goal parameter. In this case, the goal parameter is to either hire or not hire the applicant.

Figure 9.1 shows how the initial parameters, procedural rules, and goal parameter would be documented using a PERSONAL CONSULTANT worksheet. In practice, the knowledge engineer would use this, or similar, worksheets to document relevant knowledge during knowledge discovery and acquisition phases; these worksheets would be added to *The Knowledge Handbook* and used for computer entry.

STAGE 3: CONSTRUCTION OF THE EXPERT SYSTEM

Once a prototype is adequately constructed and running, the knowledge engineer then attacks the complete system. For simple applications, prototyping is usually not necessary. The knowledge engineer will develop the same hiring expert system five times, each time using one of the following tools: (1) 1ST CLASS, (2) PERSONAL CONSULTANT, (3) EXSYS, (4) GURU, and (5) KES.

Certainty factors provide clarification by allowing distinguishable degrees of confidence for some of the more subjective or fuzzy parameters, such as attitude and references. Certainty factors provide one method of dealing with knowledge uncertainty. Certainty factors will be illustrated in the first and third examples only (1ST CLASS and EXSYS), noting that certainty factors could be employed in the other three development tools.

In rule-based systems, rules may be inputted into the system in two ways: (1) entering the actual production rules (*rule-based systems*), or (2) entering a series of examples which give a representation of the decisions (*example-based systems*). In an example-based system, once the examples have been entered, the development engine proceeds to interpret the examples and generate rules using various induction techniques. The rule or rules are generated differently by each development tool. For example, 1ST CLASS generates a single optimal production rule, analogous to an elaborate decision tree, using inductive classification. During this transformation process from examples to rules, if for some reason the development engine cannot arrive at an optimal production rule (due to missing information or not fully representative examples), the knowledge engineer returns to the development engine to add more examples or manually edit the production rule(s). Another development tool, EXPERT-EASE, enters the examples into a decision table (in spreadsheet format) and works through the table to inductively infer rules. Example-based systems are often used when the knowledge engineer, or expert, cannot formally identify the rules, but can illustrate representative examples. Example-based systems are by nature most appropriate for smaller applications.

Rule-based and example-based systems employ different formats. Rule-based systems use production rules; example-based systems use parameters and values. The following is an example of how a rule-based system represents a convertible bond:

IF   the instrument is a debt instrument issued by a corporation, *AND* the instrument pays regular, semiannual coupon payments, *AND* the instrument can be converted into stock shares of the same issuing corporation,
THEN   the instrument is a convertible bond.

An example-based system expresses the same information as

INSTRUMENT	Debt
CASH FLOW STREAMS	Semiannual
SUBSTITUTIONS	Stock
CONCLUSION	Convertible bond

Now the groundwork is laid; next begins the actual development of the expert system. The remaining stages in the development process will be repeated five times using the five development tools.

1ST CLASS

1ST CLASS, developed by Programs In Motion, Inc., is an example-based expert system development tool. Once inputted, these examples are transformed into a single optimal production rule.

To begin, the knowledge engineer identifies the problem, defines the parameters, then feeds the examples or sample decisions into the system by answering simple multiple-choice questions. 1ST CLASS will generate one optimal rule based on what it learns from the examples.

STEP 1. The first step in constructing an expert system using 1ST CLASS is to define a dictionary of parameters. The goal parameters (goal states) are "hire" and "don't_hire" (the underscore "_" combines two words to create one variable). The parameters are attitude, references, education, and experience.

STEP 2. The second step involves defining the possible values of the above parameters:

Attitude	Good, poor
References	Good, poor
Education	adequate, inadequate
Experience	0, 1.0, 1.5, ..., n (years)

1ST CLASS will generate an input screen based on the parameters defined in Step 1. The following is the columnar input screen generated by 1ST CLASS for entering the parameter values. The parameters are listed across the top of the screen. The possible values for each parameter are listed below the parameter label in column fashion. Experience is identified in terms of quantitative values; their exact values will be determined by the examples inputted in Step 3. Boldface denotes computer prompts; nonboldface denotes user input.

Attitude	References	Education	Experience	Result
Good	Good	Adequate	#.#	Hire
Poor	Poor	Inadequate	#.#	Dont_hire

STEP 3. The next step is to enter examples of hiring situations. 1ST CLASS takes the information entered in Steps 1 and 2 and assists in

creating examples by asking the knowledge engineer multiple-choice questions. It is not necessary to give every possible example—just representative ones. However, it is important to enter a broad range of examples, some of which are to hire, some not to hire. If the knowledge engineer later finds an example of importance has been omitted, the example can be added, and the inference engine will recalculate the optimal production rule. The following illustrates six examples to be inputted. Notice that not every parameter value is entered. In these instances, the inference engine will base its reasoning solely on the parameter values supplied.

	Attitude	*References*	*Education*	*Experience*	*Result*	*Weight*
1.	Good	Good			Hire	3.00
2.	Good	Poor	Adequate	2.0	Hire	2.00
3.	Good	Poor	Adequate	2.0	Hire	1.00
4.	Good	Poor	Inadequate	2.0	Dont_hire	1.00
5.	Good	Poor		0	Dont_hire	2.00
6.	Poor				Dont_hire	3.00

Certainty factors are added for each example. In 1ST CLASS, certainty factors are defined as weights that assist in identifying the strength of the result. A high weight implies a high strength in the overall parameter values, and vice versa. They are not probabilities. The weights are assigned by the user and are subjective. Weights are a ranking scheme; they are not proportional; that is, a weight of 2.0 is not necessarily twice as strong as a weight of 1.0. Here, the first three examples result in a hire decision. In other words, if there were three applicants that exactly mirrored these examples, the program would recommend to hire the first applicant based upon a higher weight.

STEP 4. Now that the examples have been entered, the knowledge engineer instructs the inference engine to generate one optimal rule. 1ST CLASS uses a technique known as inductive classification to construct the one rule that encompasses all of the examples. If the inference engine encounters discrepancies among the examples entered, it will either prompt the knowledge engineer for the missing information or conclude that one optimal rule cannot be constructed. If a rule cannot be inducted, the knowledge engineer can revise the examples and, once again, attempt to construct one optimal rule. The constructed rule can also be directly modified using an external text editor.

The program is now ready to use. This is what the completed 1ST CLASS rule looks like for the hiring model. Notice the similarities in the structure of the following rule to that of a decision tree (Figure 9.2).

```
———— start of rule ————

attitude??

good: references??

    good:                                      hire

    poor: education??

            adequate: experience??

                        less than one year:    dont_hire

                        at least one year:     hire

            inadequate:                        dont_hire

poor:                                          dont_hire

———— end of rule ————
```

Personal Consultant

PERSONAL CONSULTANT, from Texas Instruments, Inc., is a rule-based, backward-chaining development tool. The basic flow of operation is to first design the root context (the primary structure and focus of the problem) along with the parameters, and second, input the production rules which outline the reasoning process. For more discussion on context data structures, see Chapter 3.

STEP 1. The first step is to define the parameters and their values for this problem. Since they have already been defined, this step will not be repeated.

STEP 2. The next step is to define and create the knowledge base and to establish the overall structure of the problem by creating a root context. A context is like a self-contained expert system. Contexts can be

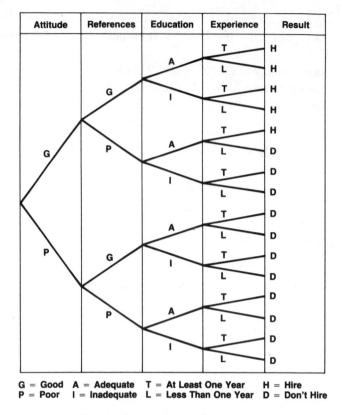

Attitude	References	Education	Experience	Result

G = Good   A = Adequate   T = At Least One Year   H = Hire
P = Poor   I = Inadequate   L = Less Than One Year   D = Don't Hire

Figure 9.2. The Hiring decision tree.

linked together to form a larger expert system. The linking structure of
these contexts is stored in a "context tree" (similar to a decision tree
of contexts vs. a decision tree of production rules). The "root context"
is the master organizer of all these contexts, tracking such items as
context names.

In this example there will be only one context, called HIRING.
Consequently, there will be no need for a context tree (the root context
and the context will be called by the same name in this example). All
of the generated rules will be stored in one HIRING rule group. The
parameters, and their values, will be stored in one HIRING parameter
group. Both groups belong to the one HIRING context.

The following is a series of detailed prompts by PERSONAL CON-
SULTANT which creates the knowledge base and root context. Fol-

lowing each prompt is the reply by the knowledge engineer and a discussion (in italics) of the prompt. Literal responses are required to be enclosed in parentheses.

(a) Knowledge base heading (DOMAIN):

HIRING MODEL

This asks for the title of the knowledge base.

(b) Root context name:

HIRING

This is the name of the root context—the primary context identifying the problem's context tree. There is one, and only one, root context for each expert system.

(c) PROMPTEVER of HIRING:

(This consultation session will provide a recommendation of whether or not to hire the applicant,

This is an introductory text to the user when running the Hiring Model expert system.

(d) SVAL of HIRING:

Select 'YES'

This prompt asks for the synonym of hiring. A response of yes means the synonym will be equivalent to the definition of hiring.

(e) TRANS of HIRING:

(Whether or not to hire the applicant)

This is the translation of the root context name hiring.

(f) PRINTID of HIRING

Select 'YES'

This prompt indicates the print identification of this model to be hiring.

(g) PARMGROUP of HIRING:

Select 'YES'

This prompt questions whether the parameter information will be stored in the hiring parameter group (for the HIRING context) or in another parameter group (for another context).

(h) List of INITIALDATA parameters

(ATTITUDE REFERENCES EDUCATION EXPERIENCE)

At this prompt the knowledge engineer defines the parameters that the expert system will ask the user at the beginning of the session. Above are the four parameters we have identified in our example.

(i) List of GOALS parameters:

(DECISION)

Here the knowledge engineer identifies all goal parameters for the example (in this case, one).

(j) DISPLAYRESULTS of DECISION:

Select 'YES'

This prompt questions whether or not the expert system is to display the results of the session on the screen.

The next seven prompts create a loop through which the development engine defines and describes each of the four initial parameters and the one goal parameter. For brevity, the five parameter responses are listed together for each of the seven prompts. The corresponding responses are represented by numbers: ATTITUDE will be represented by (1), REFERENCES by (2), EDUCATION by (3), EXPERIENCE by (4), and DECISION by (5). At any of the prompts, **[parameter name]** signifies that during the development cycle the name of the parameter will appear. During the actual development, this loop of prompts would be executed five times (once for each of the five parameters).

(k) Type of [parameter name]:

(1) SINGLEVALUED
(2) SINGLEVALUED
(3) SINGLEVALUED
(4) SINGLEVALUED
(5) SINGLEVALUED

This prompt asks how many values for each parameter will be allowed. In each of these cases, all of the responses will be single valued, of either numeric (quantitative) or alphanumeric (qualitative) nature.

(l) PARMGROUP OF [parameter name]:

(1) Select 'YES'
(2) Select 'YES'
(3) Select 'YES'
(4) Select 'YES'
(5) Select 'YES'

This prompt questions whether these types [from the prompt (k)] are to be stored in the HIRING parameter group.

(m) EXPECT of [parameter name]:

(1) Select 'ANY'
(2) Select 'ANY'
(3) Select 'ANY'
(4) Select 'POSNUMB'
(5) Select 'ANY'

This prompt asks what type of value can be expected for the parameter response. Each of the above parameters would expect an alphanumeric (qualitative) response, with the exception of EXPERIENCE, which would expect a positive numeric (quantitative) response.

(n) TRANS of [parameter name]:

(1) (The personality and congeniality of the applicant.)
(2) (The personal recommendations on behalf of the applicant.)

(3) (The extent of public/private education of the applicant.)

(4) (The amount of time spent doing similar job tasks.)

(5) (The recommendation of whether or not to hire the applicant.)

This prompt asks for the translation of the parameter. The translation is used when the user requests on-line assistance.

(o) PROMPT of [parameter name]:

(1) Enter T

(2) Enter T

(3) Enter T

(4) Enter T

(5) Press [return]

This prompt indicates whether or not the knowledge engineer wants the system to build a prompt for the translation of the parameter (for on-line assistance). According to the responses above, the knowledge engineer wants prompts for all of the initial parameters, but not for the goal parameter.

(p) REPROMPT of [parameter name]:

(1) (What is the applicant's attitude?)

(2) (What is the quality of the applicant's references?)

(3) What is the extent of the applicant's education?

(4) (How many years does the applicant have of similar work experience?)

This is the prompt to the user during the hiring session. The goal parameter is not included because it is a derived parameter, based on the values of the initial parameters and the production rules.

(q) DICTIONARY of [parameter name]:

(1) Select 'Parameter name'

(2) Select 'Parameter name'

(3) Select 'Parameter name'

(4) Select 'Parameter name'

(5) Select 'Parameter name'

This prompt asks for the dictionary of the parameter. By selecting the parameter name, the dictionary value is set equal to the definition of the parameter.

The remaining questions continue after the knowledge engineer has defined all of the parameters. If any of the parameters have not been defined, the knowledge engineer will be prompted to do so during the construction of the rules.

(r) Synonym of HIRING:

Press [return]

The knowledge engineer presses return to skip defining a synonym of HIRING.

(s) Descendant context of HIRING:

Press [return]

This provides the linking of the HIRING context to other contexts to form a context tree hierarchy. Again, there is only one context in this model and thus no linking of contexts.

STEP 3. The knowledge engineer proceeds to create the rule base of the system. The rules are entered using a BASIC-like language called ARL (Abbreviated Rules Language).

The easiest way to design the rules is to first identify the minimum value requirements of the given parameters to attain the goal. The minimum requirements of the applicant are

- If the attitude is good but the references are poor, the applicant must also have adequate education and at least one year of experience in a similar job position.
- If both the attitude and references are good, nothing else is of any consequence.

Given the first requirement, the first rule would be

(1) IF   the applicant's ATTITUDE is good, *AND*
             the REFERENCES are poor, *AND*
             the EDUCATION is adequate, *AND*
             there is at least one year EXPERIENCE,
     THEN   HIRE.

Given the second requirement, a second rule would be

(2) IF   the ATTITUDE is good, *AND*
             the REFERENCES are good,
     THEN   HIRE.

Now that we have taken into consideration all of the requirements and situations to hire an applicant, the knowledge engineer deduces the final rule:

(3) IF   the first rule is not activated, *AND*
             the second rule is not activated,
     THEN   DONT-HIRE.

Now that the rules are sketched out in English, they are ready to be encoded into the expert system.

(a) Name of rule:

Press [INsert]

This instructs the development engine to insert a new rule into the rule base.

(b) PREMISE of RULE001:

(IF ATTITUDE = GOOD AND REFERENCES = POOR AND EDUCATION = ADEQUATE AND EXPERIENCE GE 1)

Enter the premise of the first rule.

(c) ACTION of RULE001:

(DECISION = HIRE)

Enter the action of the first rule.

(d) Subject of RULE001:

Select 'HIRINGRULES'

This directs the development engine to store this rule in the HIR-INGRULES group.

(e) Name of Rule:

Press [INsert]

This instructs the development engine to insert a new rule into the rule base.

(f) PREMISE of RULE002:

(IF ATTITUDE = GOOD AND REFERENCES = GOOD)

Enter the premise of the second rule.

(g) ACTION of RULE002:

(DECISION = HIRE)

Enter the action of the second rule.

(h) Subject of RULE002:

Select 'HIRINGRULES'

This instructs the development engine to store this rule in the HIR-INGRULES group.

(i) Name of Rule:

Press [INsert]

This instructs the development engine to insert a new rule into the rule base.

(j) PREMISE OF RULE003:

(IF DECISION IS UNKNOWN)

Enter the premise of the third rule. UNKNOWN is a system function that questions if the premise parameter (DECISION) has been defined thus far. The interpretation is "If the parameter DECISION has not yet been assigned a value by any other rule, then ..."

(k) ACTION of RULE003:

(DECISION = DONT_HIRE)

Enter the action of the third rule.

(l) Subject of RULE003:

Select 'HIRINGRULES'

This directs the development engine to store this rule in the HIRINGRULES group.

The knowledge base has now been constructed. The hiring expert system is ready for use.

EXSYS

EXSYS, from Exsys, Inc., is a rule-based, backward-chaining expert system development tool. The same three basic rules identified in the last example (PERSONAL CONSULTANT) will be used again, as will the same four initial parameters (attitude, references, education, and experience) and the two goal parameters (hire and don't hire). The values for each of the parameters also remain the same.

STEP 1. The creation of the expert system begins by defining the system—what EXSYS terms the *text base*. There are nine parts to this initial step. To start, run the development engine EDITXS.

(a) Subject of knowledge base:

HIRING MODEL

The subject line defines the name of the expert system being constructed.

(b) How do you wish the data on the available choices structured:

1—Simple yes or no.

2—A range of 0–10 where 0 indicates absolutely not and 10 indicates absolutely certain. 1–9 indicate degrees of certainty.

3—A range of −100 to +100 indicating the degree of certainty.

Input the number of selection of [H] for help:

1

This allows the selection of a certainty factor scheme to be used in the inferencing process. In this example the knowledge engineer elects the first scheme. It is equivalent to a 0,1 scheme or an absolute yes or no—where the values and responses are absolute.

(c) Number of rules to use in data derivation:

1. Attempt to apply all possible rules

2. Stop after first successful rule

Select 1 or 2 (Default = 1):

Press [return]

The knowledge engineer directs the inference engine to apply all possible rules in deriving the data. The first choice provides the most effective solution; the second choice provides the most efficient solution.

(d) Input the text you wish to explain how to run this file. This text will be displayed at the start of EXSYS.

This session provides a recommendation of whether or not to hire the applicant.

(e) Input the text you wish to use at the end of the EXSYS run. This will be displayed when the rules are done, but before the choices and their calculated values are displayed.

The following is the recommendation as to whether or not to hire the applicant.

(f) Do you wish the user running this expert system to have the rules displayed as the default condition? **(The user will have the option of overriding this option) (Y/N)(Default = N):**

Press [return]

A response of Y would allow visual tracing of the inferencing process during execution.

(g) Do you wish to have an external program called at the start of a run to pass data back for multiple variables or qualifiers? (Other external programs may also be used to get data for single variables or qualifiers) (Y/N) (Default = N):

Press [return]

(h) Input the choices to select among. Input just [ENTER] when done. Additional choices can be added later.

1 HIRE
2 DONT_HIRE
3 Press [return]

Here the knowledge engineer enters the goal parameters.

(i) The function that checks new rules against the previous ones does NOT check the validity of mathematical formulas. If you predominantly use formulas, it may be more convenient to switch this option off.

Do you wish new rules checked against the previous rules? (Y/N)(Default = Y):

Press [return]

This internal function is analogous to that of a validator. It checks that the reasoning employed by the rules maintains its validity.

STEP 2. Once the text base has been constructed, the next step is to build the rule base. To build the rule base, the knowledge engineer uses the basic relationships of the following rules that were developed in the previous examples, but modifies the third rule according to the particulars of this development tool. To reiterate the rules for this expert system.

(1) IF   the ATTITUDE is good, *AND*
              the REFERENCES are poor, *AND*
              the EDUCATION is adequate, *AND*
              there is at least one year EXPERIENCE,
     THEN   HIRE.

(2) IF   the ATTITUDE is good, *AND*
              the REFERENCES are good,
     THEN   HIRE.

(3) IF   the first rule is not activated, *AND*
              the second rule is not activated,
     THEN   DONT_HIRE.

The way that rules are built in EXSYS is different from that in most other development tools. The conventional method is to literally type in the rule "if attitude = good and references = good then hire." Instead, the knowledge engineer creates what EXSYS calls *qualifiers* and their respective values. Think of a qualifier as a parameter. These qualifiers are then used to construct rules. Once qualifiers are created, they can be used repeatedly by simple recall. This saves many keystrokes over the conventional method of entering the full premise and action of every rule. The following summarizes the qualifiers and their values:

Qualifier (1)	*Values*	*Qualifier* (2)	*Values*
The attitude is	(1) Good	The references are	(1) Good
	(2) Poor		(2) Poor

Qualifier (3)	*Values*	*Qualifier* (4)	*Values*
The education is	(1) Adequate	The experience is	(1) Less than one year
	(2) Inadequate		(2) At least one year

STEP 3. Upon defining the qualifiers, the rules can then be constructed. The premise of the first rule is a combination of all four qualifiers:

1. Qualifier 1: value 1
2. Qualifier 2: value 2
3. Qualifier 3: value 1
4. Qualifier 4: value 2

producing the following premise:

RULE NUMBER 1:

IF

    (1) the ATTITUDE is good,

and (2) the REFERENCES are poor,

and (3) the EDUCATION is adequate,

and (4) the EXPERIENCE is at least one year

To complete the action ("Then") part of the rule, the knowledge engineer assigns a probability value (1 or 0) to the choices designated in Step 1. Remember that in the initial step the knowledge engineer elected to have absolute yes/no (1, 0) probabilities. Thus, in the action part of the rule the knowledge engineer assigns the choice HIRE a probability of 1 (absolute truth) and the choice DONT_HIRE a probability of 0 (absolute falsity).

The last step is to assign a flag variable that indicates whether or not a rule was activated. Unlike in the last example, there is no built-in function to determine whether a variable has been assigned (in PERSONAL CONSULTANT this function was called UNKNOWN). Therefore, the knowledge engineer defines a flag variable that changes when a rule is activated.

In this example the flag variable is defined as [PASSED_RULE]. This flag variable is initialized to zero at the beginning of the session. As in PERSONAL CONSULTANT, the third rule checks the value of the variable DECISION; in EXSYS it will check the value of the flag variable [PASSED_RULE]. Upon reaching the third rule, if the value for [PASSED_RULE] is still zero, then neither of the previous two rules was activated. This indicates that the applicant did not satisfy either of the hiring rules. The completed first rule is

RULE NUMBER 1:

IF

    (1) the ATTITUDE is good,

and (2) the REFERENCES are poor,

and (3) the EDUCATION is adequate,

and (4) the EXPERIENCE is at least one year

THEN
>   (1) HIRE—Probability = 1,
> and (2) DONT_HIRE—Probability = 0,
> and (3) [PASSED_RULE] IS GIVEN THE VALUE 1

The second rule is constructed in the same format as the first rule. The premise is a combination of qualifier 1: value 1 and qualifier 2: value 1. The action part of the second rule is identical to the action of the first rule.

RULE NUMBER 2:

IF
>   (1) the ATTITUDE is good,
> and (2) the REFERENCES are good

THEN
>   (1) HIRE—Probability = 1,
> and (2) DONT_HIRE—Probability = 0,
> and (3) [PASSED_RULE] IS GIVEN THE VALUE 1

The purpose of the third rule is to assign the value of DONT_HIRE to all other scenarios NOT falling under the first two rules. Here the flag variable is checked. The third rule is summarized as

RULE NUMBER 3:

IF
>   (1) [PASSED_RULE] = 0

THEN
>   (1) HIRE—Probability = 0,
> and (2) DONT_HIRE—Probability = 1

The expert system is now in place. As the user progresses through the session, he answers questions about the parameters. Unlike PERSONAL CONSULTANT, which asks the user literal questions, EXSYS asks the user questions in the form of the qualifiers. The user responds by entering a number which corresponds to the appropriate value of the qualifier. This makes it easier for the user, who enters the number (a single keystroke) versus keying in the full parameter value. Upon completion of calculation, EXSYS displays all goal parameters and their respective resultant probabilities (1 or 0).

GURU

GURU is different from other development tools. Micro Data Base Systems, Inc. (MDBS), the developer of the software, calls GURU "synergistic" software. The MDBS maintains that GURU is an inclusive, holistic philosophy which integrates all of the well-known business computing methods into a unified AI environment of expert systems and natural language processing.

Guru's features include:

Business graphics	Multifunction calculator
Communications	Relational database
Complete structured programming	Split-screen spreadsheets
Custom report generator	Standard structured query
Forms management	language
General-purpose text processor	Statistical analyses

Synergism—the whole is greater than the sum of the parts—results because GURU eliminates all conventional barriers between expert systems and the business computing applications aforementioned.

A second distinction is that GURU is a compiled system, whereas the others are interpreted systems. GURU comes complete with an internal C compiler. Although development time is slowed due to repeated compilings, run time is enhanced. Again, the expert system will have the same parameters, values, and rules (with some variation to adapt the third rule).

STEP 1. When GURU is run, the main menu is presented:

Expert Systems
Natural Language

Information Manager
Change Environment
Quit

The knowledge engineer selects the first option and moves into the expert system environment:

Build an Expert System
Consult an Expert System
Explain Reasoning
Previous Menu

To build the expert system, GURU begins by asking for the name of the expert system. The name of the expert system is HIRING MODEL. It then prompts whether to use an existing rule set or build a new one. The knowledge engineer begins by building a new rule set, called HIRING.RSS (Rule Set Source).

The five steps to building an expert system are shown below. Print and Exit commands are also provided:

Definition
Initialization
Rules
Variables
Completion
Print
Exit

STEP 2. In the Definition section the knowledge engineer identifies the goal parameter—DECISION. By identifying that a goal parameter exists, the knowledge engineer is instructing GURU to reason using backward chaining, which is a goal-directed technique.

STEP 3. In the Initialization section the variables are defined to "unknown" or an initial value. Initial prompts to the user are also identified. Environment variables—variables that remain constant throughout an entire session—are defined at this time. An environment variable is a variable that remains constant throughout the entire session. Environment variables are prefaced with an "E." The predefined GURU system environment variables used in this example are

E.SORD. This determines the order for firing a number of rules if several rules yield the desired variables. The choices are "c" (fires rules according to cost), "f" (fires rules in order from first to last), "h" (fires the most certain rule first, i.e., the highest certainty factor), "r" (fires in random order), "p" (fires by priority assigned to the rule in development), and "u" (fires the rules with the least number of unknowns in the premise first).

E.RIGR. This determines how to find the value of an unknown variable. The choices are "a" (fires all the rules), "m" (fires as many rules as needed to give the variable minimum certainty), and "c" (fires rules until minimum certainty is reached, then fires all other rules which can be fired and still have all the variables needed).

E.TRYP. This determines the general aggressiveness of the inference engine with respect to unknown variables in a premise. The choices are "e" (for eager, and tests the premise after each variable becomes known), "s" (for strict, and tests the premise only if all variables are known), and "p" (for prudent, and finds as many variables as possible).

E.TRAC. Turns on a verbose mode to explain which rules are examined and fired (a trace mode). The choices for trace mode are "n" (no tracing), "f" (displays rules being fired), "c" (displays rules being considered and fired), and "v" (displays both rules and variables being considered).

When finished, the initialization screen will appear as

```
E.SORD = "f"
E.TRAC = "n"
E.RIGR = "m"
E.TRYP = "e"
DECISION = UNKNOWN
ATTITUDE = UNKNOWN
REFERENCES = UNKNOWN
EDUCATION = UNKNOWN
EXPERIENCE = UNKNOWN
```

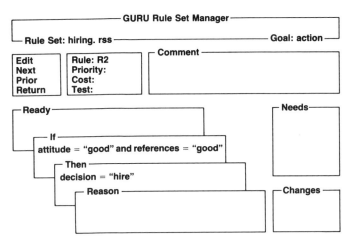

Figure 9.3. Illustration of a GURU rule.

STEP 4. The third section entails building the rules. As in the previous examples, the first two rules stay the same; the third rule is modified according to the particulars of this development tool. Following are the three rules in GURU. Figure 9.3 illustrates the second rule as it appears on the GURU screen.

```
R1:  IF    ATTITUDE = "good" and
           REFERENCES = "poor" and
           EDUCATION = "adequate" and
           EXPERIENCE > 1
     THEN  DECISION = "HIRE"

R2:  IF    ATTITUDE = "good" and
           REFERENCES = "good"
     THEN  DECISION = "HIRE"

R3:  IF    true
     THEN  DECISION = "DONT_HIRE"
```

STEP 5. The Variables section identifies and defines all of the variables. These variables include the four initial parameters and the goal parameter. The purpose of the variables section is two-fold. One purpose is to provide an area for the knowledge engineer to enter descriptive text for better understanding (and definition) of the variable. This is accessed by the user via the on-line help mode. A second purpose of the Variables section is to provide an area for instructing the expert system how to find a variable's value. For example, if the system encounters a rule which uses a variable in the premise that has not yet been defined, this section would identify where to find the value. This could be a prompt to the user for the value of the variable or it may be a call to an external subroutine; there are numerous sources available to the knowledge engineer to determine a variable's value.

The primary reason why variable prompts are found in the Variables section is that, in the Initialization section, *all* of the prompts would be asked for the user, regardless of whether or not the variable was encountered. By placing the prompt in the Variables section, the prompt is executed only if the variable is encountered during the execution. Therefore, only relevant questions are asked of the user during a session. This reasoning applies not only to prompts, but to any procedure executed for the purpose of determining a variable's value.

The variables, and corresponding prompts, are as follows (note there is no prompt for the goal parameter DECISION):

DECISION
: *Although there is no prompt, the rigor of the variable is set to "m." This means that only a minimum number of rules is to be fired in order to find any value for this unknown variable.*

ATTITUDE
: **Input attitude str with "The applicant's attitude is:"** (*"str" identifies the variable ATTITUDE to be a string variable.*)

REFERENCES
: **Input references str with "The applicant's references are:"**

EDUCATION
: **Input education str with "The applicant's education is:"**

EXPERIENCE
: **Input experience num with "The applicant's experience is:"** (*"num" identifies the variable EXPERIENCE to be a numeric variable.*)

STEP 6. The Completion section details the output screen to the user upon completion of the session, displaying the output variable DECISION and its value.

The output screen would appear as

Output "The recommendation for action is:", decision

STEP 7. Now that the expert system is built, the knowledge engineer must save and compile the source code, creating a compiled file called HIRING.RSC (Rule Set Compiled).

KES

KES, by Software Architecture & Engineering, Inc., provides both an IQLISP and a C-based microcomputer expert system development tool. KES offers three reasoning strategies: hypothesize-and-test, Bayesian statistics, and production rules. Because the parameters, values, and rules have already been formulated in previous examples, Step 1 will begin with creating the knowledge base. KES does not include an internal development engine; therefore, the knowledge base must be created using an external text editor.

STEP 1. There are "potentially" seven section of a KES knowledge base. "Potentially" means that some of the sections are not necessary for simpler applications. The seven sections are

1. *Constants.* This allows the knowledge engineer to associate text strings with names so that subsequent usage of the names in the knowledge base is equivalent to usage of the strings.
2. *Text.* This provides the means to create textual information which can be presented to the end user through the use of the display command, that is, the interface.
3. *Pattern.* This allows the knowledge engineer to define string pattern-matching facilities.
4. *Attributes.* This contains information about each attribute (also referred to as parameters)—information such as possible values of the attribute, explanation of the attribute, and a question to prompt for the attribute value. This and the Actions section are the only sections of the knowledge base that are required (except when using production rule-based reasoning—then the Rules section is also required). When the knowledge engineer enters the

attributes into the knowledge base, the attribute type must be specified. This indicates to KES the nature of the value that the attribute can represent. Legal types include

sgl   Denotes that an attribute can have only a single value at any one time

mlt   Indicates an attribute can have one or more values simultaneously

truth   An abbreviation for a dichotomous "sgl"-valued attribute whose value set consists of "true" and "false"

int   Indicates an attribute with an integer numeric value

real   Indicates an attribute with a real numeric value

str   Denotes an attribute having a value represented by a string of characters

Within the attributes section, the knowledge engineer can also specify constraints for the attribute (see the attribute "experience" in the knowledge base construction following) and default values.

5. *Externals.* This allows the expert system to communicate with other executable programs. These programs may affect the values of attributes in the expert system.

6. *Rules.* This contains the rules needed in a KES production rule-based system and is not necessary in the other two reasoning methodologies (hypothesize-and-test and Bayesian statistics). Each rule contains a name, a set of conditions (assertions involving attribute values), and a set of actions that occur if the conditions are true (assignment of values to attributes, plus certain other KES commands).

7. *Actions.* This executes KES commands in the sequence in which they appear. These commands include displaying messages to the user and obtaining attribute values, which in turn initiates the inferencing process. This section is required in order to impose the execution process of the expert system.

For this example the knowledge engineer requires the Attributes, Rules, and Actions sections to be included in the knowledge base. The knowledge base HIRING appears as follows:

```
attributes:
  attitude: sgl
    (good,
     poor)
    [explain: "The personality and congeniality of the applicant."]
    [question: "What is the applicant's attitude?"].
  references: sgl
    (good,
     poor)
    [explain: "The personal recommendations on behalf of the
      applicant."]
    [question: "What is the quality of the applicant's references?"].
  education: sgl
    (adequate,
     inadequate)
    [explain: "The extent of public/private education."]
    [question: "What is the extent of the applicant's education?"].
  experience: int
    [constraint: experience ge 1]
    [explain: "The amount of time spent doing similar job tasks."]
    [question: "How many years experience does the applicant
      have?].
  decision: sgl
    (hire,
     dont_hire).
  menu: sgl
    (quit
     [question: "Leave KES?"],
     anothercase
     [question: "Evaluate another case?"])
    [question: "What would you like to do now?"].
%
```

```
rules:
  one:
    if
      attitude = good and
      references = poor and
      education = adequate and
      experience ge 1
    then
      decision = hire
    endif.
  two:
    if
      attitude = good and
      references = good
    then
      decision = hire.
    endif.
%


actions:
    message        "The Hiring Consultant Expert System",
                   " ",
                   "This consultation session will provide",
                   "a recommendation of whether or not to",
                   "hire the applicant.",
    menu = another case
    while menu # quit do
      erase.
      obtain decision.
      if
        decision = hire
      then
        message    " ",
                   "The recommendation is to hire the applicant.",
                   " ".
      endif.
      if
        status (decision) = unknown
```

```
then
     message     " ",
                 "The recommendation is not to hire the
                   applicant.",
                 " ".

     endif.
     endwhile.
     stop.
%
```

The knowledge base is constructed and maintained under the file name HIRING. As with each of the previous development tools, the third rule, taking all other scenarios of don't hire results into consideration, is coded differently. The knowledge engineer need only include the first two rules identifying hire results into the Rules section of the knowledge base. Then, in the Actions section, the first step is to obtain the value of DECISION using the existing Rules section. The Actions section then checks the value of DECISION through KES built-in function called "status." If DECISION is known, then the inference engine has fired one of the two rules in the Rules section and displays the message to hire the applicant. Conversely, if the "status" of DECISION is unknown, then the inference engine has not fired either of the two rules in the Rules section and displays the message not to hire the applicant.

STEP 2. The second step is to run a KES parser to build an internal representation for the knowledge base. A parser is a transformation program that takes an ASCII text file, as created in Step 1, and transforms it into another file which the KES inference engine can understand. During this process, the parser also performs syntax checks. If there are parts that it cannot decipher, it will identify them to the knowledge engineer for correction. The instruction step is to enter the name of the parser (called KESP), the name of the knowledge base text file (HIRING), and an options code. The options code is an optional identifier to KES which can do several things:

-1   The knowledge base is displayed on the terminal screen as it is parsed into an internal representation. Any errors encountered will be identified.

-o   This option allows the parsed knowledge base name to be different from the text file name. The default parsed knowledge base name is the text file name with the trailer ".pkb" attached.

-s   This instructs the parser to generate a script, or record of parsing, to an indicated script file name.

-m   This allows the knowledge engineer to specify the number of bytes of memory to be allocated to create the parsed knowledge base, in case the default size is insufficient for the application.

The literal instruction to run the parser for this example is KESP HIRING -1.

The result is a parsed knowledge base named HIRING.pkb which can then be run by the KES inference engine.

STEP 3. If, during the parsing process in Step 2, no errors are encountered, the knowledge engineer proceeds to run the parsed file through the inference engine. The instruction step is to enter the name of the run-time program (called KESR), the name of the parsed knowledge base file (called HIRING.pkb), and an options code (if desired). For this example, none of the options is necessary, making the instruction to run the hiring expert system KESR HIRING.pkb.

The expert system is now complete.

STAGE 4: TESTING AND EVALUATING OF THE EXPERT SYSTEM

Once the knowledge base has been constructed, the expert system is ready to be tested and evaluated to determine whether the system has achieved its initial objectives. There are primarily two methods used in testing and evaluating an expert system.

The first method is to have the expert pose hypothetical situations to the system and analyze the answers determined by the system. The expert will be able to evaluate the correctness of the expert system responses immediately. The major drawback of the method is that the expert may be subconsciously influenced, either positively (overwhelmed) or negatively (threatened), by the system into giving a biased evaluation. The major advantage, of course, is the ease and speed with which evaluations can take place.

The second method of testing is to pose hypothetical situations to both the expert and the expert system. A comparison of their responses will indicate the closeness of the expert system problem-solving capabilities to those of the expert. Although lengthier and more complex, this method overcomes many of the bias problems.

Modifications to refine the knowledge base, that is, adding, modifying, and deleting rules, are done through the development engine (or external text editor). Editing methods closely parallel the steps executed in developing the knowledge base, with the testing stage also repeated. Upon modification of the knowledge base, it is important, and sometimes difficult, to test all of the implications of the modifications. Radical modifications require extensive testing.

STAGE 5: INTEGRATION AND IMPLEMENTATION OF THE EXPERT SYSTEM

The integration and implementation of an expert system is often a stage of frustration and patience. When the completed expert system is introduced into the mainstream operation of the organization it is often met by resistance from the intended users. This resistance is a natural reaction. Many organization members do not understand the complexities of an expert system and are thereby intimidated by its power. Their initial fear is that the expert system has arrived to replace them.

In order to effectively manage this emotion, and to initiate a smooth and effective integration, the knowledge engineer (along with any others involved with the development) must educate and enlighten the total organization as to the intended use of the expert system. Training classes, support groups, and clear documentation should also be developed in order to support the transition. Managing the integration of expert systems is an important topic of Chapter 10.

STAGE 6: MAINTENANCE OF THE EXPERT SYSTEM

Maintenance of an expert system is done by the knowledge engineer. The knowledge engineer may be external or internal to the organization. Oftentimes, the initial development stages are done by an external knowledge engineer who is concurrently training an internal staff member to replace the external knowledge engineer. Maintenance of the expert system is a continual and ever-changing task. Additional knowledge is forever being discovered, while reasoning and problem-solving methods are ever being refined.

SUMMARY

The five examples of the HIRING expert system are a fair representation of the variety of microcomputer-based tools. They illustrate different methodologies for creating an expert system which will perform the exact same application. Some tools are easier to use than others, and some are more sophisticated than others. Each tool requires some education—education about its own built-in functions, limitations, and construction techniques.

For example, 1ST CLASS requires some practice in devising appropriate and representative examples of input. PERSONAL CONSULTANT requires some understanding of contexts and how they are linked to form larger systems. EXSYS offers three types of certainty factor schemes which demand some investigation to determine which is best for each application. GURU, the most complex tool, requires a fair amount of time to understand how all of the components interact and interface with each other. KES requires an external text editor for the knowledge base development. Each of these software packages is useful and a powerful business tool in its own realm of applications, but each requires time to learn its idiosyncrasies.

All of the development tools satisfactorily solve the application. Classification-type applications, such as the HIRING MODEL, are ideally suited to backward-chaining, rule-based development tools. Each tool has its strengths and weaknesses. Some tools are easier to learn, thus minimising start-up time; some tools are compiled, thus enhancing run time, but slowing development time; some tools require additional software; and some tools are better documented than others. Unfortunately, this example does not illustrate the full potential of any of the development tools (although this chapter's intention was to illustrate differences in *building* the same expert system using different tools).

PART FIVE

CONCEPT TO REALITY

It is common knowledge that man is influenced by technology, and that should he fail to consciously adapt to changing technology he will unconsciously be consumed by it. Technology, certainly in the long run, is an irresistible force, creating as all forces do, a special law of evolution—those that adapt more perfectly to changing technology will more readily survive, and those that do not adapt will be displaced by others. History has taught us that there are few, if any, exceptions to this rule. *Ceterus paribus*, technology, when properly applied, will crush even the most motivated opponent in the competitive arena, regardless of the institutional setting. Thus, the Luddites gave way to the automated spinning wheel, Harold of England lost a country, and his life, to the longbow at the battle of Hastings, and the great clipper ship fleet rapidly retired in the face of the new steamship.

Social and organizational adaptation to technological change, such as expert systems and AI, is a managed process, however: good management begets technological adaptability, poor management discourages it. The underlying theme of Part Five is the management of expert system technology within the larger setting of organizations and society, and what the future holds. Chapter 10 discusses several important issues related to the integration of expert systems into organizations. Chapter 11 paints a future for expert systems, where they are going, and how fast.

10

The Integration of Expert Systems

Expert systems, as well as the whole of AI, represent a fundamental shift in information technology—the computerization of knowledge and decision-making. Like with any other major or radical innovation, certain patterns of acceptance and adaptation are likely to occur. Examining previous innovations, and how organizations have dealt with the innovations, both successfully and unsuccessfully, suggests a number of recurring patterns of behavior or "laws" that management must understand. The following discussion points out certain principles of innovation and suggests opportunities for successfully integrating expert system technology into organizations.

THE NATURE OF INNOVATION

Industry Principle 1: A New Technology Is Both Expensive and Relatively Crude at First

This usually leads to a sense of disappointment in the new technology following the initial euphoria and hype, and often results in predictions that the new technology will only have limited appeal after the initial "fad" phase. For example, when ball-point pens were first introduced, they enjoyed extraordinarily high initial fad sales, only to be followed by consumer dissatisfaction; they had to be withdrawn from the market until certain engineering problems were solved (skipping ink). Only then were the pens successfully reintroduced. A similar phenomenon is already apparent with expert systems. Just five years ago many writers in the popular press were predicting extraordinary and sensational applications of expert systems, fifth-generation computers, and "thinking machines" in the near future; venture capital companies, in a frenzied attempt to hop on the "high-tech bandwagon," were searching for start-up firms specializing in expert system development. In fact, several start-up companies were promoted and subsequently funded by uninformed (and subsequently poorer) venture capitalists as "expert system" technology firms when their programs were based on nothing more than simple LOTUS spreadsheets.

Now the pendulum is beginning to swing. Confronted with the fact that many of the more sensational predictions have not come to pass and that expert systems are still in their infancy, more and more writers (particularly those not really familiar with expert system technology) are now ridiculing earlier expectations as being "outrageous" and "flights of fantasy"; history has taught us, however, that the long-run truth lies somewhere in between the sensationalism of the initial euphoria and "I-told-you-so" attitude of the following disappointments.

Industry Principle 2: A New Technology Usually Invades Traditional Markets in a Sequential Manner

New technologies gain commercial acceptance by initially capturing a few submarkets and then going on to others as quality and price factors improve. Thus, some areas using older technology can be insulated from the new technology for extended periods of time. Current limitations of expert systems have been clearly discussed throughout this book; these constraints make expert systems well suited for only a limited set of domains, typically those of classification-type problems. In the near future, advances are likely to be relatively incremental, improving on the cost, complexity, and flexibility problems of existing system architectures. In the more distant future, however, as additional innovations are made, such as higher-level representation of domains, developing strategies by analogies from other domains, and interacting different domain structures, new markets/applications will be captured.

Industry Principle 3: A New Technology Will Often Create New Markets and Uses

New technologies usually beget new, previously undiscovered applications, which, in turn, lead to the development of new products and services previously not imagined. It has been estimated, for example, that 50% of all the transistors manufactured were used in equipment that was made possible by the very invention of transistors. The same phenomenon is likely to be seen with expert systems. Extensive technological forecasting and technology assessment techniques need to be applied to better understand the range of possible applications and pinpoint areas where resources should be expended.

Industry Principle 4: For Long Periods of Time Both New Technology and Old Technology Can Prosper Side by Side

Both new and old technology can grow until finally the new technology overtakes the old way of doing things. For example, it took 11 years from their introduction before sales of transistors equaled those of vacuum tubes and 14 years from introduction before diesel–electric locomotives sales equaled those of steam locomotives. Oftentimes, the threat of new technology, like expert systems, results in the ill-advised, knee-jerk reaction of quickly abandoning traditional methods, when in fact these traditional methods and technologies may still have long and profitable futures. Typewriters and word processors peacefully coexist, as do the pencil/paper and the computer. Even with expert systems, pilots will still sit in jet cockpits, physicians will still diagnose, and geologists will still drill for oil—at least for the foreseeable future.

Industry Principle 5: Usually, an Innovation or New Technology Is Introduced from a Source Outside the Traditional Industry

For example, the timing applications of integrated circuits (ICs) and quartz crystal technology did not originate from within the traditional clock/watch industry, but rather from the large IC houses; these applications were first disseminated in the IC/EE literature—literature not actively read by the traditional watch industry. Thus monitoring the environment for new developments is essential. For example, medical applications of expert systems, certainly among the most successful to date, were discussed in AI circles long before these applications were introduced in the traditional medical forums. Because of this knowledge lag, the application industry must often initially "purchase" experience from the originating industry, rather than develop it internally.

Industry Principle 6: Unsuccessful Organizations Will Usually Only Marginally Recognize the Value of a New Technology

Corporate culture is extremely potent, built up over years of doing things a particular way. Then a new technology, like expert systems, appears—the traditional organizational culture often endures, and little commitment is made to the new technology. For example, a review of the annual reports of U.S. mechanical watch firms in 1971 reveals that most recognized electronic watch technology, but almost all stated that they saw its usefulness limited to simply fad or novelty products. Not surprisingly most of these firms subsequently filed for bankruptcy or were acquired by other non-U.S. firms. Successful organizations, while also having powerful cultures, have cultures positively grounded in innovative and entrepreneurial behavior.

Industry Principle 7: By the Time Most Unsuccessful Organizations Realize the Importance of a New Technology, and Try to Participate in It, It Is too Late

High technology, by its very nature, follows an exponentially declining learning curve (the cost of production decreases by a constant percentage each time production experience doubles). One phenomenon of learning curves is that the higher the labor content, the steeper the learning curve—people learn fast. Expert systems have a very high labor content; development costs, staff time, and knowledge engineering effort currently constitutes the greatest cost component in expert system development. Because of this rapid learning curve, decisive action by management is required. Early participation in expert systems, combined with a realistic view of their current limitations, will set the organizational stage for future acceptance.

Following a "wait-and-see" strategy has sounded the death knell for more than one high-tech organization in the past.

MANAGING INNOVATION

Organizations will inevitably resist the introduction of a new technology or innovation. For a variety of reasons—organizational inertia, entrenched production and marketing systems, individual career and prestige factors, union activity—most of the individuals in an organization will view the new technology as a threat. The military institution provides numerous examples of organizational barriers to technological acceptance—automatic weapons, air-strike capability, and continuous-aim naval firing were all effectively delayed years beyond their successful invention. While the previous section discussed certain recurring patterns of behavior, and characteristics of new innovations, this section discusses the management of these innovations within an organization.

Management Principle 1: Many Barriers Are Created by Individuals in High Management Positions Who Have Power over Resources

Usually, these managers, who are typically skilled or trained in old technological ways, are well meaning in their obstructioness behavior, honestly believing that they are performing a service to the organization. Oftentimes, true acceptance of an innovation results only after a key management change (or retraining)—the U.S. Army, for example, adopted autoloading rifles only after General Stephen Vincent Benet, Chief of the Army Ordnance Department, retired in 1891, after he had effectively blocked their introduction for 20 years; he believed that the use of single-shot weapons fired in volley was a more effective battle strategy. One result of this folly was that in 1876, General Custer's men, armed with single-shot breech-loading rifles, were effectively outgunned by their Indian counterparts.

Top management commitment is key in determining the level of integration and focus of expert systems in an organization. If management commitment is low, expert systems are usually transferred into an organization in an exploratory manner with one or two small,

well-defined projects, usually developed on a microcomputer or purchased commercially. Integration will only occur after management
has been shown that expert systems are a viable technological alternative. If top management commitment is medium, the technology
transfer is usually on a project-by-project basis. The application is
often a six-month (or so) prototype project with management dedicat-
ing personnel, hardware, and software resources. These projects have
high management visibility and some risk of technical failure. When
management commitment is high, the transfer can still be on a project-by-project basis, or it can be integrated at a strategic level where
an overall knowledge engineering group provides the organization
with a knowledge engineering service in identifying and implementing various small to large expert system projects.

Management Principle 2: Successful Integration of New Technology into an Organization Almost Always Requires an Internal "Champion"

This requires somebody who is willing to sell the innovation internally, oftentimes at risk to career advancement. Successful champions,
in order to succeed in what may become an openly hostile environment, have been described as internal entrepreneurs (or "in-
trapreneurs" to use a currently popular label)—tenacious, persistent,
and even abrasive at times, acting as if the innovation's acceptance
were a form of "religious" quest. Effective technology champions have
many of the same aptitudes that successful entrepreneurs have: good
physical health, superior problem-solving abilities, broad generalist
thinking, high self-confidence, strong drive and work tenacity, a will-
ingness to take personal and career risks, a realistic viewpoint regarding the usefulness of the technology, and good interpersonal skills. In
fact, frustrated internal technology champions often become the CEOs
of small spin-off companies.

When discussing the skills of the knowledge engineer, consideration must be given to the role the knowledge engineer will play in
encouraging the organization to accept expert systems. Will the
knowledge engineer act the role of the technology "champion," or will
this role be given, either explicitly or by natural evolution, to other
management personnel? Whatever the decision, it is clear that some

form of skilled championing is requisite for successful integration of expert systems and other AI technologies.

Management Principle 3: Acceptance and Ultimate Integration of a New Technology Usually Occurs "Under Fire"

In order to be successfully integrated, any new technology must quickly prove its worthiness to the overall organization in general, and to users and top management specifically; when this happens, then the new technology becomes an integral part of the corporate culture. Expert systems are no exception, and this should be a critical concern in selecting a domain for prototype development. Prototypes should have a direct and immediate "stand-alone" performance ability upon completion.

Management Principle 4: Many Successful Organizations Institutionalize Entrepreneurial Behavior by Developing Internal Venture Programs

An internal expert system venture program is a quasi-independent organization established under the corporate umbrella which is funded and allowed to develop a particular technology, in this case, an expert system, without interference from the established bureaucracy. After a period of time the venture program is evaluated and either integrated into the larger organization, spun off and sold, or disbanded. The advantages of internal venture programs are (1) it provides insulation from "obstructionness" behavior of the larger bureaucracy and "hides" from the larger organization the normal failures and frustrations of initial development, (2) it helps reduce the frustration of interested employees, particularly the technology champions, thus reducing the chance of team members resigning, and (3) it establishes a subculture based on innovativeness that can later be integrated into the umbrella organization.

There are many forms of internal venture organizations, the exact structure being dependent on the size, culture, and structure of the organization and the complexity of the expert system project. A number of recent publications have appeared in journals such as *R & D Management* and the *Harvard Business Review* which discuss ways of institutionalizing innovative behavior and compare alternative forms of internal and joint venturing.

SOCIAL IMPACTS

On a larger scale, expert systems will have profound impacts on society, more in some areas, less in others. By their very nature, expert systems compete with human experts, or some combination of human expertise and other information technology such as decision support systems. As previously discussed, some domains, such as those that involve classification-type problems, are better suited for current expert system development than others. It is in these areas that the greatest success has been achieved—in medicine, geology, and legal and financial advice. The most immediate social impact will be on these professions, and their respective institutions.

Consider the case of the medical specialty anesthesiology. In the near future, expert systems in combination with sophisticated patient monitoring and automated anesthesia administering devices could probably perform the essential diagnostic, prescriptive, and delivery functions required during surgery more efficiently and effectively than current delivery methods. Backup support could be provided by a general practitioner, nurse, or some other technician. The necessary technology is already here; only the knowledge base and procedural rules need to be acquired and integrated with the appropriate expert system hardware/software/equipment combinations. Before a knowledge base can be built, of course, procedural rules must be elicited. The medical profession, as have many other professions, has historically resisted establishing strict rules or procedures prescribing action and standardizing behavior, preferring to skillfully educate its professionals in basic theory and encourage them to act independently, using expert judgment given the case at hand. Slowly, the medical profession is changing. Recently, for example, anesthesiologists at Harvard University Medical Center have begun to develop and document procedural rules prescribing action by anesthesiologists under different conditions; this was done according to press releases to standardize delivery in light of the increasing number of deaths while under anesthesia. Although not their stated intent, these procedural rules can also provide the working framework of an expert system prototype. How will the patient respond to computerized medical delivery? Nobody really knows, but Feigenbaum and McCorduck (1983) report:

> If the idea of a mechanical doctor repels you, consider that not everyone feels that way. Studies in England showed that many humans were much

more comfortable and candid with an examination by a computer terminal than with a human physician, whom they perceived as somehow disapproving of them.

Other medical specialties, particularly those involving a high degree of diagnostic responsibility within a tight, well-defined domain, are also likely candidates for viable commercial expert systems in the near future. The social impacts of such developments on the medical profession will be tremendous. The social image of the specialist may be affected as less-trained individuals use expert systems to aid in patient care. As the general population relies less on human experts, the power, prestige, and probably remuneration to the impacted profession will be reduced. In addition, legal and administrative responsibility for medical decisions will likely be assigned differently—for example, when an expert system is employed, who is ultimately responsible for good, or bad, decisions?

The medical profession does not stand alone; many professions—legal, educational, scientific, financial, and technical—will be similarly affected. A natural reaction from these professions (particularly the more organized groups) will be to discourage, by various legislative, legal, and public relations means, the proliferation of competing expert systems, or they will at least insist that the application of such systems be under the direct supervision of the profession. Remember, the Luddites, who now have been memorialized as symbols of technology obstructionism, were simply unemployed textile workers without legal access to union representation and with a flair for the dramatic. If this attitude persists in the long run, it will certainly be counterproductive to society in general. For the immediate future, professional skepticism of expert systems may serve a very useful, socially beneficial service; it will discourage the premature application of ill-prepared, improperly structured, and inadequately tested expert systems. This skepticism will also serve as a social buffer until the required legal, ethical, and administrative constructs of society are revamped to catch up with the new technology.

In the end, technology will prevail, the social relationships of professions and institutions will be affected, and ultimately some jobs, previously insulated from creeping technology, will be radically altered or even disappear. This is not new, of course. Since the industrial revolution, the work endeavors of humans have been replaced by technology. In the past, however, it was the physically skilled—the craftsmen and factory workers—who were susceptible to the advancement of "thinking machines." In the future, it will be the mentally skilled, the trained and educated expert. For today, however, Dr. Neil Pessal of Westinghouse Electric Research and Development Center in Pittsburgh, Pennsylvania, states,

> Our approach to the development of expert systems is aimed *not* at replacing the expert, but at developing an environment that will make him more efficient and his knowledge more accessible to others. The process forces the expert to organize his knowledge and logic, which in turn can indicate critical gaps in the knowledge base and trigger new ideas. (Artificial Intelligence Letter, Texas Instruments Data Systems Group, Dec. 1985, p. 4)

This joint decision-making responsibility between the human expert and the expert system will be the norm in the near future for several reasons:

1. Human expertise can be added to the total decision's domain knowledge base, augmenting the expert systems knowledge base, which can only contain a limited percentage of the total domain knowledge.
2. Human experts are able to draw on first principles, metaknowledge, analogies, and higher-order reasoning during problem solving: aspects in which expert systems are currently weak.
3. Group, or joint, consensus with human input overcomes much of the bias that professionals hold against computer solutions to problems in their area of expertise.

Toffler, in *The Third Wave* (1980), convincingly argues that a new wave of change is upon society, rending apart and making useless the institutions and mores of the second wave, industrial society. Our centralized, standardized, large-scaled mass institutions are becoming obsolete in the face of the changing technology of the third wave and must be replaced with a new set of smaller, decentralized, demassified institutions. Expert systems are only one of these third wave technologies, yet it indicates that this new age has arrived. Studies have shown that computers have forced a revolutionary change in the workplace, many workers moving from productive and manufacturing activities into service industries. Expert systems will have a similar effect, only here it will be to open up new vistas for creative thinking and the creation of computer–human relationships never before seen. Other futurists, such as John Naisbitt in *Megatrends* (1982), have presented similar scenarios.

Society, like any large organization, develops an inertia, a culture which is inexorably intertwined with the successes of the past. Society's natural reaction is to resist change not associated with past successes and to protect the existing institutions and bureaucracies which support and feed the populace. Yet society, like any organization, can be strategically managed into the future—witness the relative success of Japan in moving from a feudal society to a leading high-technology country in less than 50 years. It is interesting to note that Japan had to undergo the "removal" of top old-line executives and the interjection of "outside-the-industry" influence in the name of General MacArthur's administrative and rebuilding efforts after World War II—activities that closely parallel the requirements for technological adaptation suggested earlier in this chapter. Great Britain, on the other hand, has yet to make this transition. Toffler, in his *Previews and Premises*, compares Japan and Great Britain:

> Japan has several powerful advantages—its embrace of computer technology, its willingness to accept high technology. Over and above this, it has a degree of future-consciousness that is astonishing. The British— also an island people—are forever wallowing in the past, mourning their lost empire, engaging in jingo theatrics, putting on magnificent television programs about the Age of Elizabeth or the Victorian era, and filling their bookstores and magazines with nostalgia. The Japanese like nothing better than to think, talk, debate, imagine, quarrel about, and stimulate each other with images of the future. This doesn't mean they have lost their past. I dare say the past is far more present in Japan, even today, than in Britain. But the public is more attuned to the future and to change. The key to this, I think, is their collective sense of insecurity—even paranoia.
>
> The British have displayed the reverse—numb complacency in the face of looming disaster. The Japanese, by contrast, tend to be great worriers. I think a great deal has to do with Britain's colonial successes in the past, which give the present generation of British leaders an inflated sense of Britain's power and significance. (Toffler, 1983, pp. 67–68)

This is a reminder to management that it must realistically evaluate any new technology like expert systems and manage the integration of innovation into the overall purpose of the organization—whether that organization is a small corporation or a broad society.

11

The Future

In the past, most expert system development efforts by the Fortune 500 companies were funded by government agencies as internal research and development projects since widespread commercial use was not viewed as a viable short-term objective. Today, both AI and its offspring, expert systems, are unquestionably growth industries with far-ranging, and immediate, commercial applications. The present use of expert systems outside the realm of government and academic institutions is still a relatively new phenomenon, however; the majority of current expert systems are either in development or prototyping stages, and many questions still remain as to their ultimate utility. It will take probably a full five to ten years to see the true impact of expert systems within the corporate realm.

COMMERCIAL SUCCESS

Over the next several years many changes will become visible as modern managers are challenged by this new technology. Organizations currently participating in expert system applications will have definite advantages over those who are not yet using these systems; benefits of increased productivity, decreased production costs, increased efficiency, and better decision-making are already accruing. Almost all organizations of the future, in order to maintain a competitive edge, will need to find ways to incorporate expert systems into their day-to-day operations. This force, driven by intense competition, will create increasing demands for higher software productivity and reliability, better identification of "true" expertise, establishing more knowledge bases, developing systems capable of addressing more complex problems, and inventing faster processors. Management information systems (MIS), computer sciences (CS), and electrical engineering (EE) departments at universities and colleges across the country are continuously adding research programs, courses, and specialties addressing these issues. Many computer companies are in the process of changing their corporate identity and strategic focus from the business of "information systems" to "intelligent processing."

The overall AI market for 1986 was estimated to be worth about $700 million in sales and will probably surpass $1 billion in 1987. Most estimates of the combined size of the AI market in 1990 range from $2 billion to $3 billion; expert systems will likely account for about 20–30% of this total. Other researchers predict that within 10 years more than 80% of the Fortune 500 companies will be actively engaged in some form of AI (Harmon and King, 1985).

HAL, the *2001, A Space Odyssey* electronic nemesis, is not seen as a threat today. The difference between the "strongly interactive" nature of the brain and the noninteractive character of the machine organization suggests that, insofar as arguments from biology are relevant, the evidence is against the possibility of using digital computers to replicate intelligence in the foreseeable future. Computers are not able to make inferences based upon the amount of information they contain or have learned; the counterpoint is the ability to "teach" the computer hundreds of thousands of situations and decision rules so that it can solve all of the problems a human can.

Other issues and questions stand out. What is a practical AI language with which to communicate with the computer? Is English too sophisticated a language to program? Currently, the majority of the world's programming languages are modeled after the English syntax and thought processes. Possibly, expert systems will be more powerful when AI programming languages are developed in a non-English syntax, such as Chinese or Japanese, where symbolic relationships are incorporated into the language itself. Maybe AI languages need to be more "low-level" and rudimentary; or is trying to communicate in a natural language too limiting for AI advancements altogether? Some experts suggest we are at the forefront of a true AI language discovery.

Most current expert systems are essentially very fancy, extremely complex decision trees—"Give me information and I will give you an answer." This is a perfect relationship if what is desired is simply a tool to enhance the decision-making process rather than replace it. Here, the computer is modeled after an expert and is expected to produce an answer similar to what the expert would conclude—as long as the domain boundaries are not compromised. Granted, any expert system will likely be modeled after someone or something; the real long-run test will come, however, when there is a dynamic control and feedback system capable of rapidly informing the computer that an incorrect response was given and then adjusting its reasoning strategies and knowledge to better conform with reality. This requires time; time to both understand higher-level reasoning processes and construct symbolic representations of them. Humans are often informed of their errors, but even then it seems many humans do not really learn—Can we honestly ask computers to do better?

Implied computer learning is an emerging field today and is called *metaknowledge*, that is, "gaining knowledge about knowledge." Examples of metaknowledge may be being able to (1) detect simple bugs in rules, (2) justify rules, (3) record needed facts about knowledge, (4) select appropriate rules, (5) justify the program's architecture, or (6) model the program's abilities and limitations.

A key to the commercial success of any innovation is how the leading companies respond to it. With expert systems there is no question about the response. We offer several examples of the dedication of large companies across several industries that are contributing to the advancement of AI and expert systems. Highlights of 1985 and 1986 include

1. A $14 million contract was reached between Ford Motor Company and The Carnegie Group, Inc. It is a long-term technology licensing agreement that will focus on the production of expert diagnostic systems for Ford's electrical, electronics, engine, parts, and service divisions. Also included are applications designed to improve customer service and diagnostics. Ford purchased a 10% equity position in The Carnegie Group, Inc.

2. A $14 million contract was reached between Ford Motor Company and Inference Corporation. Inference will be involved in building a number of expert systems for Ford's business operations in the areas of manufacturing, design of vehicle assemblies, and financial services. Ford purchased a 10% equity position in Inference Corporation.

3. A $42 million contract was reached between Sperry Corporation and Texas Instruments, Inc. The purpose is for Sperry to resell Texas Instruments Explorer LISP machine as a platform for their expert system software. Sperry will bundle and market the system with the Intellicorp KEE development tool.

4. A $50 million AI program was established by Hewlett-Packard in conjunction with other computer companies and leading universities to deliver a natural-language system within the next five years.

5. FMC Corporation, a major international producer of machinery and chemical products for industry, agriculture, and government, NYNEX Corporation, a provider of communications services to the Northeast, and Procter & Gamble Corporation have established "strategic relationships" with Teknowledge, Inc.

6. Texas Instruments donated the PERSONAL CONSULTANT development tool to 13 universities to develop expert systems. Universities selected for this project include Johns Hopkins University, Carnegie-Mellon University, Carleton College, Colorado School of Mines, Duke University, North Carolina State University, North Texas State University, the University of Delaware, Ohio State University, Texas A & M University, The American University, the University of Texas at Dallas, and Drexel University. IBM and Hewlett-Packard have similar programs under study.

7. The U.S. Department of Defense awarded Teknowledge, Inc. a $1.75 million contract to develop next-generation software tools. The project, code-named ABE, represents the largest contract between the U.S. Department of Defense and an independent commercial AI software company for research into new tools. Under the contract, Teknowledge is developing a new architecture for knowledge systems that will make it possible to reuse and assemble existing software modules as required for specific applications and treat these software modules as linked external subroutines. This approach should dramatically increase knowledge engineering productivity.

8. CDC acquired a 20% equity position in Software Architecture & Engineering, with an option to acquire an additional 10%.

9. Texas Instruments announced it had purchased an equity interest of approximately 10% in the Carnegie Group, Inc., a privately held Pittsburgh-based corporation specializing in research and development of AI software.

10. There has been increasing participation in annual conferences such as the National Conference on AI, the Conference on AI Applications, the International Joint Conference of AI, and various IEEE workshops on expert systems.

11. November 13, 1985 was the day of the Texas Instruments Satellite Symposium on Knowledge-Based Systems. More than 30,000 people viewed the symposium, which was beamed via satellite from Texas Instruments facilities in Dallas to 476 sites around the country. Texas Instruments sponsored the symposium to help increase understanding of the value and power of knowledge-based AI systems. It included presentations by distinguished experts in AI, question-and-answer periods, and information on specific AI applications. The guest presenters were Dr. Edward Feigenbaum and Dr. Bruce Buchanan (Stanford University), Dr. Randall Davis (M.I.T.), and Dr. Mark Fox (Carnegie-Mellon University).

12. A second satellite symposium took place June 25, 1986. Titled "Knowledge-Based Systems: A Step-By-Step Guide to Getting Started," it was broadcast throughout the United States, Canada, and western Europe. It was downlinked to approximately 850 sites and seen by more than 50,000 viewers. Guest lecturers included Dr. Edward Feigenbaum (Stanford University), Dr. John McDermott (Carnegie Group, Carnegie-Mellon University), Dr. Thomas Kehler (Intellicorp), and James Williams (Inference Corporation).

It is important to note that all the above activities, while extremely significant in their contribution to the field, pale next to the total government funding of AI and expert system research and development. All branches of the military have their own research systems groups, with annual budgets ranging upwards of $40 million. Perhaps the largest government agency is DARPA and its Strategic Computing Program; it initiated a 10-year $1 billion Strategic Computing Program. Its 1986 budget is designated to be around $142 million; much of this funding will be in hardware development.

HARDWARE OF THE FUTURE

As future expert systems become more complex and integrated, severe demands will be placed on current hardware technology. Current technology must be improved, or new technology must be developed, to accommodate the seemingly insatiable demands for faster and cheaper hardware. One way to improve current technology is to reduce the paths in the hardware components over which the electronic pulses travel. If the distance is shortened, so is execution time. However, since just about everything today is reduced to a chip or wafer, it is physically impossible to reduce these distances much further. In some ways, today's hardware employing today's technology is simply reaching its processing limits.

What is emerging, particularly from the government's DARPA contracts, are two research areas foretelling new technological answers: VLSI (Very Large Scale Integration) chips and sophisticated parallel processing machines.

In 1984, Texas Instruments was awarded a contract to develop a Compact Lisp Machine (CLM), based on high-performance semiconductor technology, as a key element in the DARPA Strategic Computing Program. The first CLM was delivered to DARPA in 1986. The custom VLSI LISP processor chip, called the Explorer MegaChip LISP processor, will execute a superset of COMMON LISP dialect which is compatible with Texas Instruments Explorer LISP and is being designed to provide significantly greater processing power than today's commercial symbolic processors.

According to the Director of Texas Instruments Computer Science Laboratory, Floyd Hollister,

> The importance of this is it offers the potential to reduce the size and increase the speed of LISP processors by an order of magnitude. This will be a real enabler of applications. There are a lot of places where people want to put expert systems where the environment is too hostile for current machines, or where current machines are inappropriate because of their size, speed, or ruggedness. This machine should be able to fit into those places. (*AI Interactions*, Texas Instruments Data Systems Group, Jan. 1986, p. 1)

Ideal locations for these machines will be in aircraft cockpits, robotic vehicles, and industrial environments such as power plants, steel mills, and automobile assembly plants.

The CLM consists of four electronic modules: a processor, a combination data cache/memory mapper, two megabytes of memory, and a multibus interface. The heart of the CLM system is the Explorer MegaChip LISP processor. This 32-bit VLSI chip is 1 cm^2, contains more than 550,000 transistors, and consumes approximately 1 W of power. The chip design is memory intensive, with more than 114 kbits of RAM. It features the powerful bit manipulation and branching capabilities required for efficient implementation of LISP. It has approximately two and a half times the density of the Motorola 68020 chip, with a clock speed better than double that of the MC68020, and will be more than five times as powerful as the Explorer.

This technological leap, represented by the Explorer MegaChip LISP processor, is dramatic. The CADR, the first of the family of LISP machines (originating at M.I.T. in the late 1970s), was approximately 6 ft high and 20 in. wide, containing half a dozen circuit boards that were welded together to make one large circuit board—the CPU of the system. The Texas Instruments Explorer, introduced in 1984, measured in at 1 by 2 ft, about one-quarter of the CADR's size, and used 30% fewer integrated circuits. The power consumption was reduced by 50%, and performance increased by a factor of 3. The Explorer MegaChip LISP processor will further reduce the footprint of the CLM to that of a shoebox.

Bell Laboratories announced in late 1985 that it had developed an expert system on a computer chip: not a conglomeration of boards, but on a chip. It was designed using advanced parallel processing computer architecture and metal-oxide chip technology. It will be ideal for specialized applications requiring real-time response such as missile command, manufacturing, and robotics. Integrating the expert system instructions into the chip's circuitry will avoid time-consuming retrieval of information from the computer's peripheral memory devices. Bell Labs estimates the processing power to be about 10,000 times faster, and the system uses only one-quarter of the available surface of the chip.

The function of parallel processing machines is as follows: given multiple CPUs, simultaneously attack a single problem, that is, in parallel. Current hardware technology, created years ago by Von Neuman, processes programs serially: one input, one processor, and one output. This means that the program is broken up into independent tasks and processed simultaneously to provide an answer in much less time.

Another advantage of parallel processor machines is their expandability. Given the addition of more processors, these machines can theoretically grow from a microcomputer, to a minicomputer, to a superminicomputer, to a mainframe, to a supercomputer, and maybe beyond.

BBN Laboratories, Inc. of Cambridge, Massachusetts, has developed a parallel processing machine around its BBN Butterfly parallel processor. Funded by a DARPA contract, this machine is a true virtual memory machine and can expand up to 256 processors. Each processor has the capability to contain 4 megabytes of memory, therefore making the potential main memory capacity of the machine equal to 1 gigabyte (256 processors × 4 megabytes of memory each). Some of the features special to parallel processing machines (and in some cases, special to the Butterfly processor itself) are as follows:

Homogeneity. Each Butterfly processor board contains its own power supply. Therefore, if one processor board becomes inoperable, the rest of the system will continue to operate, minus one processor. All of the processor boards are identical and fully interchangeable.

Modularity. Due to the simplicity and independence of the number of boards to the type of system, processors can be added easily (up to 256 boards). This modularity allows the "stepping stone" effect of a core hardware system that, by adding additional processors, can expand its processing power from that of a microcomputer up the scale to that of a supercomputer.

Shared Memory System. All processors have access to the full amount of memory provided by all of the processors.

Open Communication System. All processors can communicate with each of the other processors.

Linear One-for-One Progression. There is no degradation of processing power due to linking additional processors. The total processing power of the system is equal to the sum of the individual processor's power. The total memory of the system is equal to the sum of the individual processor's memory.

According to BBN Labs Chairman Gary Schmidt, the above features make the Butterfly processing machine more cost effective in price per mips (million instructions per second) than IBM (4300 Series), Digital

Equipment Corporation (VAX Series), Prime (Series 50), DGN (MV Series), and Wang (VS Series). Much of this power will be wasted unless the programs are geared to take advantage of the parallel processing capacity. This is not an easy task and requires a shift in thinking on the part of the software developer.

WHAT LIES AHEAD FOR EXPERT SYSTEMS?

Expert systems are becoming commercially more prominent and available as the breadth of applications contines to expand. Parallel with the refinement of expert systems comes the refinement of other areas of AI, such as robotics. Eventually, expert systems will affect almost every area of operations of an organization—from "what-if" scenario analysis that is used in high-level corporate strategic decision making, to automating production facilities, to sophisticated CAD/CAM and CAE programs, to fighting in "armed conflicts." Expert systems could very well become the most integral part of an organization's normal operations in the future.

As previously discussed in Chapter 1 expert systems are best used for decision-making in the areas of interpreting and identifying, predicting, diagnosing, designing, planning, monitoring, debugging and testing, instruction and training, and controlling. Although most applications have been in the manufacturing and engineering areas, several companies are moving expert systems into management. Tactical operating plans in accounting, operations, finance, sales, marketing, data processing, and human resources lend themselves to expert systems. Current expert system applications include credit analysis, claim estimation, tax advising, software service consulting, financial statement analysis, financial planning, bond analysis, shop floor scheduling, optimal loading, order checking, and personnel planning. Potential applications range from management, to production, to operations, to finance, to marketing and sales. Specifically, problems of productivity, lack of expertise availability, training, market analysis, hardware and software configurations, portfolio analysis, and research (allowing the expert system to analyze vast amounts of complex information simultaneously, making inferences and conclusions) are prime applications for expert systems.

As organizational management responsibilities move away from the tactical operational level, towards corporate strategic decision-making, the decision environment becomes much more dynamic, intuitive, and ill-defined. At this level, decision making is more complex, spanning multiple domains and environments. The difficulty resides in properly representing and capturing strategic level domains. Although some subdomains can be modeled, general strategic and policy-level decision-making expert systems will be difficult to implement with current technology. But, while not actually making decisions, expert systems can still analyze plans for logical consistency and completeness, thus challenging the planner by suggesting alternative paths of analysis when forming a strategic plan or policy. Currently, several "planning analyzer" expert systems are in development or prototype stages.

Another step towards integrating expert systems into the field of management would be a knowledge-based office system.

> A knowledge-based office system contains knowledge about the structure and functioning of an office. It transcends the functionality of classical office systems in that it not only stores the application information needed to carry out the office tasks, but also provides "metainformation" on the structure and functioning of the office as an organization. (Maes, 1984)

Some of the functions this office system would address are

- To serve as an information source by providing a descriptive framework, specifying what tasks are to be done, who is responsible for their execution, and how they are to be executed
- To aid in analyzing and monitoring the execution of these tasks and track the progress
- To serve as a communication device for supporting the interaction between the people executing complex, interdependent office tasks (i.e., somewhat like a coordinator)
- To do planning and problem solving to determine what actions must be taken to accomplish a goal; for example, to assist the manager in organizing the work within the limits of time, manpower, and budget

GURU is a step in this direction; GURU, from Micro Data Base Systems, combines many of the tools needed by management, housing an expert system shell, a relational database, a spreadsheet, a word processor, and telecommunication features. This synergism provides more power to the managers through the easy access among all of the previously named features. As expert systems become more sophisticated hardwarewise, thus bringing the cost down, more and more integrated applications, such as GURU, will be developed. This will enhance the managerial uses, making organizations much more cost effective and decision-making efficient.

With the increased applicational use of expert systems, more powerful systems will be demanded. This demand will pull the economic forces of research to develop more sophisticated hardware. We are already seeing this through the advancements of parallel processing machines. When demand is matched with funding, then innovation occurs. In addition to the demand for hardware technology advancements, there will be a demand for better algorithms, better inference engines, and better tools for managing knowledge bases and extracting expertise. We are almost at the point where the limitation to an expert system will be human knowledge and understanding—not the hardware and software.

With the integration of computers into organizational areas such as data processing, word processing, robotics, and expert systems, the reliance upon these systems will increase tremendously. Computers will solve many problems and improve many processes, but new problems will be created. One problem is the strong dependence of an organization upon the computer and its systems. When the computer is down, the organization stops: no information can be added to or queried from the databases. What is going to happen when the entire organization relies on computers? From these new problems are born new industries, such as "disaster recovery."

One emerging research trend may be to move away from spot applications, such as production scheduling, and move towards "design fusion"—to determine how to take downstream knowledge and put it into a machine. The end result would be a machine with the full span of production knowledge that can then analyze the optimization of the product's production. This could totally revolutionize manufacturing processes.

Expect to see the prominent emergence of expert systems throughout government branches—particularly in the military. The projects that have been funded by government agencies such as AFIT and

DARPA over the past decade are beginning to become visible as realistic applications. Programs such as the ALV, Pilot's Associate, Battle Management, and Strategic Defense Initiative will play a major part in non-human-aided land exploration, aeronautical emergency assistance, strategic military planning, and early missile warning systems.

Here, at the forefront of a new computer thrust, futurists have applied various labels—the "information age," the "postindustrial society," and the "third wave"—to the upcoming era. In this age, applications will become phenomenally complex, and the determining factor of success of expert systems will be their ability to manage this information. The growth of information is exponential; the more that is known, the more that will be invented, making it easier to know still more, and invent still more. There is no foreseeable upper limit to the growth of knowledge—Forrester's "Limits to Growth" argument does not apply to mental activities. The growth, recording, and subsequent computerization of knowledge is irreversible.

Indeed expert systems represent just one of many recent developments that thrust modern society into Toffler's "third wave." The success of organizations in this third wave is based upon knowledge of third wave tools, such as expert systems, but probably even more importantly, on proper use and integration of these techniques into organizations.

KNOWLEDGE ENGINEERING

"WE'RE A LITTLE BEHIND ON THIS PROJECT...
COULD YOU TELL ME EVERYTHING YOU KNOW IN 5 MINUTES"

Companies Working With Expert Systems

The following is a list of companies currently working with expert systems either in prototype mode, in field testing, or in regular use. It is impossible to include all companies engaged in expert systems development, but this list will illustrate the breadth of companies/industries actively engaged in the field.

It was compiled to give the reader a feel for what types of industries/companies are already working with expert systems in the commercial environment. Unfortunately, the level of expertise of their expert systems and usage is unknown in many cases because the information is proprietary.

Aerospace

Boeing Corporation

Ford Aerospace & Communications

Hughes Aircraft—Space & Communications

Lockheed

Martin-Marietta Denver Aerospace

McDonnell-Douglas

Pratt and Whitney

Rockwell International Science Center

United Technologies

Automotive

Ford Motor Company

General Motors Company

Airlines
Northwest Orient Airlines

Chemical Engineering
Allied Corporation

Bendix Field Engineering

DuPont

Eastman Chemicals Division

ICI

Rohm & Haas Corporation

Union Carbide Corporation

Communication
Bell Communications Research

GTE Data Services

ITT

Computer (Hardware, Software and Research)
Apollo Computer

Applied Expert Systems

Artificial Intelligence

Carnegie Group, The

Cognitive Systems, Inc.

Control Data Corporation

Data General

Digital Equipment
   Corporation

Expertelligence

Expert Software International

Expert Systems, Inc.

Expert Systems Ltd.

Franz, Inc.

Gold Hill Computers, Inc.

Hewlett-Packard

Honeywell

IBM

Inference Corporation

Informat Resource Center

Intellicorp

Level Five Research

Lisp Machine, Inc.

Logicware, Inc.

Micro Data Base Systems, Inc.

NCR Corporation

Radian Corporation

Rand Corporation

Smart Systems Technology

Software Architecture &
   Engineering, Inc.

Sperry

SRI International

Symbolics, Inc.

Teknowledge, Inc.

Tektronix

Texas Instruments, Inc.

Xerox

Consumer Goods
Procter & Gamble

Education
Carnegie-Mellon University
Dartmouth College
Georgia Institute of
    Technology
Georgia State University
Harvard Business School
M.I.T.
North Carolina State
    University
Stanford University
Tulane University

University of California, Irvine
University of Colorado
University of Illinois
University of Maryland
University of Massachusetts
University of South California
University of Texas, Austin
Utah State University
Washington University

Electrical Equipment
Babcock and Wilcox
General Electric Company

Westinghouse Research

Electronic
Delco Products

Hitachi

Financial
American Management
    Systems
Arthur D. Little
AVCO
Chemical Bank
First National Bank of
Chicago

First Wachovia Bank
Lehman Brothers
Peat, Marwick & Mitchell
Security Industry Automation
Wells Fargo Bank

Food
Campbell Soup

Forest Products
Weyerhaeuser Company

Government Agencies
Department of Health Systems Management

Environmental Protection Agency

NASA

National Archives & Records Administration

National Weather Service

Naval Ocean Systems Command

U.S. Air Force

U.S. Army

U.S. Army Engineering Topographic Laboratory

U.S. Navy

U.S. Navy Research Personnel Development Center

Heavy Equipment
Caterpillar Tractor Company

Insurance
American International Group (AIG)

Metropolitan Life Insurance

Mutual Life of Canada

Prudential Insurance Company

St. Paul Companies, The

Travellors Corporation

Wausau Insurance

Medicine
Various medical schools for MYCIN training

Oil and Gas
Atlantic Richfield

British Gas

Elf-Acquitaine

Gearhart Industries

Mobil E & P Services

Phillips Petroleum Company

Schlumberger

Shell Petroleum

Standard Oil Company

Service
Federal Express Corporation

Expert System Consultants

Following is a partial list of companies who consult on expert systems. Many, if not all, of the vendors who sell commercial tools also offer consulting services.

Company	*Area of Expertise*
Advanced Information & Design Systems	Large AI expert systems
Applied Expert Systems, Inc.	Financial
Arthur Andersen	Financial
Arthur D. Little	Financial
Brattle Research Corporation	Electronic publishing, financial
California Intelligence	Financial, insurance, manufacturing
Carnegie Group, The	General
Cognitive Systems	Portfolio management
Computer Thought Corporation	Education
Henry Firdman & Associates	General
International Computer Ltd. (ICL)	General

Company	*Area of Expertise*
Jeffrey Perrone & Associates	General
Teknowledge, Inc.	General
Texas Instruments, Inc.	General

NAMES AND ADDRESSES

AI Mentor

1000 Elwell Court, Suite 205
Palo Alto, CA 94303
(415) 969-4500

Aion Corporation

101 University Avenue, 4th Floor
Palo Alto, CA 94301
(415) 328-9595

Aldo Ventures

525 University Avenue, Suite 1206
Palo Alto, CA 94301
(415) 322-2233

American Association
for Artificial
Intelligence

445 Burgess Drive
Menlo Park, CA 94025
(415) 328-3123

Analytic Investment Management

2222 Martin Street, Suite 230
Irvine, CA 92715
(714) 833-0294

Apollo Computer

330 Billerica Road
Chelmsford, MA 01824
(617) 256-6600

Apple Computer

20525 Mariani Avenue
Cupertino, CA 95014
(408) 996-1010

Applied Expert Systems

Five Cambridge Center
Cambridge, MA 02142
(617) 492-7322

Arity Corporation	358 Baker Avenue Concord, MA 01742 (617) 371-1243
Artelligence, Inc.	14902 Preston Rd, Suites 212–252 Dallas, TX 75240 (214) 437-0361
Automated Reasoning Corporation	290 W. 12th Street, Suite 1D New York, NY 10014 (212) 206-6331
BNN Laboratories, Inc.	10 Moulton Street Cambridge, MA 02238 (617) 491-1850
Borland International	4585 Scotts Valley Drive Scotts Valley, CA 95066 (408) 438-8400
California Intelligence, Inc.	912 Powell Street, #8 San Francisco, CA 94108 (415) 391-4846
Carnegie Group, The	650 Commerce Court Station Square Pittsburgh, PA 15219 (412) 642-6900
Cognitive Science Journal	Academic Press, Inc. 111 Fifth Avenue New York, NY 10003 (800) 346-8648
Data General	4400 Computer Drive Westboro, MA 01580 (617) 366-8911
Decision Support Software	1300 Vincent Place McLean, VA 22101 (703) 442-7900

Digital Equipment Corporation	AI Technology Center 75 Reed Road Hudson, MA 01749-2809 (617) 568-4000
Expertelligence	559 San Ysidro Road Santa Barbara, CA 93108 (805) 969-7871
Expert Systems International	1700 Walnut Street, Suite 1024 Philadelphia, PA 19103 (215) 735-8510
Exsys, Inc.	P.O. Box 75158 Albuquerque, NM 87194 (505) 836-6676
Franz, Inc.	1141 Harbor Bay Parkway Alameda, CA 94501 (415) 769-5656
Galbraith Forensic & Management Sciences, Ltd.	701 "B" Street, Suite 1300 San Diego, CA 92101 (619) 235-8802
General Research Corporation	7655 Old Springhouse Road McLean, VA 22102 (703) 893-5900
Gold Hill Computers, Inc.	163 Harvard Street Cambridge, MA 02139 (617) 492-2071
Harmon & Associates	151 Collingwood San Francisco, Ca 94114 (415) 861-1660
Hewlett-Packard	3000 Hanover Street Palo Alto, CA 94304 (415) 857-5069
Honeywell	Systems & Research Center 3660 Technology Drive Minneapolis, MN 55418 (612) 782-7432

Human Edge Software	1875 S. Grant Street, Suite 480 San Mateo, CA 94402-2669 (415) 493-1593 (800) 624-5227 (outside CA) (800) 824-7325 (inside CA)
IBM	Old Orchard Road Armonk, NY 10504 (914) 765-1900
	Palo Alto Scientific Center 1530 Page Mill Road Palo Alto, CA 94304 (415) 855-3117 (800) IBM-3333 (information)
IEEE Computer Society	10662 Los Vaqueros Circle Los Alamitos, CA 90720
Inference Coporation	5300 W. Century Boulevard, Suite 700 Los Angeles, CA 90045 (213) 417-7997
Institute of Artificial Intelligence	1888 Century Park East, Suite 1207 Los Angeles, CA 90067-1716
Integral Quality	P.O. Box 31970 Seattle, WA 98103 (206) 527-2918
Intellicorp	1975 El Camino Real West Mountain View, CA 94040 (415) 965-5500
Intelligence Ware, Inc.	9800 S. Sepulveda Boulevard, Suite 730 Los Angeles, CA 90045 (213) 417-8896

Jeffrey Perrone & Associates

3685 17th Street
San Francisco, CA 94114
(415) 431-9562

KDS Corporation

934 Hunter Road
Wilmette, IL 60091
(312) 251-2621

Level Five Research, Inc.

503 Fifth Avenue
Indialantic, FL 32903
(305) 729-9046

Lisp Machine, Inc.

3601 Aviation Boulevard,
Suite 3000
Manhattan Beach, CA 90266-3706
(213) 643-8833

Building Four
Andover Tech Center
6 Tech Drive
Andover, MA 01810
(617) 682-0500

Logicware, Inc.

5915 Airport Road, Suite 200
Mississauga, Ont.,
Canada L4V 1T1
(416) 665-0022

McDonnell-Douglas

20705 Valley Green Drive
Cupertino, CA 95014
(408) 446-6324

Micro Data Base Systems, Inc.

P.O. Box 248
Lafayette, IN 47902
(317) 463-2581

Microsoft

16011 N.E. 36th Way
Box 97017
Redmond, WA 98073-9717
(800) 426-9400

Microtex Industries, Inc.

2091 Business Center Drive,
Suite 100
Irvine, CA 92715
(714) 476-0777

Miller Microcomputer Services

61 Lake Shore Road
Natick, MA 01760-2099
(617) 653-6136

Palladian Software

Four Cambridge Center,
11th Floor
Cambridge, MA 02142
(617) 661-7171

Portable Software, Inc.

9550 Skillman, L.B. 125
Dallas, TX 75243
(214) 341-7531

Production Systems
Technologies, Inc.

642 Gettysburg Street
Pittsburgh PA 15206
(412) 362-3117

Programs In Motion, Inc.

10 Sycamore Road
Wayland, MA 01778
(617) 653-5093

Quintus Computer Systems

2345 Yale Street
Palo Alto, CA 94306
(415) 494-3612

Radian Corporation

8501 Mo-Pac Boulevard
P.O. Box 9948
Austin, TX 78766
(512) 454-4797

Rand Corporation

1700 Main Street
P.O. Box 2138
Santa Monica, CA 90406

Scientific DataLink

150 E. 52nd Street, 23rd Floor
New York, NY 10022
(212) 838-7498

Silogic

9841 Airport Boulevard, Suite 600
Los Angeles, CA 90045
(213) 337-7477

Smart Systems Technology

7700 Leesburg Pike,
Central Tower
Falls Church, VA 22043
(703) 448-8562

Software Architecture &
Engineering, Inc.

1600 Wilson Boulevard,
Suite 500
Arlington, VA 22209-2403
(703) 276-7910

Software Intelligence Laboratory

1593 Locust Avenue
Bohemia, NY 11716
(516) 589-1676

Spang Robinson Report

3600 West Bayshore Road
Palo Alto, CA 94303
(415) 424-1447

SRI International

Artificial Intelligence Center
333 Ravenswood Avenue
Menlo Park, CA 94025
(415) 326-6200

Symbolics, Inc.

11 Cambridge Center
Cambridge, MA 02142
(617) 577-7500

Syntelligence

1000 Hamlin Court
Sunnyvale, CA 94088
(408) 745-6666

Systems Designer Software

444 Washington Street, Suite 407
Woburn, MA 01801
(617) 935-8009

Teknowledge, Inc.

1850 Embarcadero Road
Palo Alto, CA 94303
(415) 424-0500

Tektronix   Tektronix Industrial Park
                                   Beaverton, OR 97077
                                   (503) 682-3411

Texas Instruments, Inc.   Data Systems Group
                                   P.O. Box 809063
                                   Dallas, TX 75380-9063
                                   (800) 527-3500

                                   Data Systems Group
                                   17891 Cartwright Boulevard
                                   Irvine, CA 92714
                                   (714) 660-8150

Thoughtware, Inc.   2699 S. Bayshore Drive,
                                   Suite 1000A
                                   Coconut Grove, FL 33133
                                   (305) 854-2318

VERAC, Inc.   9605 Scranton Road, Suite 500
                                   San Diego, CA 92121
                                   (619) 457-5550

Xerox Corporation   Palo Alto Research Center
                                   333 Coyote Hill Road
                                   Palo Alto, CA 94304
                                   (415) 494-4000

                                   Artificial Intelligence Systems
                                   250 N. Halstead Street
                                   P.O. Box 7018
                                   Pasadena, CA 91107
                                   (818) 351-2351

Discussion of Commercial Expert System Tools and Shells

Within the past several years, many expert system development tools and shells have become commercially available. The tools were first available for mainframes, and within the last couple years have filtered down to minicomputers and microcomputers. What follows is a brief discussion of various tools and shells and their features, such as search and reasoning techniques, knowledge capacity, and data representation methods. The noted features are the standard functions; additional functions may be able to be added.

DEVELOPMENT TOOL	1ST CLASS	ADS
Company	Programs In Motion, Inc.	Aion Corporation
Source Language	Pascal	Pascal
External Language Required	None	None
Control Strategy	Forward & Backward Chaining	Backward Chaining
Search Technique	Inductive Classification	Least-Cost Path Algorithm
Data Representation	Rules	Production Rules
If Production Rule-Based: Maximum Number of Rules	None	None
Input Rules or Examples	Rule or Examples	Rules
Internal Development Engine	Yes	Yes
Method to Manage Uncertainty	Weights for each example	None
Compiled or Interpreted	Interpreted	Interpreted
Internal Compiler	N/A	N/A
External Interface Hooks	Yes	Yes
Hardware Company: Microcomputer	IBM	IBM
Mini/Mainframe		IBM

DEVELOPMENT TOOL	ARITY EXPERT SYSTEM DEVELOPMENT PACKAGE	ART (Automated Reasoning Tool)
Company	Arity Corporation	Inference Corporation
Source Language	Prolog	Common Lisp
External Language Required	None	None
Control Strategy	Backward Chaining	Forward & Backward Chaining
Search Technique	Depth-First Exhaustive	Can be modified to use any technique, default is Depth-First
Data Representation	Production Rules & Frames	Production Rules & Frames
If Production Rule-Based: Maximum Number of Rules Input Rules or Examples	20,000 Rules	None Rules or Examples
Internal Development Engine	None	Yes
Method to Manage Uncertainty	Certainty Factors, Confidence Factors & Probabilities	None
Compiled or Interpreted	Compiled or Interpreted	Compiled
Internal Compiler	None	Yes
External Interface Hooks	Yes	Yes
Hardware Company: Microcomputer Mini/Mainframe	IBM	DEC, Lisp Machine, Sun Microsystems, Symbolics, Texas Instruments

DEVELOPMENT TOOL	ESP ADVISOR	EXPERT-2 IN MMSFORTH
Company	Expert Systems International	Miller Microcomputer Services
Source Language	Prolog-2	MMSFORTH
External Language Required	None	MMSFORTH System
Control Strategy	Backward Chaining	Consequent Reasoning
Search Technique	Hashed Depth-First	Sequence of Rules
Data Representation	Production Rules	Production Rules
If Production Rule-Based: Maximum Number of Rules Input Rules or Examples	3,000 Rules	None Rules
Internal Development Engine	None	Yes
Method to Manage Uncertainty	None	None
Compiled or Interpreted	Compiled	Compiled
Internal Compiler	Yes	Yes
External Interface Hooks	Yes	Yes
Hardware Company: Microcomputer	IBM	IBM, Radio Shack
Mini/Mainframe	DEC	

DEVELOPMENT TOOL	EXPERT CHOICE	EXPERT-EASE
Company	Decision Support Software	Jeffrey Perrone & Associates
Source Language	Basic & Machine Language	UCSD Pascal
External Language Required	None	None
Control Strategy	Backward Chaining	Backward Chaining
Search Technique	Inductive Classification	Inductive Classification
Data Representation	Production Rules	Production Rules
If Production Rule-Based: Maximum Number of Rules Input Rules or Examples	None Examples	None Examples
Internal Development Engine	Yes	Yes
Method to Manage Uncertainty	None	None
Compiled or Interpreted	Interpreted	Compiled
Internal Compiler	N/A	Yes
External Interface Hooks	None	None
Hardware Company: Microcomputer Mini/Mainframe	IBM	IBM

DEVELOPMENT TOOL	EXPERT EDGE	EXSYS
Company	Human Edge Software	Exsys
Source Language	C	C
External Language Required	None	None
Control Strategy	Backward Chaining	Backward Chaining
Search Technique	Depth-First	Depth-First
Data Representation	Production Rules	Production Rules
If Production Rule-Based: Maximum Number of Rules Input Rules or Examples	500 Rules	5,000 (Microcomputer Version) Rules
Internal Development Engine	Yes	Yes
Method to Manage Uncertainty	Probabilities	Certainty Factors
Compiled or Interpreted	Interpreted	Interpreted
Internal Compiler	N/A	N/A
External Interface Hooks	Yes	Yes
Hardware Company: Microcomputer	IBM	IBM
Mini/Mainframe		DEC

DEVELOPMENT TOOL	EX-TRAN 7	GURU
Company	Jeffrey Perrone & Associates	Micro Data Base Systems
Source Language	Fortran 77	Lattice C
External Language Required	None	None
Control Strategy	Forward Chaining	Forward & Backward Chaining
Search Technique	Depth-First	Hybrid—User Defined Default is Depth-First
Data Representation	Production Rules	Production Rules
If Production Rule-Based: Maximum Number of Rules Input Rules or Examples	None Rules or Examples	None Rules
Internal Development Engine	Yes	Yes
Method to Manage Uncertainty	None	Certainty Factors
Compiled or Interpreted	Compiled	Compiled
Internal Compiler	None	Yes
External Interface Hooks	Yes	Yes
Hardware Company: Microcomputer	IBM	IBM
Mini/Mainframe	DEC, IBM, Sun Microsystems	DEC

DEVELOPMENT TOOL	IN-ATE (Intelligent Automatic Test Equipment)	IKE (Integrated Knowledge Environment)
Company	Automated Reasoning Corporation	Lisp Machine, Inc.
Source Language	C & FranzLisp	Common Lisp
External Language Required	None	None
Control Strategy	Backward Chaining	Forward & Backward Chaining
Search Technique	Best-First determined heuristically	Depth-First
Data Representation	Production Rules & Frames	Production Rules & Frames
If Production Rule–Based: Maximum Number of Rules Input Rules or Examples	None Schematic Diagrams	None Rules
Internal Development Engine	Yes	Yes
Method to Manage Uncertainty	Probabilities	Certainty Factors
Compiled or Interpreted	Interpreted & Compiled	Compiled
Internal Compiler	Yes	None
External Interface Hooks	Yes	Yes
Hardware Company: Microcomputer	Apple	
Mini/Mainframe	DEC, Lisp Machine, Symbolics, Texas Instruments	Lisp Machine

DEVELOPMENT TOOL	INSIGHT 2+	KDS DEVELOPMENT SYSTEM
Company	Level Five Research	KDS Corporation
Source Language	Turbo Pascal	Assembler
External Language Required	None	None
Control Strategy	Forward & Backward Chaining	Forward & Backward Chaining
Search Technique	Breadth-First or Exhaustive	Matrix Search
Data Representation	Production Rules	Production Rules & Frames
If Production Rule-Based: Maximum Number of Rules Input Rules or Examples	None Rules	None Examples
Internal Development Engine	Yes	Yes
Method to Manage Uncertainty	Confidence Factors	Confidence Factors
Compiled or Interpreted	Compiled	Compiled
Internal Compiler	Yes	Yes
External Interface Hooks	Yes	Yes
Hardware Company: Microcomputer Mini/Mainframe	IBM DEC	IBM

DEVELOPMENT TOOL	KEE	KES
Company	Intellicorp	Software Architecture & Engineering
Source Language	Common Lisp	C
External Language Required	None	None
Control Strategy	Forward & Backward Chaining	Backward Chaining
Search Technique	User defined among: Depth-First, Best-First, & Breadth-First	Hypothesize & Test
Data Representation	Production Rules, Frames & Semantic Nets	Production Rules
If Production Rule-Based: Maximum Number of Rules Input Rules or Examples	None Rules	None Rules
Internal Development Engine	None	None
Method to Manage Uncertainty	None	Certainty Factors
Compiled or Interpreted	Compiled	Interpreted
Internal Compiler	None	N/A
External Interface Hooks	Yes	Yes
Hardware Company: Microcomputer		IBM
Mini/Mainframe	Apollo, DEC, Hewlett Packard, IBM, Lisp Machine, Symbolics, Sun Microsystems, Texas Instruments, Xerox	Apollo, DEC, NEC, Sperry, Sun Micro-systems, Tektronix

DEVELOPMENT TOOL	KNOWLEDGE CRAFT	M.1
Company	Carnegie Group	Teknowledge
Source Language	Common Lisp	C
External Language Required	Yes	None
Control Strategy	Forward & Backward Chaining	Forward & Backward Chaining
Search Technique	User Defined	Depth-First
Data Representation	Production Rules, Frames & Semantic Nets	Production Rules
If Production Rule-Based: Maximum Number of Rules Input Rules or Examples	None Rules	None Rules
Internal Development Engine	Yes	None
Method to Manage Uncertainty	Certainty Factors, Confidence Factors, & Probabilities	Certainty Factors
Compiled or Interpreted	Compiled	Interpreted
Internal Compiler	None	N/A
External Interface Hooks	Yes	Yes
Hardware Company: Microcomputer Mini/Mainframe	Apollo, DEC, Hewlett Packard, IBM, Lisp Machine, Sun Microsystems, Symbolics, Texas Instruments	IBM Deliverable on IBM

DEVELOPMENT TOOL	PICON	PERSONAL CONSULTANT
Company	Lisp Machine, Inc.	Texas Instruments, Inc.
Source Language	Common Lisp	IQLISP
External Language Required	None	Yes
Control Strategy	Forward & Backward Chaining	Backward Chaining
Search Technique	Depth-First	Depth-First
Data Representation	Production Rules & Frames	Production Rules
If Production Rule-Based: Maximum Number of Rules Input Rules or Examples	None Rules	400 Rules
Internal Development Engine	Yes	Yes
Method to Manage Uncertainty	Certainty Factors	Certainty Factors
Compiled or Interpreted	Compiled	Interpreted
Internal Compiler	None	None
External Interface Hooks	Yes	Yes
Hardware Company: Microcomputer		IBM, Texas Instruments
Mini/Mainframe	Lisp Machine	

DEVELOPMENT TOOL	PERSONAL CONSULTANT PLUS	RULE MASTER
Company	Texas Instruments, Inc.	Radian Corporation
Source Language	PC scheme	C
External Language Required	Yes	None
Control Strategy	Backward Chaining	Forward & Backward Chaining
Search Technique	Depth-First	Sequence of Rules
Data Representation	Production Rules & Frames	Production Rules
If Production Rule-Based: Maximum Number of Rules Input Rules or Examples	1,000 Rules	None Examples or Rules
Internal Development Engine	Yes	Yes
Method to Manage Uncertainty	Certainty Factors	Probabilities, Certainty Factors, & Fuzzy Logic
Compiled or Interpreted	Compiled	Compiled
Internal Compiler	Yes	None
External Interface Hooks	Yes	Yes
Hardware Company: Microcomputer	IBM, Texas Instruments	A T & T, IBM
Mini/Mainframe		Apollo, A T & T, Burroughs, Celerity, DEC, Gould, Hewlett Packard, Masscomp, Perkin-Elmer, Sun Microsystems, Tektronix

DEVELOPMENT TOOL	S.1	TIMM
Company	Teknowledge	General Research Corporation
Source Language	C	Fortran 77
External Language Required	None	None
Control Strategy	Forward & Backward Chaining	Analogical Partial Match
Search Technique	Depth-First	Analogical Partial Match
Data Representation	Production Rules & Frames	Production Rules & Frames
If Production Rule-Based: Maximum Number of Rules	None	5,000 (mainframe version) 500(TIMM-PC)
Input Rules or Examples	Rules	Rules or Examples
Internal Development Engine	Yes	Yes
Method to Manage Uncertainty	Certainty Factors	Certainty Factors & Probabilities
Compiled or Interpreted	Interpreted	Compiled
Internal Compiler	N/A	None
External Interface Hooks	Yes	Yes
Hardware Company: Microcomputer	Deliverable on IBM, A T & T	IBM
Mini/Mainframe	Amdahl, Apollo, DEC, Hewlett Packard, IBM, Motorola, NCR, Sun Microsystems	Amdahl, DEC, IBM, Prime

DEVELOPMENT TOOL	WIZDOM	XSYS
Company	Software Intelligence Laboratory	California Intelligence
Source Language	C	IQLISP
External Language Required	None	IQLISP
Control Strategy	Forward & Backward Chaining	Forward, Backward, & Bidirectional Chaining
Search Technique	(not available)	Depth-First
Data Representation	Semantic Nets & Frames	Production Rules
If Production Rule-Based: Maximum Number of Rules Input Rules or Examples		None Rules
Internal Development Engine	Yes	Yes
Method to Manage Uncertainty	Certainty Factors & Fuzzy Logic	Certainty Factors
Compiled or Interpreted	Compiled	Compiled
Internal Compiler	Yes	Yes
External Interface Hooks	Yes	Yes
Hardware Company: Microcomputer	IBM	IBM
Mini/Mainframe	Apollo	

References

Barr, A., Cohen, P.R., and Feigenbaum, E. (Eds.), *The Handbook of Artificial Intelligence*, Vols. 1 and 2, and Cohen, P.R., and Feigenbaum, E., Vol. 3, William Kaufmann, Los Altos, CA, 1981.

Davis, D.B., "Artificial Intelligence Enters the Mainstream," *High Technol.*, pp. 16–23, July 1986.

Hayes, J.R., "Issues in Protocol Analysis," in Ungson, G., and Braunstein, D. (Eds.), *Decision Making: An Interdisciplinary Inquiry*, Kent Publishing, 1982.

Feigenbaum, E., and McCorduck, P., *The Fifth Generation: Artificial Intelligence and Japan's Computer Challenge to the World*, Addison-Wesley, Reading, MA, 1983.

Forsyth, R. (Ed.), *Expert Systems: Principles and Case Studies*, Chapman and Hall Computing, New York, 1984.

Harmon, P., and King, D., *Expert Systems*, Wiley, New York, 1985.

Hayes-Roth, F., "The Knowledge-Based Expert Systems: A Tutorial," *IEEE Computer*, pp. 11–28, Sept. 1985.

Hayes-Roth, F., Waterman, D.A., and Lenat, D.B., *Building Expert Systems*, Addison-Wesley, Reading, MA, 1983.

Hill, R.H., "A Knowledge Engineering Bibliography," Microelectronics and Computer Technology Corp. Austin, TX, Tech. Rep. AI-119-85, 1985.

Naisbitt, J., *Megatrends*, Warner Books, New York, 1982.

Maes, P., "Steps Towards Knowledge-Based Office Systems," paper presented at the First Conf. Artif. Intell. Appl., Boston, 1984.

Ritti, R., "Work Goals of Scientists and Engineers," *Ind. Relations*, Vol. 7, pp. 118–131, 1968.

Texas Instruments Data Systems Group, *AI Interactions*, pp. 2–5, Dec. 1985.

Toffler. A., *The Third Wave*, William Morrow, New York, 1980.

Toffler, A., *Previews and Premises*, Bantam Books, Toronto, Canada, 1983.

Williamson, M., "Made-to-Order Mentors," *PC Products*, pp. 43–76, Dec. 1985.

Winston, P.H., *Artificial Intelligence*, Addison-Wesley, Reading, MA, 1979, p. 99.

Bibliography

Books

Dreyfus, H.L., *What Computers Can't Do*: *The Limits of Artificial Intelligence*, Harper & Row, New York, 1979.

Hayes, J.E., and Michie, D. (Eds), *Intelligent Systems*: *The Unprecedented Opportunity*, Ellis Horwood Limited, New York, 1983.

O'Shea, T., and Eisenstadt, M., *Artificial Intelligence*: *Tools, Techniques & Applications*, Harper & Row, New York, 1984.

Rose, F., *Into the Heart of the Mind*: *An American Quest for Artificial Intelligence*, Harper & Row, New York, 1985.

Scown, S.J., *The Artificial Intelligence Experience*: *An Introduction*, Digital Equipment Corp., Maynard, MA, 1985.

Winston, P.H., and Pendergast, K.A., *The AI Business*, M.I.T. Press, Cambridge, MA, 1984.

Articles

Adelson, B., and Soloway, E., "The Role of Domain Experience in Software Design," *IEEE Trans. Software Eng.*, pp. 1351–1360, Nov. 1985.

"AI Goes Commercial," *Ind. Week*, pp. 58–59, Feb. 3, 1986.

"A Maintenance Expert That Never Sleeps," *High Technol.*, pp. 48–49, Nov. 1985.

Alexander, T., "The Next Revolution in Computer Programming," *Fortune*, pp. 81–86, Oct. 29, 1984.

Alexander, T., "Why Computers Can't Outthink the Experts," *Fortune*, pp. 105–118, Aug. 20, 1984.

"Artificial Intelligence Is Here: Computers That Mimic Human Reasoning Are Already at Work," *Business Week*, pp. 54–62, July 9, 1984.

"AT & T Develops Natural Language Interface," *Comput. Syst. News*, p. 22, Oct. 21, 1985.

Barstow, D.R., "Domain-Specific Automatic Programming," *IEEE Trans. Software Eng.*, pp. 1321–1336, Nov. 1985.

Benoit, E., "Filling the Gap," *Forbes*, pp. 166–170, Mar. 11, 1985.

Borgida, A., Greenspan, S., and Mylopoulos, J., "Knowledge Representation as the Basis for Requirements Specifications," *IEEE Computer*, pp. 82–91, Apr. 1985.

Bridger, M., and Frampton, J., "Creating a Standard LISP," *PC Tech J.*, Vol. 3, No. 12, pp. 98–117, Dec. 1985.

Brown, J.S., and Moskovitz, G., "AI: Windows of Opportunity in Office Automation," Xerox Corp. pp. 1–13, July 1985.

Buchanan, B.G., "Expert Systems: Working Systems and the Research Literature," Knowledge Syst. Lab., Dep. Comput. Sci., Stanford Univ., Stanford, CA, Rep. No. KSL-85-37, pp. 1–55, Oct. 1985.

Conlon, T., "Expert Systems in the Economy Size," *Comput. Decisions*, pp. 32, 33, May 21, 1985.

Cooper, A.C., and Schendel, D., "Strategic Responses to Technological Threats," *Business Horizons*, pp. 61–69, Feb. 1986.

Covington, M., "Programming in Logic: Part 1," *PC Tech J.*, Vol. 3, No. 12, pp. 83–95, Dec. 1985.

"DARPA'S Pilot Associate Program Provides Development Challenges," *Aviation Week Space Technol.*, pp. 45–52, Feb. 17, 1986.

Davis, R., "Amplifying Expertise with Expert Systems," Sloan M.I.T., Cambridge, MA, pp. 2–10, Summer 1985.

Derfler, F.J., "Expert-Ease Makes Its Own Rules," *PC Mag.*, pp. 119–124, Apr. 16, 1985.

"AI VAX Station, Dedicated AI Computing Plus Superior Power at Your Desk," Digital Equipment Corp. pamphlet, Maynard, MA, 1985.

Doyle, J., "Expert Systems and the 'Myth' of Symbolic Reasoning," *IEEE Trans. Software Eng.*, pp. 1386–1390, Nov. 1985.

Emrich, M., "Artificial Intelligence: Expert Systems Hardware, Part II," *Manufact. Syst.*, pp. 28–33, Apr. 1985.

Emrich, M., "Artificial Intelligence: Software for Expert Systems, Part III," *Manufact. Syst.*, pp. 38–43, May 1985.

Emrich, M., "Artificial Intelligence: Expert Systems in the Real World, Part IV," *Manufact. Syst.*, pp. 26–27, June 1985.

Emrich, M., "Artificial Intelligence: Experts on Expert Systems, Part V, Conclusion," *Manufact. Syst.*, pp. 24–31, July 1985.

"Expert System Is Built into a Chip," *Ind. Week*, p. 64, Feb. 3, 1986.

Fikes, R., and Kehler, T., "The Role of Frame-Based Representation in Reasoning," *Commun. ACM*, pp. 904–920, Sept. 1985.

Friedland, P., "Acquisition of Procedural Knowledge from Domain Experts," *Proc. IJCAI-81*, Vancouver, BC, Canada, pp. 856–861.

Friedland, P., "Special Section on Architecture for Knowledge-Based Systems," *Commun. ACM*, p. 903, Sept. 1985.

Hadden, W.J., and Hadden, S., "Expert Systems for Environmental Regulations," Dep. Mech. Eng., pamphlet, Texas A & M Univ.,

Hartley, R.T., "CRIB: Computer Fault-Finding Through Knowledge Engineering," *IEEE Computer*, pp. 76–83, Mar. 1984.

Hass, J., "LISP on the Move," *UNIX Rev.*, pp. 51–57, Sept. 1985.

Hawkins, W.J., "Expert Systems Promise Supersmart PCs," *Popular Sci.*, pp. 83–116, Mar. 1986.

Hayes-Roth, F., "Knowledge-Based Expert Systems," *IEEE Computer*, pp. 263–273, Oct. 1984.

Hayes-Roth, F., "Rule-Based Systems," *Commun. ACM*, pp. 921–932, Sept. 1985.

Hill, R.H., "Automating Knowledge Acquisition from Experts," Microelectronics and Computer Technology Corp., Austin, TX, Tech. Rep. AI-082-86, 1986.

Hirsch, A., "Tagged Architecture Supports Symbolic Processing," *Comput. Des.*, pp. 75–80, June 1, 1984.

Hirsch, A., "Toolkit Extends the Benefits of LISP-Based Computer to Fortran Programming," *Electron. Des.*, pp. 193–202, May 31, 1984.

Horwitt, E., "Exploring Expert Systems," *Business Comput. Syst.*, pp. 48–57, Mar. 1985.

Hunter, P., "Sperry Brainstorms AI Effort on Both Sides of the Atlantic," *Information-Week*, p. 12, Nov. 4, 1985.

Johnson, W. L., and Soloway, E., "PROUST: Knowledge-Based Program Understanding," *IEEE Computer*, pp. 267–275, Mar. 1985.

Kahn, G., Nowlan, S., and McDermott, J., "A Foundation for Knowledge Acquisition," *Proc. IEEE Workshop Principles Knowledge-Based Syst.*, Denver, CO, Dec. 1984.

Keller, E. L., "Artificial Intelligence Starts Punching into Factory Applications," *Comp. Syst. News*, p. 8, Oct. 28, 1985.

Kent, E., "Understanding: Automating Algorithm Design," *IEEE Trans. Software Eng.*, pp. 1361–1374, Nov. 1985.

Kinnucan, P. "Software Tools Speed Expert System Development," *High Technol.*, pp. 16–20, Mar. 1985.

Klausmeier, R., and Allen, W., "An Expert System for Diagnosing Electronically Controlled Automobiles," Radian Corp., Austin, TX pamphlet, June 1985.

Kobler, V.P., "Overview of Tools for Knowledge Base Construction," *Proc. CAIA*-84, pp. 282–285.

LaPlante, A., "Human Edge Certification Program Gives Lift to AI Systems," *InfoWorld*, Vol. 8, Iss. 8, p. 10, Feb. 24, 1986.

Linden, E., "Intellicorp: The Selling of Artificial Intelligence," *High Technol.*, pp. 22–25, Mar. 1985.

"Management, Not Technology, Is the Problem," *Ind. Week*, editorial, p. 7, Jan. 20, 1986.

Manuel, T., "What's Holding Back Expert Systems?" *Electron.*, pp. 59–63, Aug. 7, 1986.

McWilliams, G. "TI's AI Workstation to Share Files with Apollo, Sun Products," *Comput. Syst. News*, pp. 30, 33, Mar. 17, 1986.

Neches, R., Swartout, W.R., and Moore, J.D., "Enhanced Maintenance and Explanation of Expert Systems Through Explicit Models of Their Development," *IEEE Trans. Software Eng.*, pp. 1337–1351, Nov. 1985.

Nii, H.P., "The Blackboard Model of Problem Solving," *AI Mag.*, Vol. VII, No. 2, pp. 38–53, Summer 1986.

Nofel, P.J., "There's Nothing Artificial About AI," *Modern Office Technol.*, pp. 41–44, Feb. 1985.

Petrosky, M., "Expert Software Aids Large Systems Design," *InfoWorld*, Vol. 8, Iss. 7, pp. 1, 8, Feb. 17, 1986.

Quinlan, J.R., "Discovering Rules by Induction from Large Collections of Examples," in Michie, D. (Ed.) *Expert Systems in the Microelectronic Age*, Edinburgh University Press, Edinburgh, UK, 1979.

"Researchers Channel AI Activities Toward Real-World Applications," *Aviation Week Space Technol.*, pp. 40–41, Feb. 17, 1986.

Richer, M.H., "Evaluating the Existing Tools for Developing Knowledge-Based Systems," Knowledge Syst. Lab., Dep. Comput. Sci., Stanford Univ., Stanford, CA, pamphlet, May 1985.

Riese, C., "Transformer Fault Detection and Diagnosis Using RuleMaster by Radian," Radian Corp., Austin, TX, Paper, Jan. 1985.

Scannell, T., "Expert Systems Have yet to Arrive," *PC Products*, p. 13, Dec. 1985.

Shamoon, S., "AIG's Smart Software: The 'Expert' That Thinks Like an Underwriter," *Management Technol.*, Feb. 1985.

Shannon, T.C., "AI at Work," *Digital Rev.*, pp. 62–69, May 1986.

Sheil, B., "Power Tools for Programmers," *Datamation*, pp. 131–144, Feb. 1983.

Slagle, J.R., and Hamburger, H., "An Expert System for a Resource Allocation Problem," *Commun. ACM*, pp. 994–1004, Sept. 1985.

Smith, D.R., Kotik, G.B., and Westfold, S.J., "Research on Knowledge-Based Software Environments at Kestrel Institute," *IEEE Trans. Software Eng.*, pp. 1278–1295, Nov. 1985.

Smith, E.T., "Turning an Expert's Skill into Computer Software," *Business Week*, pp. 104–108, Oct. 7, 1985.

Sorensen, K., "Expert Systems Introduced for IBM RT PC, MacPlus," *InfoWorld*, p. 10, Feb. 3, 1986.

Stefik, M., and Bobrow, D.G., "Object-Oriented Programming: Themes and Variations," Xerox PARC, *AI Mag.*, pp. 40–62, 1984.

Stuart, J.D., Pardue, S.D., Carr, L.S., and Feldcamp, D.A., "Titan: An Expert System to Assist in Troubleshooting the Texas Instruments 990 Minicomputer," Radian Corp., Austin, TX, Tech. Rep. ST-RS-00974.

Stuart, J.D., and Vinson, J.W., "Turbomac: An Expert System to Aid in the Diagnosis of Cause of Vibration-Producing Problems in Large Turbomachinery," Radian Corp., Austin, TX, Tech. Rep. ST-RS-00968, Aug. 1985.

Subrahmanyam, P.A., "The 'Software Engineering' of Expert Systems: Is PROLOG Appropriate?" *IEEE Trans. Software Eng.*, pp. 1391–1399, Nov. 1985.

"Teknowledge Transfer," Teknowledge, Inc., Palo Alto, corporate newsletter, Fall 1985.

Teresko, J., "AI Moves into Industrial Control Area," *Ind. Week*, pp. 70–78, Nov. 25, 1985.

Teresko, J., "Delivering Desktop Decision Support," *Ind. Week*, pp. 333–335, Aug. 5, 1985.

Teresko, J., "TI Is Mounting a Push for AI," *Ind. Week*, p. 67, Jan. 20, 1986.

Texas Instruments Data Systems Group, *AI Interactions*, pp. 2–5, Dec. 1985.

Texas Instruments Data Systems Group, *AI Interactions*, p. 1, Jan. 1986.

Texas Instruments Data Systems Group, artificial intelligence letter, p. 2, Sep. 1985.

"Texas Instruments Nears Completion of LISP Language Microprocessor," *Aviation Week Space Technol.*, pp. 57–61, Feb. 17, 1986.

Tucker, M., "Expert Systems Blaze Trails to AI Success," *Mini–Micro Syst.*, pp. 69–78, Mar. 1986.

Wates, R.C., "The Programmer's Apprentice: A Session with KBEmacs," *IEEE Trans. Software Eng.*, pp. 1296–1320, Nov. 1985.

Weizenbaum, J., "The Myths of Artificial Intelligence," in Forester, T. (Ed.), *The Information Technology*, Basil Blackwell, Oxford, UK, 1985.

Wyland, K., "Artificial Intelligence: Strategic Military Applications," *Professional Careers*, pp. 16–19, Aug./Sept. 1986.

Zubrick, S.M., and Riese, C.E., "An Expert System to Aid in Severe Thunderstorm Forecasting," Radian Corp., Austin, TX, Tech. Rep. ZU-RS-00025, Oct. 1985.

Interviews

Arthur Anderson, N. Skorus

CH2M-Hill, R. Halm, Regional Computer Coordinator

Digital Equipment Corp., F. VanDerMolen, Corporate Consultant

Exsys, Inc., D. Huntington, President

KDS, B. Wallace, President

McDonnell-Douglas, W. Brown, Senior Staff Engineer

NOSC, R. Camen, B.D. Fraser

Naval Weapons Center, J. Lind

Syntelligence, S. Breiner, President

Texas Instruments, J. Maginnis, Branch Sales Manager, Data Systems Group

Glossary

Action The "then" part of a production rule, which contains "action" if the premise is true.

Algorithm A step-by-step procedure for solving a well-defined problem in a finite number of steps that frequently involves repetition of the operation (e.g., loan interest calculation).

Arcs (See Links.)

Artificial Intelligence (AI) (broad definition) Computer problem-solving techniques developed to imitate human thought or decision-making processes.

Attribute Describes a property of an object. For example, a particular stock is an attribute in the calculation of the *Standard & Poor's* 500 stock index.

Audit Trail An expert-system generated documentation showing the reasoning steps used by the expert system when solving a particular problem.

Backtracking Returning back to a known step during a search procedure, making guesses at specified times during the problem-solving program. If a guess leads to an unacceptable result the program returns to the previous specified point and opts for another guess.

Backward Chaining A control (also auditing) procedure that attempts to repeat the resulting goals through iterations, starting at the desired solution, working towards the initial conditions.

Systems employing backward chaining are also called goal-directed systems.

Bidirectional Search A search technique that most opportunistically combines forward and backward chaining *within one session.*

Blackboard Architecture A system design where independent data bases and knowledge bases share a common working memory, called a blackboard.

Boolean Developed around 1860 by George Boole, Boolean is a logical combinatorial system that represents relationships symbolically. Examples include AND, OR, and NOT.

Breadth-First Search A search technique which evaluates every item at a given level of the search space before proceeding to the next level.

Certainty Factor A number entered into the expert system by the user that indicates the level of certainty regarding the uncertainty of inputted information. For example, on a scale from -1 to $+1$, a certainty factor of $+1$ would indicate absolute certainty. Likewise, a factor of -1 would indicate absolute uncertainty. Areas of uncertainty range in level of difficulty from knowledge uncertainty, to knowledge relevance, to multiple instances, to multiple experts, to exploratory programming, to deep reasoning and pushing knowledge to its limits of hypothesization.

Concurrent Protocols Recording, or protocol, of information simultaneously as the task is being performed.

Confidence Factor A confidence factor is a number supplied by the expert system that indicates the level of the system's confidence in its conclusion.

Context A structure that organizes the information in a knowledge base according to subproblems. A problem addressed by a knowledge base can be separated into subproblems which, when solved, contribute to the solution of the problem as a whole.

Context Tree An organizational structure used to define the relationships among the different contexts in a knowledge base.

DARPA (Defense Advanced Research Projects Agency) An agency in the Department of Defense that finances high-technology research projects with potential military application.

Database   The storage area for the facts of the problem, which may or may not be related.

Data Structure   (See Structure).

Decision Support System   A passive software tool used to model/ forecast various problems to assist in the decision-making process, typically using matrix-type data structures.

Declarative Statement   A fact; an assertion that is true.

Deduction   The deriving of a conclusion by reasoning. An inference process in which the conclusion follows necessarily from the premises.

Depth-First Search   A search technique that evaluates only one item at a given level of the search space before proceeding to the next level.

Development Engine   The part of an expert system that enables the knowledge engineer to build, update, and save a knowledge base.

Development Tool   A programming system that simplifies the work of building an expert system; development tools contain a prespecified range of reasoning techniques and knowledge representations, but are missing the knowledge base. The knowledge base is added by the knowledge engineer or expert. Development tools are sometimes called "shells."

Domain   The universe of data and knowledge contained in the expert system, usually related to a common set of problems or tasks.

Dynamic   Marked by continuous activity or change.

Editor   A development engine.

Epistemology   The study or a theory of the nature and grounds of knowledge, especially with reference to its limits and validity.

Example Based   An expert system structure whereby the knowledge base is entered into the system through examples. The inference engine then deciphers these examples by means of induction to form the rule base. The development tool 1ST CLASS is an example of this structure methodology.

Expert   An individual, who by training, education, experience, or insight, is able to solve a particular type of problem that most other people cannot solve nearly as efficiently or effectively. Experts typically have expertise in a particular domain (sometimes called domain experts).

Expert Reports A knowledge acquisition technique where the expert is asked to write down rules, data, and strategies for solving a problem.

Expert System A computer system, comprising both hardware and software, which models and/or mimics an expert's thought process to solve a complex problem in a given field.

Eye-Movement Protocol A record of the eye fixes as the expert solves a problem, usually used to supplement verbal protocol analysis (see Protocol).

Forecast An estimation or prediction of a future event or condition.

Forward Chaining A control (also auditing) procedure that produces new goals iteratively by affirming the consequent propositions associated within an inferential rule. It is logical reasoning from data to hypothesis. Systems employing forward chaining are also called data-driven systems.

Frame Representation "Frame of reference." A knowledge representation matrix that associates expert system features with an object in terms of "slots" and "slot values" (see Slot).

Fuzzy Logic When no clear concise boundary exists between situations where a concept applies and situations where it does not apply, fuzzy logic is a gradual transitioning where a network of assertions controls the success or failure of subsequent logic. For example, the statement "X is a large number" would be represented as the following in fuzzy logic:

Fuzzy proposition: X is a large number

Fuzzy set: $[X \in (0,5), 0.05]$

$[X \in (5,5000), 0.10]$

$[(X > 5000), 0.85]$

The interpretation of the proposition is that there is a 5% probability that X is less than 5, a 10% probability that X is between 5 and 5000, and an 85% probability that X is greater than 5000.

Garbage Collection A set of methods for recovering areas of address space that are no longer being used. Once the memory is recovered, it can be reused to represent new objects. Garbage collection can be done parallel to program processing (real time) or can interrupt program processing (see Stop-and-Copy Storage Management).

Heuristics "Private knowledge" that is composed of rules of thumb that enable experts to make educated guesses. This approach does not guarantee a solution to a specific problem. This knowledge is often judgmental, experimental, and uncertain.

Heuristic Rule A procedural tip or incomplete method for performing some task.

Heuristic Search A procedure by which a computer attacks problems by a trial-and-error method and which frequently involves the act of learning.

Induction The act, process, or result or an instance of reasoning from a part to a whole, from particulars to generals, or from the individual to the universal.

Inference An implied relationship of one object to another, allowing new facts to be derived from existing facts.

Inference Engine The "driver" of an expert system that selects, searches, and manipulates the database and knowledge base for a solution.

Inheritance A feature of semantic network data structures. It is the ability of one node to inherit characteristics of other nodes that are related to it.

Instantiation The fulfilling of values from a particular context or situation during an expert system session (see Slot Filling).

Interface An area of communication of knowledge between two or more parties or systems.

Iterative Repetitious; executing over and over again.

Knowledge Acquisition The process of identifying, documenting, and analyzing the information processing behavior of the expert.

Knowledge Acquisition Tools A special computer program designed to extract the knowledge base directly from the expert, without the intervening step of using human knowledge engineers. Knowledge acquisition tools use either induction or rule-elicitation techniques.

Knowledge Base   The storage area of an expert system that includes the relationships and heuristics of the database.

Knowledge Discovery   The first stage of knowledge acquisition. It is the process of defining the domain boundaries, the range of knowledge needed, and typical reasoning scenarios, including metarules. Knowledge discovery usually involves archival background research, and initial consultation with experts.

Knowledge Engineering   The area of expertise that assumes the overall task of building expert systems using the tools and methods that support the development of an expert system.

Knowledge Handbook   A compendium of all knowledge acquired by the knowledge engineer during archival research and expert consultations. Major sections include a comprehensive domain listing (descriptions of domains and subdomains), descriptive (object-related) knowledge, procedural (rule-oriented) knowledge, and glossary. It is the primary source of information for entering knowledge into the expert system.

Knowledge Representation   A structure (format) in which knowledge is stored that allows the system to understand the relationships of the data in the knowledge base.

Lexicon   A dictionary that contains the list of words that are understood by the natural language system and their meaning to the underlying application.

Links   Are used in semantic network data structures and relate objects (nodes) and descriptors. They are also called "arcs."

LISP   A computer programming AI language having a unique recursive structure. LISP stands for LISt Processing.

Logic   A technique for drawing inferences that relies on formal rules for manipulating symbols.

Metaknowledge   Knowledge about knowledge.

Metarules   The implementation of metaknowledge to supply information on how to best apply the other forms of knowledge—particularly rules. In operation, the system often must choose an order in which to consider several rules that could determine the value of a parameter. With metarules the developer can specify how this ordering should be performed. Metarules can be used to specify rules to be considered based on parameter values or parameters mentioned in the rule's premise or action clauses. Metarules provide a clean way of specifying interrelationships between rules. The following illustrates a metarule from PERSONAL CONSULTANT PLUS (by Texas Instruments) that might be part of a computer fault diagnosis application.

| MetaRule 001 | If: | the computer does not initialize properly, and there are rules which mention in their premise disk drive errors, and there are rules which mention in their premise processor logic errors, |
| | Then: | the former should be used before the latter. |

Monotonic   Repetitive; always utilizing the same path of process.

Monotonic Reasoning   Where all values concluded for an attribute remain true for the duration of the program run. MYCIN is a monotonic system.

Motor Protocol   A record of the physical actions taken during a task.

Natural Language   The branch of AI that studies methods of communicating with the user at a conversational level. The interface is a conversation in English rather than menu driven or static questions programmed as in a computer language like BASIC or FORTRAN.

Nonmonotonic Reasoning   Any facts that once defined (true or false) may be retracted. The retraction process can be expensive and confusing, both computationally and conceptually.

Object–Attribute–Value Triplets (O–A–V)   Objects may be physical entities such as a car, or they may be conceptual entities such as a bank loan. Attributes are characteristics of the objects (like the interest rate for a bank loan). Values identify the specific nature of an attribute (such as an 8% interest rate). Thus, in this type of data structure, for each piece of information in the knowledge base there exists an object, attribute, and value.

Open-Ended System   Means that the expert system tool allows the invoking of programs, external to the system, during development.

Ordered State-Space   The evaluation sequence or arrangement of all of the states, based on some sorting order.

Paradigm   A pattern, model, or example.

Parallel Processing   An advanced computer processing technique that allows the computer to perform multiple processes at the same time, "in parallel."

Parameter   A fact or piece of information used by an expert system to infer conclusions or recommendations.

Parser   A translation program that converts an input file into an output file which can then be interpreted by a program.

Pattern Matching   An AI technique which recognizes similarities between patterns and objects or events.

Plausible Reasoning   A guess that is made when attempting to cope with incomplete knowledge, when solutions are plentiful and any path will do, or when trying to limit the scope of the domain and converge upon the solution rapidly.

Predicate Calculus   A knowledge representation model based on logic. The elementary unit is an object. Statements about objects are called predicates. For facts stated in predicate calculus, their predicates must be either true or false (i.e. true or false that the interest rate is 8%).

Premise   The "if" part of a production rule. If the premise of a rule being tested is true, the action ("then") part of the rule is evaluated.

Probes   Questions asked during the collection of protocols or during interviews with the expert.

Problem Solving   The process of starting in an initial state and searching through a problem space in order to identify the sequence of operations or actions that will lead to a desired goal. Weak problem-solving techniques are domain independent. Strong problem-solving techniques are domain dependent and exploit knowledge to achieve greater performance.

Procedural Attachment   Used in frame representation, it is a set of instructions to be executed for slot filling.

Production Rule A condition/action rule that produces changes that result in a new state for another condition/action rule to be applied, and so on. The most common format of this data structure is *If-Then*. A production rule typically represents a single heuristic.

Prolog A computer programming AI language. It stands for PROgramming in LOGic.

Protocol A record of the mental and physical actions taken when accomplishing a task. There are verbal, eye-movement, and motor protocols. Protocols need to be analyzed to determine relevant knowledge and reasoning strategies.

Protocol Analysis The analysis of protocols for expert system development. Protocol analysis includes transcription, phrase indexing, coding, and documentation.

Pruning The process where one or more branches of a decision tree are erased from consideration. The purpose is to reduce the problem search space as soon as possible to "zero in" on the goal in the most efficient manner.

Readthrough A knowledge acquisition technique where the expert shows the knowledge acquirer how to read complex or confusing documents, manuals, and reports.

Reasoning Strategies Strategies used to analyze, infer, think logically, or draw conclusions from facts explicitly or implicitly expressed, including forward and backward chaining. Reasoning strategies are expressed in expert systems within the inference engine.

Recursive Nested iterations—a procedure that is able to call itself to solve a subprocess.

Retrospective Protocol Information gathered after the fact, but still during the knowledge engineering phase (see Protocol).

Rule-Based An expert system structure whereby the knowledge base is entered into the system through production rules. The rules are generally of the form *If–Then*. The development tool EXSYS is an example of this structure.

Rule Set A collection of rules that constitutes a module of heuristic knowledge.

Rule of Inference Modus ponens, modus tolens, resolution; various techniques used by logicians to determine the truth or falsity of a statement.

Search The process of attempting to proceed from an initial state to a goal state by systematically evaluating possible alternative solution paths.

Search Space All of the possibilities that might be evaluated during a search. The search is often represented by a tree structure, called a search tree. The search space is not necessarily the same as the domain.

Semantic Network (Semantic Net) A data structure where information is stored in nodes and the nodes are then connected with arcs or links (see Links).

Semantics Rules that govern what constitutes a meaningful statement in a language. The sentence "Colorless green ideas sleep furiously" does not make sense and therefore is not semantically correct.

Sequential Processing The traditional computer processing technique of performing actions one at a time, that is, in sequence.

Session The contiguous time spent with an expert system solving a particular problem.

Slot A feature or description of an object in a frame. Slots may correspond to intrinsic features, such as names and definitions, or to derived features, such as numeric values.

Slot-Filling During a session, values are attached to slots in a frame representation (see Instantiation).

Sorting Order The procedure that determines the next state to evaluate in a state-space representation model.

State-Space Representation The set of all attainable states describing the environment under varying conditions, used to model the problem including its initial condition and goal state.

Static A situation where the environment does not change. All conditions remain the same during the session.

Stop-and-Copy Storage Management During the garbage collection process within the execution of the program, processing is suspended. Processing is resumed after the garbage collection is finished.

Structure (as in data structure)   The organization or systematization of data for representing knowledge in a usable fashion for various applications.

Symbolic   Expressing an object, event, action, relationship, or value by the use of alphanumeric variable names.

Symbolic Pattern Matching   The matching of new information to that which the system already knows or wants to know.

Symbolic Processing   The manipulation of symbolic knowledge.

Syntax   The set of rules that govern the legal order of words within a language. The sentence "The is house blue" is syntactically incorrect and therefore not a legal sentence.

Tagged Memory Architecture   Uses part of each memory word to convey information about the data stored in the remaining bits of that word, including the data type and format.

Taxonomy   A classification of objects, a system of arrangement of objects, based on some common factor.

Teachthrough   A knowledge acquisition technique where the expert instructs the knowledge acquirer, as a teacher would a student.

Thrashing   As the size of working memory use grows, the efficiency of non-real-time garbage collection (Stop-and-Copy Storage Management) declines as more and more time is spent scrounging less and less memory. This will cause a significant increase in disk access and a significant decrease in program efficiency.

Translator   The component of the natural language software that changes the natural language sentence entered by the user into a command understood by the application. The translator consults the lexicon to translate the input into a command that is meaningful to the application.

Verbal Protocol   The record of problem solving based on the expert "thinking aloud," or verbalizing, while accomplishing a particular task. It is the most widely used form of protocol for detailed knowledge acquisition (see Protocol).

Virtual Memory   From the programmer's viewpoint, it is the space in which programs and data are stored; from the system's viewpoint, it is the collection of pages of information, some of which reside in physical main memory and some of which reside on disk. Since programs can be run only when they are resident in physical main memory, the hardware automatically swaps between the physical main memory and the pages on the disk.

Very Large Scale Integration (VLSI)   The process of combining several hundred thousand electronic components into a single integrated circuit.

Walkthrough   A knowledge acquisition technique where the expert "walks" the knowledge acquirer through a typical task, describing problem-solving behavior. It is not a "real-time" process like protocols.

Index